Contents at a Glance

Contents

About the Authors

Keith Franklin is the president and senior architect of Empowered Software Solutions (ESS) based in Naperville, IL. He is the author of *VB.NET For Developers* from Sams Publishing, a regular contributor to *Visual Basic Programmers Journal* and *Visual Studio Magazine*, and a speaker at VBITS. Keith is the director of the Chicago.NET Users Group and one of the featured architects of www.dot-netrocks.com, which he created with Rocky Lhotka. As an architect for ESS, Keith consults, teaches, and architects solutions for clients building highly scalable Internet, e-Commerce, and Distributed Client/Server applications. Keith and ESS have been building applications for clients with the .NET Framework, ASP.NET, and VB.NET since Beta 1 was released. You can contact Keith via ESS (www.empowered.com) or via e-mail at ka_franklin@empowered.com.

Rebecca M. Riordan has almost 20 years of experience in software design and has earned an international reputation as a consultant, systems analyst, and designer of database and work-support systems. Her experience includes leading development projects in the United States, Australia, and Europe, managing the professional services department of one of Australia's largest computer retailers, and serving as a senior technical engineer for Microsoft. Currently living in New Mexico, she is the author of *Designing Relational Database Systems*, *SQL Server 2000 Programming Step by Step*, and the upcoming *ADO.NET Step by Step*.

Dedication

I dedicate this book to my wife and children. I have driven them crazy (especially Tami) over the past six months as I poured over documentation (especially when the information sometimes seemed hidden from view). Tami, you make everything worthwhile and I love you with all of my heart; you are my soul. You have created a warm, happy family, and I treasure that more then anything else; without you nothing would be worthwhile.

I have two wonderful little boys and a third child on the way. Scottie and Jeffie make the sun seem to shine so much brighter whenever I hear them laugh. Scottie, when I see you race past your first base coach (totally ignoring his desperate pleas for you to stop), I can't help but laugh and cry. I laugh because you are so much fun to love and cry because you are growing up so fast. Jeffie, you are Daddy's little comic; although you may look more like your mom, your wit and sarcasm are certainly mine. When I see you give me your little mischievous smirk, I grow just a little bit younger. You guys are Daddy's heart.

I would also like to dedicate this to my father, mother, brothers, and sister. Especially my father: Dad, you never realize how much of the intelligence and compassion that all of your children share comes directly from you. No matter how much we may argue with you about Chicago sports teams, we all love and respect you and your intelligence. But most of all because of you we all grew to be compassionate and kind people. I love you Dad, and your grandchildren adore you.

Acknowledgments

To produce a book based on a product that is being built as you write is a difficult thing to accomplish. It takes a number of dedicated people to accomplish this and I would like to acknowledge a few. First, I would like to acknowledge Neil Rowe, my acquisitions editor, who kept all this organized and moving forward. I would like to acknowledge Rebecca Riordan, my development editor, for helping structure the book to keep the message clear.

In addition, I need to acknowledge Microsoft for building such a fantastic product. In particular I need to acknowledge the Visual Studio.NET and .NET Framework development teams. This development platform and development tool is heads and shoulders above anything else ever developed. Particular attention needs to be given to the Authors team who shared so much time and energy sharing information with me.

Finally, I need to acknowledge my fantastically talented partners and the great developers of Empowered Software Solutions: This is just the beginning of the proof that our goal of building an extremely high-quality oriented consulting company dedicated to developers was the right mission.

Tell Us What You Think!

As the reader of this book, *you* are our most important critic and commentator. We value your opinion and want to know what we're doing right, what we could do better, what areas you'd like to see us publish in, and any other words of wisdom you're willing to pass our way.

As an Associate Publisher for Sams, I welcome your comments. You can fax, e-mail, or write me directly to let me know what you did or didn't like about this book—as well as what we can do to make our books stronger.

Please note that I cannot help you with technical problems related to the topic of this book, and that due to the high volume of mail I receive, I might not be able to reply to every message.

When you write, please be sure to include this book's title and author as well as your name and phone or fax number. I will carefully review your comments and share them with the author and editors who worked on the book.

Fax: 317-581-4770

Email: feedback@samspublishing.com

Mail: Jeff Koch, Associate Publisher
         Sams
         201 West 103rd Street
         Indianapolis, IN 46290 USA

Introduction

Since the introduction of Visual Basic 1.0 in 1991, Windows application development has been dominated by a RAD-based development metaphor. But as we move into the maturing age of Internet-based application development, the need for a more efficient programming model for Windows and Internet development is clearly needed.

In an effort to capitalize on the Internet, Microsoft changed the meaning and the technical architecture of ActiveX to make the technology more lightweight for embedding in browsers. For client-side development Microsoft produced a lighter weight version of Visual Basic known as VBScript. Work was also done on Visual Basic to make it a premier component development tool.

Work was already in progress on the second wave, which included updated tools for Java and Active Server Page development. At the same time, Microsoft began work on a radically different programming model for both Windows and Internet development. The outcome of this effort was the .NET Framework, introduced at the Microsoft Professional Developers Conference in July 2000.

The .NET Framework is a comprehensive platform for building applications for the Internet age that still allows developers the option of building complete feature-rich applications that use the Windows platform. The .NET framework includes an extremely comprehensive class framework to provide services for the most common tasks that application developers do. In addition, the .NET framework provides integrated services for security, cross-platform communication, resource management, and extensibility.

With .NET as the chosen platform for the future of Windows development and Microsoft as the chosen methodology for building Internet applications, Visual Basic.NET was rewritten from the ground up. Visual Basic developers will find this to be both exciting and a little unsettling. As Yoda said in *Star Wars Episode V: The Empire Strikes Back*, "You must unlearn what you have learned."

In many cases, this is not the issue. The .NET Framework in nearly all cases will provide a more logical elegant method of accomplishing tasks that required hacks in previous versions of Visual Basic. The goal of this book is to get you up to speed with Visual Basic.NET and to point out many of the changes that have been made as Visual Basic moves into the .NET framework.

Who Should Read This Book

The primary focus of this book is to help existing Visual Basic developers get up to speed quickly with the changes introduced by the .NET Framework. In addition, developers with experience in Java, C++, Delphi, or other application-development tools who are interested in Visual Basic or the .NET Framework will also find this book of interest.

Although this book concentrates on Visual Basic.NET, it's primary goal is to introduce you to how Visual Basic and the .NET framework work together. It will introduce you to the new development paradigms introduced by the .NET Framework, including ASP.NET, Windows Forms, and Web Services.

What You Will Need to Get Started

To start developing applications with Visual Basic.NET, you will need Visual Studio.NET Beta 2. Visual Studio.NET Beta 2 is available for download for MSDN Universal Subscribers or can be ordered on CD from Microsoft.

My recommendation is to run the product on a Windows 2000 or Windows Whistler machine, and prior to the actual release run it on a machine suitable for testing beta products.

Although the .NET Framework is still in Beta, many companies are choosing to deploy applications with it today. Bill Gates said that this is the most solid Beta he has ever seen at the June 2001 TechEd in Atlanta.

CHAPTER 1

The .NET Framework

In the mid-1990s, development paradigms across the industry changed rapidly primarily because of the drastically reduced cost of computing hardware and the explosion of the Internet. In response to these changes, Microsoft changed the development paradigm for the Windows platform. This decision ultimately led to the development of the .Net Framework.

The very first form of runtime environment for objects from Microsoft became available in 1997 when Microsoft introduced *Microsoft Transaction Server (MTS)*. Shortly thereafter, they began talking about Windows NT 5, which became Windows 2000, and the next version of COM, which they called COM+.

COM+ originally consisted of two components: COM+ Services, which allowed services to be provided via an administrative tool rather than through coding directly to an API; and COM+ Runtime, which would move all the COM plumbing code away from the developers and into the operating system.

At the same time, Microsoft was actively at work exploring a number of technologies such as Java and XML. Realizing that they aren't the only developers that have good ideas, Microsoft looked at what others had done, chose the good ideas, and expanded on them.

All of this eventually merged into what was known as *Next Generation Web Services (NGWS)*, which ultimately became the .NET Framework.

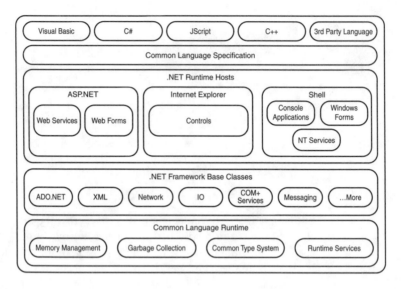

Figure 1.1

Components of the .NET Framework.

Assemblies

There have always been problems deploying applications in the Windows environment. One of the most common problems is DLL Hell.

There are actually a couple of versions of DLL Hell. The first and most serious version of the problem occurs when an application overwrites an existing DLL with an older version, causing other applications to break. The other version of DLL Hell occurs when a new version of a COM DLL breaks older applications because the actual implementation of the component works differently then a previous version.

The first, non-COM problem is exacerbated by the fact that non-COM DLLs can be loaded from anywhere on a system. If multiple versions of the DLL are on a given machine, one application might load it from one location and another might load it from a different location. However, because Windows tries to use a loaded DLL before it loads another, applications can break at nonpredictable times depending on the order in which they are loaded.

In COM, Microsoft attacked the DLL Hell problem in two ways. First, all COM components need to be registered so that they are only loaded from one location. Second, when COM components are changed to add functionality, they should implement new interfaces and still support the old interfaces. But problems have still occurred, most often because a newer version of the component "fixes" behavior that older clients depend on.

In Windows 2000, Microsoft introduced the concept of side-by-side deployment to fix DLL Hell problems. Windows 2000 also protects system DLLs so that bad installation programs can't replace system DLLs with older versions. The .NET Framework takes side-by-side deployment and versioning to a new level.

In the .NET Framework, managed code is deployed in the form of *assemblies*. You can think of assemblies as analogous to DLLs or EXEs in VB, but assemblies are a great deal more than a simple DLL or EXE, which are basically just binary files.

Unlike traditional DLLs and EXEs, assemblies can be broken up into multiple DLLs. This can be used to separate the frequently and rarely used parts of an application. This technique is beneficial for applications delivered over the network or Internet because parts that are rarely used won't be downloaded until needed.

In the COM world, components are accessed through type libraries, which describe the objects and the interfaces that they implement down to the method level. Type libraries are written in a language called *Interface Definition Language (IDL)*, which is very much like C/C++. One of the problems of COM is that the type libraries and the DLL or EXE that it describes are kept separate from each other.

Assemblies, on the other hand, are self-describing. Information contained within the assembly tells other components and the Common Language Runtime (CLR) just what the assembly can do and in what context it is allowed to do certain things.

Some of the information contained in the assembly for a component is as follows:

- Versioning information
- Information for Code Access Security
- Information to facilitate Cross language integration

There are two types of assemblies in the .NET Framework: shared and private.

Private Assemblies

Assemblies are private by default. After the .Net Framework is installed, a private assembly is only used by the application into whose directory or subdirectories it has been copied. This is a marked difference to COM, where components are registered on a system-wide basis. Private assemblies alleviate DLL Hell because two applications can use different versions of the same component without worrying about which version has been installed on a user's machine.

Shared Assemblies

A shared assembly is accessible to all applications on the machine. When an application attempts to load a component, the CLR will first attempt to find a private assembly and only look for a shared assembly if none is found.

A shared assembly must be installed into the Global Assembly Cache (GAC). Figure 1.2 illustrates a shell extension that installs with the .NET Framework and shows what is installed into my test machine's GAC. Other utilities that ship with the .NET

Framework allow you to install components into the GAC, as does the Microsoft Installer.

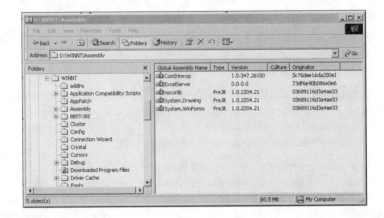

Figure 1.2

Global Assembly Cache.

In most cases you will be using private assemblies, but third-party components might be installed to the GAC. One additional capability of the GAC is the capability to hold multiple versions of the same assembly. This is so that the DLL Hell problem isn't just reinvented.

Metadata

Unlike earlier development platforms, the architects of the .NET Framework believe that all code should be self-describing; that is, it should provide information that other development tools can use to determine if and how they should interact with it. In the .NET Framework, *metadata* stored in the assembly provides this information.

Metadata plays a key role in how the design-time and runtime environments work with the assembly. Visual Studio.NET and developer's code look at the metadata of an assembly through a process called *reflection*. Included within the .NET Framework is a set of classes to facilitate reflection.

Metadata is also key to how the security system of the .NET Framework controls the ways in which types can be used in given circumstances. We'll look at this in more detail in Chapter 11, ".NET Application Development Design, Architecture, and Implementation."

Assembly metadata is contained within the assembly in a section called the *manifest*. The manifest contains the following information about the assembly:

- Identity
- File list
- Referenced assemblies and version information

- Exported types
- Declarations of the fields, methods, properties, and events of all types
- Exported resources
- Permission requests

Finally, the remoting strategy for objects is facilitated by metadata. The .NET Framework uses the metadata to determine the proper way to remote an object; should just a reference to the object be remoted, or should the object be serialized and sent across the network and deserialized on the other side.

The Common Language Runtime

Behind the .NET Framework is the idea of a *managed environment*. A managed environment acts as a runtime governor, controlling what application code is doing and what it is allowed to do. Within a managed environment, developers are relieved of the burden of building all the plumbing that ensures robust, flexible, and secure applications.

In the .NET Framework, that runtime is known as the *Common Language Runtime (CLR)*. CLR provides all the runtime services for the .NET Framework. Although a runtime is nothing new for a Visual Basic developer, the CLR for the .NET Framework is another beast entirely.

Unlike the Visual Basic runtime, the CLR is responsible for how all *managed code* interacts with the operating system. Code that doesn't operate within the CLR is called *unmanaged code*. Unmanaged code is rarely needed in business applications.

The VB.NET compiler only creates managed code. Some other compilers can choose to create managed or unmanaged code. By default, C# creates managed code but can also produce unmanaged code. On the other hand, Visual C++.NET creates unmanaged code by default, but can also produce managed code. Jscript.NET is similar to VB.NET in that it only produces managed code.

The CLR is responsible for the following tasks:

- The Common Type System
- Garbage collection
- Just-In-Time compilation
- Versioning
- Security

The Common Type System is discussed in detail in Chapter 9, "Error Handling," whereas garbage collection and security are in Chapter 10, "ADO.NET." The remaining tasks are discussed next.

Just-In-Time Compilation

In more traditional development environments, developers compile code when they are ready to deploy solutions. With the introduction of byte-code, Java delayed the compilation until execution. This made it possible for code to run on multiple platforms without requiring multiple deployment packages.

The .NET Framework takes this concept several steps further with a deployment, versioning, and security scenario built around *Just-In-Time (JIT)* compilation. When an assembly is compiled from within Visual Studio.NET, it is compiled into Intermediate Language (IL). IL is a cross-platform version of machine language. After the code is compiled into IL, it can then be JIT compiled.

JIT compilation starts when an application is executed. As code is called, the CLR first looks to see whether the function to be executed has already been compiled and placed in the cache. If the code isn't found in the cache, the CLR and the JIT compiler will examine metadata to determine whether the code is *type-safe*.

Code is type-safe if it only accesses memory locations that it has authority to use. This ensures that objects are isolated from each other and won't do anything unsafe (either inadvertently or maliciously).

After the CLR has verified the code, it can count on the following:

- References to types are strictly compatible with the type that was declared.
- Only appropriate operations can be invoked on the object.
- Identities are what they claim to be.

The .NET Framework JIT is a very robust and feature-rich compiler model. It offers multiple methods of JIT compiling through multiple JIT compilers. The .NET Framework ships with two compilers: a normal compiler and an economy compiler.

The normal compiler works by compiling IL into native code as it is executed. This is similar to a typical compiler used by traditional development environments.

The economy compiler is designed for machines with smaller memory and CPU resources such as handheld devices and smaller form factor devices such as PDAs and Cellular Phones. The economy compiler keeps track of code, and as resources become scarcer, it will throw away older compiled code that hasn't been executed. This means that the IL might need to be re-compiled if it is called after it has been discarded.

Microsoft has developed a Pre-JIT compiler, which allows a developer to compile an assembly prior to deployment. This has the benefit that the first time the code is executed it will be much faster. However, IL code must still be deployed with the application in order for the CLR to perform code verification.

The .NET Framework also solves the problem of locked files when assemblies are in use through the JIT compilers. Because the executing code is kept in the cache, the actual files aren't locked. In fact, in the case of ASP.NET, the CLR will automatically start a new process and forward all new requests to the new process if an assembly is changed. All existing requests will finish in the current process and then it will be killed.

Versioning

In the .NET Framework, versioning is used for more than just documentation; it is actually part of the deployment and execution model. Each assembly has a four-part version number, as shown in Figure 1.3.

Major	Minor	Build	Revision
2	0	2	11

Figure 1.3

Version Number.

When an assembly is built, it records within its manifest the versions of other assemblies that it is using. When an application is deployed, it will attempt to use versions of assemblies according to a *version policy.*

The .NET Framework provides a default version policy that can be overridden. The default version policy specifies that the assembly to be loaded must have the same major and minor version numbers and will pick up the highest build and revision numbers. The default version policy assumes the following:

- Different major version numbers aren't compatible.
- Different minor version numbers usually aren't compatible.
- Different builds should be compatible.
- Different revisions should be compatible.

In the .NET Framework, versioning can be enforced using the default version policy or custom policy can be kept in a custom version policy.

In a custom version policy, a configuration file can require that a specific version be used or not used for an application or for all applications on a machine. For an executable program, the version policy is stored in a file with the application program file but with a .config instead of .exe extension. For instance, an application called MyApplication.exe would have a .config file called MyApplication.config. Listing 1.1 is an example of the contents of a .config file. This .config file tells the CLR that it is OK to use the 2.0.0.0 version of the *DataBaseAccess* assembly instead of the 1.0.0.0 version of *DataBaseAccess*.

Listing 1.1 Application .config File

```
<configuration>
   <runtime>
      <assemblyBinding xmlns="urn:schemas-microsoft-com:asm.v1">
       <dependentAssembly>
         <assemblyIdentity name="DataBaseAccess"
                       publickeytoken="45cf3ba46e0b67b3"
                       culture="en-us" />
         <bindingRedirect oldVersion="1.0.0.0"
                       newVersion="2.0.0.0"/>
       </dependentAssembly>
      </assemblyBinding>
   </runtime>
</configuration>
```

Namespaces

Before exploring the project types available in VB.NET, it is important for developers to understand the concept of namespaces. Namespaces are used to organize components into groups based on organizational and logical reasons. In COM, you had two levels: the component name and the class name. In .NET, you can have many more levels. For instance, to use XML serialization in .NET, you use System.XML. Serialization. In that namespace, various classes can assist you with XML serialization. The .NET Framework uses namespaces to reduce confusion and ambiguity.

In COM-based applications, components are dependent on a 128-bit *Globally Unique Identifier (GUID)* to bind and organize components. Friendly names were limited to a library name and a class name, as shown here:

```
MyApplicationComponent.DataBaseAccess
```

In the .NET Framework, GUIDs are replaced by namespaces. Namespaces allow for a more logical organization of components because they eliminate the two-part friendly name limitation.

Components are now bound to namespaces after a 128-bit hash key—which you create with the Shared Name utility—is applied to the namespace to make sure that no organizations have the same components that confuse the environment. This hashing is known as creating a strong name, which ensures that the wrong component isn't used even though it might have the same Namespace and Class name. Strong names aren't required for private assemblies, but they are required for shared assemblies.

The syntax of namespaces is quite simple, as shown in the following:

```
Namespace NamespaceName
End Namespace
```

The namespace itself follows the format shown here:

```
NamePart1.NamePart2.NamePart3.....NamePartX
```

Microsoft suggests that the first part of the name should be the organization name and the second part should be the technology, such as XML, or Data, or Windows.

The same namespace name might be used in separate .VB files, and the classes will be compiled into a single namespace. This makes multi-developer environments easier to manage. In addition, namespaces can be embedded within namespaces, as shown in Listing 1.2.

Listing 1.2   Namespace Example

```
Namespace Empowered.VisualBasicDotNetForDevelopers.Samples
    Public Class Employee
        ' Employee Code here
    End Class
```

Listing 1.2   Continued

```
        Public Class Department
            ' Department Code here
        End Class
        Namespace Payroll
            Public Class PayCheck
                ' PayCheck code goes here
            End Class
            Public Class TimeSheet
                ' Timesheet code goes here
            End Class
        End Namespace
    End Namespace
End Namespace
```

Note that in Listing 1.2, *NamePart1* is the root namespace. By default, Visual Studio.NET will use the root namespace as the name of the project. To change this setting, use the project properties window and change the Root namespace property, as shown in Figure 1.4.

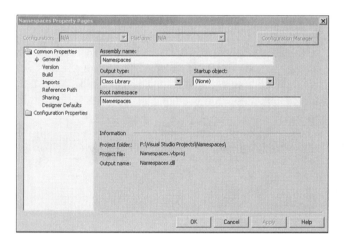

Figure 1.4

Project properties.

With deeply nested namespaces, creating an instance of a class can involve a great deal of typing. The following shows the definition of the Department and TimeSheet class:

```
Dim oDepartment as _
Empowered.VisualBasicDotNetForDevelopers.Samples.Department
Dim oTimeSheet as _
Empowered.VisualBasicDotNetForDevelopers.Samples.Payroll.TimeSheet
```

Thankfully, VB.Net has a keyword to help with this. Before all the code in a file, you can use the `Imports` command to import a namespace that you project references. Listing 1.3 illustrates the use of `Imports`.

Listing 1.3   Using Imports

```
Imports Empowered.VisualBasicDotNetForDevelopers.Samples
Imports Empowered.VisualBasicDotNetForDevelopers.HumanResources.Payroll
Public Class TestClass
    Private oDepartment as Department
    Private oTimeSheet as TimeSheet
End Class
```

This saves a great deal of typing and also makes the code easier to read.

The .NET Framework Class Library

The .NET Framework provides a large and very rich library of classes to be used and extended by application developers. Reuse and extension of these classes will allow developers to be more productive and to develop more robust and feature-rich applications in a shorter time frame because the class library provides many features that previously had to be built from scratch.

At the highest level of the class library is the System namespace, which acts as the root namespace for all classes in the .NET Framework. The System namespace contains all the base data type classes used by application developers to build frameworks and applications. Table 1.1 provides a quick reference to the high-level class namespaces in the .NET Framework.

Table 1.1   The .NET Framework Class Library by Functionality

Service	Namespace
Core	System
Data	System.Data
	System.XML
Component Model	System.CodeDom
	System.ComponentModel
	System.Core
Configuration	System.Configuration
Framework Services	System.Diagnostics
	System.DirectoryServices
	System.ServiceProcesses
	System.Messaging
	System.Timers
Globalization	System.Globalization
	System.Resources
Network and Internet	System.Net
Programming Basic	System.Collections

Table 1.1   Continued

Service	Namespace
	System.IO
	System.Text
	System.Threading
Reflection	System.Reflection
Rich Client GUI	System.Drawing
	System.Windows Forms
Runtime Infrastructure	System.Runtime.InteropServices
Services	System.Runtime.Remoting
	System.Runtime.Serialization
Security	System.Security
Web Services	System.Web

Deployment

One of the design goals of the .NET Framework was to make the deployment of applications as easy as copying files. This is how Active Server Pages and applications that are simply static linked executables are deployed.

For COM–based applications and components, registration in the Windows registry has always been a requirement. In addition, if a component was in use, it was impossible to install a newer version of the component.

The .NET Framework, on the other hand, provides zero-impact deployment and XCOPY installation. Installation of new applications will have no effect on existing applications. Applications will be very easy to re-deploy, even if existing components are used. In fact, an application will be able to use more than one version of the same component.

Because .NET applications supply a great deal of metadata, they don't require registration. If a .NET component is going to be used by COM applications, registration is required. .NET applications support several deployment scenarios with simple XCopy deployment sure to be the most common. With XCopy deployment the CLR will search through the directory and any sub-directories of the application looking for a private assembly to load.

Summary

The .NET Framework is a highly complex and robust platform for building both rich client and Internet-based applications. Microsoft has put a tremendous amount of time and effort into providing the most robust development platform ever implemented.

The .NET Framework is a shift away from the proprietary model that Microsoft has embraced in the past. It is built on standards and built to allow cross-platform execution and cross-platform interoperability.

The burden has been placed on developers to learn about how to best go about building solutions using the platform. It is crucial for developers to learn not only the development language(s) of choice, but also the platform and how to best use it.

This chapter has introduced you to the .NET Framework. It by no means is a complete description of all the facilities and capabilities that the .NET Framework provides. It is up to you to dig deeper into the .NET Framework to make sure that you can build the best applications for your problems.

CHAPTER 2

Visual Studio.NET

Microsoft has always been at the forefront of advanced development environments, and Visual Basic developers have often been the first to experience their innovations. For example IntelliSense, a revolutionary innovation that presents developers with the available properties and methods of an object, first appeared in VB 5. Visual Studio.NET (VS.NET) continues this record of innovations.

Preview of Visual Studio.NET

Visual Studio.NET is a complex development environment built to handle any language. Unfortunately, this can be confusing for developers familiar with a specific language or development environment.

The VB 5 environment was the model for the Visual Studio *Integrated Development Environment (IDE)* in Visual Studio 6, but surprisingly, VB 6 didn't share it.

The VB 6 IDE did include tools to manage projects and project groups, and its editor included extensive IntelliSense support, but the database tools didn't include extensive editors and often relied on Visual Studio 6 for database management tasks.

When you first start up Visual Studio.NET, you will see the DHTML page shown in Figure 2.1. This page contains links to recent projects, to open an existing project, to create a new project, to log a bug, to MSDN Online, to MSDN Search, to Microsoft Newsgroups, and to customize the environment.

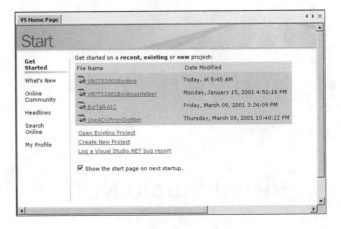

Figure 2.1

The Visual Studio Start page.

Clicking the My Profile link brings you to a page that allows you to customize the environment. In Figure 2.2, I selected Visual Basic Developer from the Profile drop-down box.

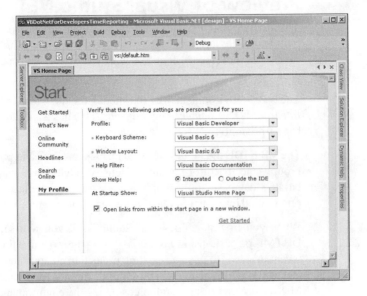

Figure 2.2

Customize Visual Studio.NET for VB development.

After creating a new Windows Application, the IDE will open with a form in the designer just as it does in VB 6. The first difference you will notice is in the toolbox. Figure 2.3 shows the Form designer and the toolbox.

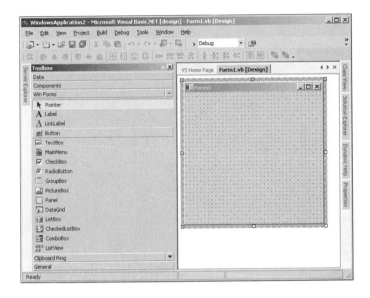

Figure 2.3

The Form designer and toolbox.

New in VS.NET is Dynamic Help. Dynamic Help is an adaptable help system that builds on context-sensitive help. A new window has been added to VS.NET, which contains links to help topics that change as what you are doing changes. Figure 2.4 shows the Dynamic Help window when the form designer is active.

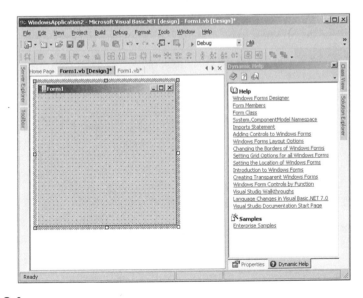

Figure 2.4

Dynamic Help for the Form designer.

Figure 2.5 shows the Dynamic Help window when the code editor is active.

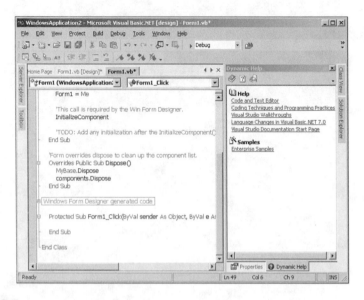

Figure 2.5

Dynamic Help for the code editor.

The Solution Explorer replaces the VB 6 Project Explorer. In addition to integrating a number of items that *should* have been included in VB 6, the Solution Explorer adds significant new functionality. Component references are now included in the Solution Explorer instead of in a separate dialog and Web References are also available here. Figure 2.6 shows the Solution Explorer with three projects in the solution.

One item that I really wish VB 6 had was the ability to view a class and all the properties, methods, interfaces that the class contained. Visual C++ and Visual J++ had this ability, and now that VB.NET is part of VS.NET, VB has this ability too. Figure 2.7 shows the Class View window.

New to VS.NET is a window called Server Explorer. The Server Explorer, which evolved from the data tools in Visual InterDev 6, allows you to design components using a drag-and-drop metaphor. Not only can you use the Server Explorer to manipulate databases, but you can also manipulate other services on a server.

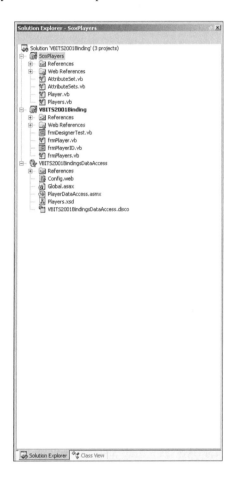

Figure 2.6

The Solution Explorer.

Figure 2.7

The Class View.

Using the Server Explorer, you can drag a stored procedure, event log, or Message Queue to the design service, and the designer will create the code necessary to use that object. Figure 2.8 illustrates the Server Explorer.

Right-clicking Performance Counters in the Server Explorer and selecting Create New Category brings up the dialog box in Figure 2.9.

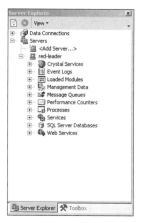

Figure 2.8

The Server Explorer.

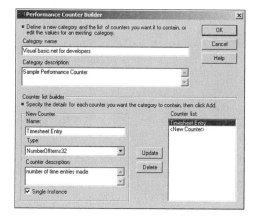

Figure 2.9

The Performance Counter Builder.

Figure 2.10 shows the Server Explorer and the Form designer after I open up the Performance Counters node in the tree and drag it over to the form.

I want to add 1 to the Performance Counter every time the form is clicked, a common operation in business applications. Figure 2.11 shows the code created by the designer and the code I added in `Form1_Click`.

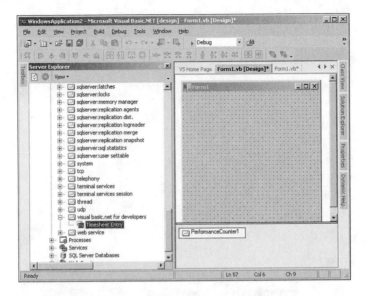

Figure 2.10

The Server Explorer open to Performance Counter.

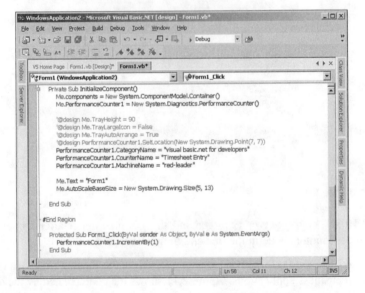

Figure 2.11

Code created by dragging the Performance Counter over to the form.

The Visual Studio.NET IDE

A number of dialogs have been changed for the better in VB.NET. One of the most requested changes is the Menu Editor. Figure 2.12 illustrates the Menu Editor from VB 6, and Figure 2.13 illustrates the menu editor in VS.NET.

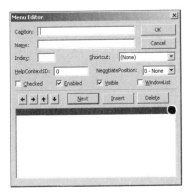

Figure 2.12

VB6 Menu Editor.

As you can see, the VS.NET Menu editor is an interactive tool on the form.

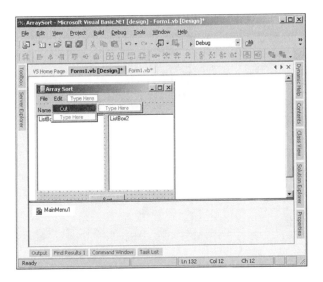

Figure 2.13

VS.NET Menu Editor.

One of the dialog boxes in VB 6 that caused me the most headaches was the References dialog box. (Figure 2.14 depicts the VB 6 References dialog box.)

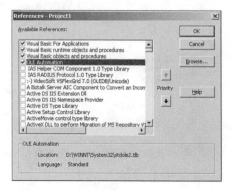

Figure 2.14

The VB 6 References dialog box.

This dialog box didn't allow for any sort of resizing, so figuring out which particular COM object you wanted to reference could be difficult, particularly if the objects used long names or were deep in subdirectories of subdirectories. Figure 2.15 illustrates the VS.NET Add Reference dialog box. Note that it includes multiple types of references—.NET Framework, COM, and Projects.

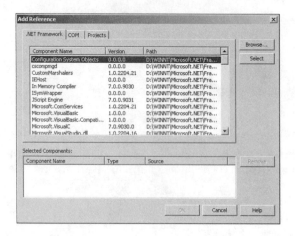

Figure 2.15

The VS.NET Add Reference dialog box.

The Visual Studio.NET Editor

The VS.NET window in which you will spend the most time is the code editor. The editor has a number of new features that make your work easier.

Collapsible Code Blocks

One of my favorite new features of the VS.NET editor is the addition of collapsible code blocks. The small square on the left side of the code window in Figure 2.16 indicates a code block.

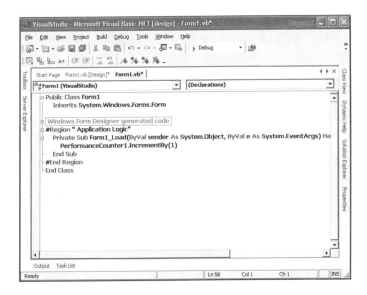

Figure 2.16

Collapsible code block.

Clicking these boxes will collapse or expand the code block. VS.NET automatically creates code blocks for every procedure and every class. In addition, one of the helpful new features is the ability to define your own collapsible code blocks with the new #Region and #End Region code editor commands, as shown in Listing 2.1.

Listing 2.1   *Use of* #Region *and* #End Region

```
#Region "My own code block"
    Private Sub DoSomething()
    End Sub
    Private Sub DoSomethingElse()
    End Sub
#End Region
```

When a code block defined by a #Region and #End Region command is collapsed, a text box with the string from the #Region will be displayed and everything else is hidden. The #Region and #End Region tags allow you to organize your code and document what a group of methods do. Figure 2.17 shows the same code as in Figure 2.16, but it is collapsed.

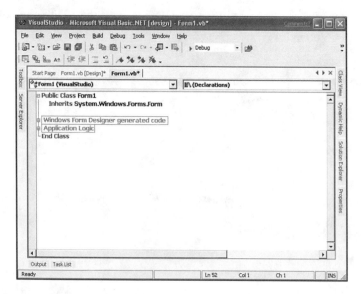

Figure 2.17

Collapsed code.

Automatic Formatting and Completion

Another new feature of the Visual Studio.NET editor is autoformatting and autocompletion of code. For example, when you type an IF statement, the VS.NET editor will insert the Else and End If portions and will also automatically indent any code that you place between the IF and the Else and between the Else and the End If.

The editor has many other formatting features:

- Line numbers can be automatically entered and renumbered as you enter code.
- Word wrap can be activated so that no code extends beyond the end of a line.
- Hovering over anything gives you information. And if the code includes XML documentation (which will be available to VB.NET as an add-in), hovering above a method will display the documentation for the method.

Embedded URLs in Code and Comments

A great new feature of the VS.NET editor is the ability to include URLs in code and comments. For example, you can add links to additional help for a section of code right in the code. Or you could place your e-mail address right in the code, and someone else looking at the code can simply click the link to send you a note. The VB 6 Migration Wizard uses this feature to link to more detailed descriptions of code issues.

Other Editors

VS.NET includes a number of other editors to assist you in development. These include a Cascading Style Sheet editor, an XML editor, an XSL editor, a Stored Procedure editor, and an HTML editor. All these editors feature IntelliSense.

The HTML editor and the XML editor are particularly interesting. The HTML editor adapts to the HTML version you choose. The XML editor will perform validation and limit what you can place in the XML based on the XML schema that you choose for the XML document.

VB and the .NET Framework

VB has been around now for 10 years and has gone through six versions. It has evolved from a simple, somewhat limited Rapid Application Development tool to a powerful development tool that is also great for building COM components.

However, despite the fact that it has become the most popular development tool in the world, VB has had to deal with a stigma of being a "toy" language. This has never been the case of course, but some people have denigrated VB for various reasons, such as

- Difficult to use the complete Windows API
- Doesn't support full object orientation
- Requires a runtime

VB also did some great things that changed the software development industry:

- Component-based development via VB controls (VBXs) and their successors, ActiveX Controls
- The Rapid Application Development model
- Visual designers
- Event-Based programming

The .NET Framework has taken all the things that VB has done right, improved on them, and exposed them to non-VB developers. Many of the design decisions within Visual Studio.Net evolved from VB. In fact, as quoted by David Mendlen of Microsoft, a major design goal of ASP.NET is to make Internet application development "as easy as VB development."

An Introduction to VB.NET

Many people believe that C# is Microsoft's tool of choice for .NET, mostly because C# has been used by Microsoft for building parts of .NET. But this is simply because C# was the first language built for .NET and has a huge head start. The .NET Framework is built to support all languages, and VB is a first-class .NET language.

Visual Basic.NET is a complete re-write of VB. Among the many changes is that VB.NET, under the covers, relies on the .NET Framework, not the Windows API. In supporting the .NET Framework, VB retains the majority of the syntax to which developers are accustomed; the new syntax additions follow the guidelines established by the existing language.

VB, unlike C/C++, has never been a standards-based language. It has been controlled by Microsoft and has never been through a standards body. This has served VB well in the past, but has also allowed Microsoft to make changes to the language that break applications built with previous versions. This will change with the .NET Framework. For Microsoft to break a VB.NET application in the future, Microsoft will have to break the .NET Framework.

As a .NET language, VB supports everything that the .NET platform provides. It is the premier tool from Microsoft to develop completely managed applications using the .NET framework.

VB.NET Design Goals

As a company, Microsoft is shifting from providing operating systems to providing services over the Internet. These services, known as Web Services, will provide the developers the ability to create widely distributed applications.

To ensure that developers support this concept, the goal is for VB.NET to do for Web Service development what the first version of Visual Basic did for Windows development. To do so, VB.NET has the following design goals:

- VB.NET will be immediately recognizable to VB developers.
- VB.NET will have a simple and straightforward syntax.
- VB.NET will allow the use of all major features of the .NET Framework.
- VB.NET will support the .NET Framework multi-language environment.
- Applications will be reasonably upgradeable from VB 6.
- VB.NET will retain the syntax of previous versions of VB as much as possible.

These design goals left the VB.NET team enough leverage to produce a world-class language that makes it easy to build .NET applications with VB.

Accessibility

Visual Basic, as a language, has always been accessible to a wide audience of developers and potential developers. It has strived to allow developers to start quickly and build up skills as they go.

VB's accessibility is both a blessing and a curse. It has brought in many people who never did development before, and many of them have been very successful; many were not so successful. Unfortunately, VB often gets blamed for some developers' lack of success.

A key feature that has attracted developers and potential developers to VB in the past has been the ease of getting started. The reasons that VB is so approachable are numerous.

VB syntax doesn't scare people away. It is quite easy for a developer to read a piece of VB code and understand what is going on. With the syntax of the language so appealing, developers can become comfortable with VB much more quickly than with more traditional languages and tools such as C/C++.

VB, similar to object-oriented programming languages, hides the implementation from the interface. One of the major ideas of object-oriented programming is encapsulation. Encapsulation simply means that you should present things that can be done but keep how it is actually accomplished a secret. For example, a Button has a click event. VB hides the message handling and message loop that cause the actual event to be raised. VB has traditionally hidden the internals of Windows programming from the VB developer. (Of course, developers have found ways to get around many of these built-in limitations.)

Another key for beginners is the ability to do typeless programming. *Typeless programming* is the ability to define variables without declaring what data type the variable will hold. This allows the variable to hold virtually any data type. Typeless programming shouldn't be encouraged because it leads to hard-to-find bugs in applications. However, it does allow programmers to get started without learning what all the types are and how to properly convert from one type to another.

VB is a language that is easy to get started with. But as easy is as it is to get started, it is very important that developers explore not only the functions and capabilities of VB, but also the best way to do tasks such as database access, string manipulation, state management, and resource management.

VB, at its core, is based on simplicity and verbosity. If VB is used correctly, the code produced is almost self-documenting. VB avoids the use of special characters and operators in favor of words and commands except when the operators are extremely common and simple. When I teach developers, I always stress that you need to write code that the next developer can work on. VB makes this very easy.

Other languages such as C/C++ and derivatives such as Java and C# rely much more on code comments. Code comments are a very good thing, but because code is maintained through the years, comments tend to be left as is. If the code itself creates the documentation, the documentation stays current.

Some developers dislike the fact that it takes more typing to achieve the same result in VB than it takes in other languages. This is one of the reasons many C/C++ developers consider VB a "toy" language, when in effect what this does is make VB easier to maintain.

OOP Support

From the very beginning, Visual Basic has been an object-based language. This means that VB has always used objects in the form of controls or other components to do development. In version 4, VB became an object-oriented language, and version 5 added several new features that increased this support. But not until VB.NET has it fully supported all aspects of object-oriented programming.

VB.NET introduces developers to Implementation inheritance in a very big way. In addition to being able to inherit from classes created with VB, VB.NET can inherit from any .NET-compliant language, including C#, JScript.NET, Managed C++, or any other language built for the .NET Framework, whether implemented by Microsoft or from another vendor.

Interface inheritance, which is still key to building flexible applications, has also been enhanced in a number of ways in VB.NET. The syntax has changed to allow one method to be the implementation of multiple interfaces.

A number of additional keywords have been added to assist in the design of flexible and powerful objects with VB.NET. This includes keywords to control how methods can be overridden and overloaded, how methods can be overloaded, and how methods and properties are protected and exposed.

With its integration into the .NET Framework, VB finally has an object-oriented method of obtaining addresses to functions through the use of delegates. A *delegate* is a very elegant method of synchronizing callbacks, events, and other methods of function manipulation.

With all the changes in VB.NET, the language is now a fully functional object-oriented language with a simple and understandable model for building applications for the .NET platform.

Although much of the procedural-based syntax of earlier versions of VB is still available in VB.NET, I suggest that when developing new applications and reworking existing code, you move away from the procedural-based methods to the newer object-oriented methods.

Modern Language Constructs

Although Visual Basic.NET has maintained legacy methods of error handling, it has added structured exception handling, which should greatly simplify and clarify exception handling.

VB.NET introduces the idea of attribute-based programming, which is part of the .NET Framework. Attribute-based programming allows developers to apply properties to methods in order to control other code interacting with the methods. This tells the runtime how to treat pieces of code.

Safety and Security

The .NET Framework brings to VB.NET a complete infrastructure for secure applications. Security in previous versions of VB was accomplished using a variety of methods, including custom code, Windows-based security, and the use of COM/MTS and COM+. In VB.NET, security mechanisms are built directly into the .NET Framework. Through the use of .NET Security, VB.NET applications can easily protect data and processes from inappropriate access.

VB.NET also adds a new feature to ensure type safety. Prior to VB.NET, VB would attempt to convert any data type to any other data type. This was affectionately called "evil type coercion" by developers who had been bitten by this functionality—it can make debugging extraordinarily difficult.

By default, VB.NET now requires explicit type casting. This functionality can be turned off, but that is only suggested for applications being ported from earlier versions of VB or for applications that must do late binding to objects.

Multi-Language Integration

Classes built in VB.NET are fully extensible and capable of extending other classes built with other languages. VB.NET classes can be used as base classes in other languages, and can use and inherit from classes built with other languages. This allows developers to choose the correct language for a particular process. If a process is formula intensive, a language built for formulas might be the best choice. If a process is string-manipulation intensive, a language built for that use might be best.

COM and Windows API Interoperability

VB.NET components can use COM components and be used by COM components and applications. Access to the Windows API has been designed into the .NET Framework through .NET Framework classes and through pInvoke, a method familiar to VB developers. Although the .NET Framework has been built so that it can be cross platform, it also allows access to the underlying platform if the developer needs to do this—a vast difference between Java technologies and the .NET Framework. We'll examine interoperability in more detail in Chapter 12, "Interoperability."

Summary

Visual Studio.NET is easily the most productive development ever developed by Microsoft and quite possibly the best tool ever developed by any vendor. VB developers should be very comfortable working within the tool, and Visual InterDev developers should feel right at home.

The Visual Studio.NET also can be thought of as the first .NET Framework application because a great deal of the IDE was actually built with the .NET Framework.

CHAPTER 3

Object-Oriented Programming Concepts

In its lifetime, VB has varied from an object-*based* development tool to an object-*oriented* development tool, but previous versions of Visual Basic had still been missing a few key features.

Using previous versions of VB, programmers have been able to create classes and use those classes in building applications. But VB was missing key object-oriented development features. This hasn't stopped developers from building robust component-based systems, but it has hampered them in building extensible frameworks.

This isn't the case with Visual Basic.NET. In fact, object-oriented programming is required in the .Net Framework, and VB has become a full-featured, object-oriented development language.

New to the language is support for inheritance, new methods of exposing objects, and support for attribute-based programming. Visual Basic.NET also has improved support for interfaces, properties, and events.

Object-oriented programming is very important when building complex applications. When using past versions of VB, many choose not to explore the use of object-oriented programming techniques. This is a mistake that cannot be repeated in VB.NET. To effectively use VB.NET, a developer must understand and apply object-oriented concepts.

Object-oriented development has four key concepts in relation to programming: abstraction, encapsulation, polymorphism, and inheritance. We'll discuss each of these in this chapter.

Abstraction in Visual Basic.NET

Abstraction is the ability to generalize an object as a data type that has a specific set of characteristics and is able to perform a set of actions. For example, you can create an abstraction of a dog with characteristics, such as `color`, `height`, and `weight`, and actions such as `run` and `bite`. The characteristics are called *properties*, and the actions are called *methods*.

Object-oriented languages provide abstraction via *classes*. Classes define the properties and methods of an object type, but it is important to remember that a developer cannot use a class directly; instead, an object must be created from a class—it must be *instantiated*.

VB has supported classes since version 4.0. Up until VB.NET, each class was implemented as a separate file that abstracted an object.

Listing 3.1 shows an instance of a VB6 class, and shows a Visual Basic.NET class. VB.NET changes the way you define your classes. First, in VB 6 a class was defined as a file with a .CLS extension: in VB.NET this is done in code. In the example in Listing 3.2, notice the `Public Class Car` and the `End Class` statements.

Listing 3.1 VB6 *Class*

```
Public MaximumSpeed as Integer
Public ModelName as String
Public Sub Accelerate()
    'Some code to make the car go
End Sub
Public Sub Stop()
        'Some code to make the car stop
End Sub
```

Listing 3.2 VB.NET *Class*

```
Public Class Car
    Public MaximumSpeed as Integer
    Public ModelName as String
    Public Sub Accelerate()
        'Some code to make the car go
    End Sub
    Public Sub Stop()
        'Some code to make the car stop
    End Sub
End Class
```

These listings show an abstraction of a very simple car. To use this abstraction, an instance of the class must be created. There were multiple ways to create an instance of a class in VB 6. Things have changed in VB.NET. Using `New` is now the preferred method of creating an object. Listing 3.3 shows three methods for creating an instance in VB 6 and Listing 3.4 shows four methods for doing so in VB.NET.

Listing 3.3   *Three Methods to Create a Class Instance in VB 6*

```
Dim oCar as New Car
Set oCar = New Car
Set oCar = CreateObject("Vehicles.Car")
```

You will notice that in Listing 3.4 I didn't include CreateObject. CreateObject has been denigrated to only create classic COM components and won't create an instance of a .NET component. The replacement for CreateObject is the System.Activator. CreateInstance method. (The Assembly.CreateInstance method maps to the System.Activator.CreateInstance method.)

Listing 3.4   *Four Methods to Create a Class Instance in VB.NET*

```
Dim oCar as New Car
oCar = New Car
oCar = Assembly.CreateInstance("Car")
oCar = System.Activator.CreateInstance("Car","URIToAssembly")
```

Encapsulation in VB.NET

Encapsulation is the exposure of properties and methods of an object while hiding the actual implementation from the outside world. In other words, the object is treated as a black box—developers who use the object should have no need to understand how it actually works.

Encapsulation allows developers to build objects that can be changed without affecting the client code that uses them. The key is that the *interface* of the object, the set of exposed properties and methods of the object, doesn't change even if the internal implementation does. VB has supported encapsulation since version 4.0.

Lets take a look at two trivial examples of a Person class. Listings 3.5 and 3.6 and implement the same functionality in two different ways.

Listing 3.5   Person *Class Implementation #1*

```
Public Class Person
        Private m_sFirstName as String
    Private m_sLastName as String
    Public Property FirstName() as String
        Get
            FirstName = m_sFirstName
        End Get
        Set(ByVal Value as String)
            m_sFirstName = Value
        End Set
    End Property
    Public Property LastName() as String
        Get
            LastName = m_sLastName
        End Get
```

Listing 3.5 *Continued*

```
        Set(ByVal Value as String)
            m_sLastName = Value
        End Set
    End Property
    ReadOnly Property FullName() as String
        Get
            FullName = m_sLastName & ", " & m_sFirstName
        End Get
    End Property
End Class
```

Listing 3.6 Person *Class Implementation #2*

```
Public Class Person
        Private m_sFirstName as String
    Private m_sLastName as String
    Private m_sFullName as String
    Public Property FirstName() as String
        Get
            FirstName = m_sFirstName
        End Get
        Set(ByVal Value as String)
            m_sFirstName = Value
            m_sFullName = m_sLastName & ", " & m_sFirstName
        End Set
    End Property
    Public Property LastName() as String
        Get
            LastName = m_sLastName
        End Get
        Set(ByVal Value as String)
            m_sLastName = Value
            m_sFullName = m_sLastName & ", " & m_sFirstName
        End Set
    End Property
    ReadOnly Property FullName() as String
        Get
            FullName = m_sFirstName
        End Get
    End Property
End Class
```

This illustrates how the internal implementation of the classes is different but the external interface encapsulates how the class works internally. That is the goal of encapsulation: to allow a developer to transparently use different implementations of the same object.

Polymorphism in VB.NET

Polymorphism is the concept that different objects have different implementations of the same characteristic. For example, consider two objects, one representing a Porsche 911 and the other a Toyota Corolla. They are both cars; that is, they both derive from the Car class, and they both have a drive method, but the implementations of the methods could be drastically different.

Polymorphism sounds a great deal like encapsulation, but it is different. Encapsulation has to do with hiding the internal implementation of an object. Polymorphism has to do with multiple classes having the same interface.

Visual Basic introduced a very limited support for polymorphism in VB 4.0 through the use of late binding. *Late binding* is the technology for code to determine at runtime what properties and methods a given object provides. This allows code to create any object and attempt to call a method or property of that object without knowing whether the object supports the method at compile time. Given two different classes with the same properties and methods, a variable of type object could be used to instantiate an object of either class. This worked, but did not provide any type safety at compile time. *Type safety* is the concept to ensure that a string is used as a string, an integer is used as an integer, and a Boolean is used as a Boolean. Without type safety, potentially more errors can occur when a user is executing a program rather than when the program is compiled. Type safety also is one mechanism to prevent hackers from overloading code with a destructive piece of code.

VB 5 introduced an additional form of polymorphism using interfaces. An *interface* defines a set of properties, methods, and events that a class implements. Any number of classes can implement the same interface. A variable that instantiates an interface can reference any class that implements that interface.

Interfaces provide early binding to an object, which can greatly improve performance and also provide type protection at compile time. Interfaces were the most important feature introduced in VB 5, but are still one of the least understood or used.

As you'll see later in this chapter, VB.NET has improved support for interfaces. The language now has direct support for interfaces creation, which was done in earlier versions either via IDL or by creating empty classes. In addition, a single method can be the implementation of methods in multiple interfaces.

Listing 3.7 illustrates polymorphism through late binding and Listing 3.8 illustrates polymorphism through early binding. Both listings show classes that implement Ride methods. As shown, whether using either late binding or early binding, a method can call either class's method without caring what kind of object it is using. This is the essence of polymorphism: It provides the ability to create code that can use different objects that implement the same interfaces.

Listing 3.7 Polymorphism Through Late Binding

```
Public Class RollerCoaster
    Public Sub Ride()
        Console.WriteLine("Here we go")
        Console.WriteLine("Click, Click ,Click")
        Console.WriteLine("Oh, *&@&#%")
        Console.WriteLine("That was great")
    End Sub
End Class
Public Class MerryGoRound
    Public Sub Ride()
        Console.WriteLine("OK will go on it")
        Console.Writeline("Nap Time")
        Console.WriteLine("Yea its over")
    End Sub
End Class
```

Some code somewhere else in the application:

```
Private Sub DayAtTheAmusementPark()
        Dim oRollerCoaster as New RollerCoaster
        Dim oMerryGoRound as New MerryGoRound
        Call GoOnRide(oRollerCoaster)
        Call GoOnRide(oMerryGoRound)
End Sub
Private Sub GoOnRide(oRide as Object)
    oRide.Ride()
End Sub
```

For better performance and to find errors at compile time, early binding is the preferred choice. Early binding can be accomplished through the use of Interfaces (see Listing 3.8).

Listing 3.8 Polymorphism Through Interfaces

```
Public Interface IAmusementParkRide
    Sub Ride()
End Interface
Public Class RollerCoaster
    Implements IAmusementParkRide
    Public Sub IAmusementParkRide_Ride()
        Console.WriteLine("Here we go")
        Console.WriteLine("Click, Click ,Click")
        Console.WriteLine("Oh, *&@&#%")
        Console.WriteLine("That was great")
    End Sub
End Class
Public Class MerryGoRound
    Implements IAmusementParkRide
```

Listing 3.8 **Continued**

```
    Public Sub IAmusementParkRide_Ride()
        Console.WriteLine("OK will go on it")
        Console.Writeline("Nap Time")
        Console.WriteLine("Yea its over")
    End Sub
End Class
```

Some code somewhere else in the application:

```
Private Sub DayAtTheAmusementPark()
        Dim oRollerCoaster as New RollerCoaster
        Dim oMerryGoRound as New MerryGoRound
        Call GoOnRide(oRollerCoaster)
        Call GoOnRide(oMerryGoRound)
End Sub
Private Sub GoOnRide(oRide as IAmusementParkRide)
    oRide.Ride()
End Sub
```

Inheritance in VB.NET

Inheritance is the idea that one class, called a subclass, can be based on another class, called a base class. Inheritance provides a mechanism for creating hierarchies of objects. For example, a dog is a mammal and a collie is a dog. Thus the dog class inherits the properties and methods of the mammal class, and the collie class inherits from both dog and mammal.

The objects in a hierarchy have two different types of relationships to one another, referred to in object-oriented parlance as HasA and IsA relationships. For example, a Collie IsA dog and HasA tail. Implementation inheritance is the object-oriented feature that supports IsA relationships. Containment supports HasA relationships. Implementation inheritance is also another way that VB.NET supports polymorphism. A function might accept a parameter typed as **mammal** and then an object that is derived from mammal can be passed in as the parameter.

Implementation Inheritance

Since version 5, Visual Basic has supported interface inheritance through the imple-ments keyword. In previous versions of VB, the idea of using an existing class as the starting point in the development of a new class wasn't possible. This language feature is known as *implementation inheritance*. Now in VB.NET, implementation inheritance has been added to the language.

Previous versions of Visual Basic were targeted to COM development, which discouraged the use of implementation inheritance. Visual Basic.NET, on the other hand, is targeted for the .Net Framework, which is based on implementation inheritance.

Support for implementation inheritance is perhaps the biggest change in Visual Basic.NET. Table 3.1 shows the new keywords that have been added along with new statements and methods.

Table 3.1   New Language Elements for Implementation Inheritance

Element	Context	Description
Inherits	Class Statement	Indicates the class from which the new class inherits
NotInheritable	Class Statement	Indicates that a class that cannot be inherited from
MustInherit	Class Statement	Indicates a class that must be inherited by another class
Overridable	Procedure	Indicates a procedure that can be overridden by a subclass
NotOverridable	Procedure	Indicates a procedure that cannot be overridden in a subclass
MustOverride	Procedure	Indicates a procedure that must be overridden in a subclass
Overrides	Procedure	Indicates that a procedure is overriding a procedure in a base class
MyBase	Code	Allows code in a class to invoke code in the base class
MyClass	Code	Allows code in a class to invoke code in itself
Protected	Function, Sub, Field, Property	Indicates that code in a child class can access this

The example in Listing 3.9 shows a number of the new keywords in action. The code describes a class with four properties and one method. Any class that inherits from this class must override the ClassName property. No class that inherits from this class can override the BaseClassName property. Any class that inherits from this class can freely override the remaining properties and methods.

Listing 3.9 Person ***Class***

```
Public Class Person
     Protected c_sFirstName as String
     Protected c_sLastName as String
     MustOverride ReadOnly Property ClassName() as String
        Get
            ClassName = "Person"
        End Get
     End Property
     NotOverridable ReadOnly Property BaseClassName() as String
        Get
            BaseClassName = "Person"
```

Listing 3.9   Continued

```
            End Get
        End Property
        Overidable Public Property FirstName() as String
        Get
            FirstName = c_sFirstName
        End Get
        Set(ByVal Value as string)
            c_sFirstName = Value
        End Set
    End Property
    Overidable Public Property LastName() as String
        Get
            LastName = c_sLastName
        End Get
        Set(ByVal Value as string)
            c_sLastName = Value
        End Set
    End Property
    Overridable Sub Speak()
        Console.WriteLine("I am " & c_sFirstName & " " & c_sLastName)
        Console.WriteLine(" and I am a Person.")
    End Sub
End Class
```

This example illustrates VB.NET's implementation of inheritance. In keeping with the language's design goals, VB requires that everything be very explicit. Table 3.2 compares some of the VB.NET keywords used to control the accessibility of classes and class members with their C# equivalents. In my opinion, the VB.NET keywords are much clearer than the C# keywords.

Table 3.2   VB Keywords Compared to C# Keywords

VB.NET	C#
NotInheritable	Sealed
MustInherit	Abstract
MustOverride	Virtual
Inherits	:

Listing 3.10 illustrates a class that inherits from the Person class.

Listing 3.10   NewPerson **Class**

```
Public Class NewPerson
    Inherits Person
    MustOverride Overrides Public ReadOnly Property ClassName() as String
        Get
            ClassName = "NewPerson"
```

Listing 3.10   Continued

```
        End Get
    End Property
    Overrides Sub Speak()
        Console.WriteLine("My name is " & c_sFirstName & " " & c_sLastName)
        Console.WriteLine(" and I am a new person.")
    End Sub
End Public
```

This class shows a number of new keywords in use. Inherits indicates the class inherited. The ClassName property accessibility is set to MustOverride and Public, indicating that any class that inherits from this class must override this property. The Overrides keyword indicates that the ClassName property and the Speak method from the base class are being overridden by the new class.

c_sFirstName and c_sLastName aren't defined in the new class. They were defined in the base class, and their accessibility was set to protected. We will examine the accessibility modifiers in more detail in Chapter 4, "Methods, Properties, and Events."

EFFECTIVE IMPLEMENTATION INHERITANCE

Analysis and design are paramount to an effective solution using implementation inheritance. VB.NET encourages developers to take time out to design because it requires developers to be very explicit about their intentions.

Class methods and properties must be marked as Overridable to allow inheritance. A class that inherits from a base class must mark methods that are being overridden with the Overrides keyword. Finally, if a class cannot be inherited from, this must be indicated with the NotInheritable keyword.

The requirement that a developer explicitly define his intentions helps to alleviate a problem known as "the fragile base class."

An example of the fragile base class problem is when a base class adds a new method that has the same name as a method name in a class that inherits from the base. The developer of the subclass never intended the method in the subclass to override the base class, but now this is exactly what has happened. This can cause problems with how clients use the class.

This problem cannot occur in VB.NET because of the declarative syntax required.

Containment

Containment, as we saw earlier, is the mechanism for implementing HasA relationships. Containment is actually rather simple, and isn't supported by anything specific within a language. In VB, for one object to have a HasA relationship to another, the first object will simply hold an instance of a object. For example, in my Person class, if I wanted to define a HasA relationship to the person's dog, I would simply add the code shown in Listing 3.11.

Listing 3.11   Containment Illustrates HasA Relationships

```
Private c_oDog as Dog
Public Property MyDog() as Dog
    Get
        MyDog = c_oDog
    End Get
End Property
Public Sub GetADog(ByVal Breed as String, ByVal Name as String)
    c_oDog = New Dog(Breed,Name)
End Sub
```

Interface-Based Programming

Building component-based solutions has a number of unique problems and benefits. One of the key benefits is the ability to build applications on a piece-by-piece basis. The whole idea is to build software in the same way industry builds other products—instead of a single monolithic system, systems are built as individual components.

This sounds great, but like so many great ideas, it's easier said than done, especially with earlier versions of Visual Basic. In theory, one should be able to take a component that does something and replace it with another component that does the same thing. But in most circumstances, this just doesn't happen.

Why? For performance reasons, developers prefer to use early binding to link components together at compile time. This causes components to be tightly coupled because in order to use early binding, components had to be explicitly referenced. This can lead to a nasty chain of recompilation, with a minor change to one component requiring recompilation of every component that depends on it, and all the components that depend on them, and so on.

With the introduction in VB 5 of the ability to keep the definition of an interface separate from the component that implements the interface, the need to tightly couple components in this way disappears. By referencing the interface rather than a class, an instance of any class that implements that interface can be created.

This technique allows a developer to continually change which component he actually uses. This is particularly important when a component and code using the component are being developed simultaneously. During the early stages of development, a simple implementation of a component can be used. Later, the completed implementation can be used, and finally some time later, a completely new implementation can be used to replace the initial implementation.

Interfaces make the complete software development process easier. They stress analysis and design, they make maintenance of applications easier, and they make deployment of applications easier. Interfaces are like car tires. How difficult would it be if you could only put one brand, style, and rating of tire on your car?

Changes to Interfaces in VB.NET

A few enhancements have been made to interfaces in Visual Basic.NET. The most important of these is that events can now be part of an interface. (In previous versions of VB, events were always late bound and never part of the interface.)

The mechanism for defining an interface has also been changed. In previous versions of VB, interfaces were created by coding a class or by using IDL. Listing 3.12 illustrates the new interface syntax with an event included in the interface. Although this is a very simple example, it is clear that interface definition in VB.NET follows the same clear Visual Basic syntax.

Listing 3.12   Define an Interface in VB.NET

```
Public Interface IEmployee
    Property FirstName() As String
    Property LastName() As String
    Function ChangeSalary(ByVal PercentageIncrease as Decimal) as Decimal
    Event Fired(ByVal ReasonCode as Integer)
End Interface
```

Interfaces in VB.NET have a number of other enhancements, including inheritance. Once an interface has been created, it can be implemented by any .NET language. To implement an interface in VB.NET, you can use the method that was introduced in VB 5 or the new method introduced in VB.NET. Listing 13 illustrates implementing an interface in VB 5 or VB 6. Listing 3.14 illustrates implementing an interface in VB.NET.

Listing 3.13   Implementing an Interface VB6 Style

```
Public Class Employee
    Implements IEmployee
    Private c_sFirstName as String
    Private c_sLastName as String
    Private c_dSalary as Decimal
    Private Property IEmployee_FirstName() as String
        Get
            IEmployee_FirstName = c_sFirstName
        End Get
        Set(ByVal Value as String)
            c_sFirstName = value
        End Set
    End Property
        Private Property IEmployee_LastName() as String
        Get
            IEmployee_LastName = c_sLastName
        End Get
        Set(ByVal Value as String)
            c_sLastName = value
        End Set
    End Property
```

Listing 3.14   Continued

```
Private Function IEmployee_ChangeSalary _
                (ByVal PercentageIncrease as Decimal) as Decimal
    Return c_dSalary * (PercentageIncrease / 100)
End Function
' In this example I will not be implementing the event…
'Although this is required…The syntax is
    ' complex and for brevity will wait for the section on events
End Class
```

VB.NET provides a cleaner, more flexible and easier to understand syntax for implementing interfaces. This can be seen in Listing 3.14.

Listing 3.14   Implementing an Interface VB.NET Style

```
Public Class Employee
    Implements IEmployee
    Private c_sFirstName as String
    Private c_sLastName as String
    Private c_dSalary as Decimal
    Public Property FirstNameofEmployee() as String _
                    Implements IEmployee.FirstName
        Get
            IEmployee_FirstName = c_sFirstName
        End Get
        Set(ByVal Value as String)
            c_sFirstName = value
        End Set
    End Property
        Public Property LastNameOfEmployee() as String _
                    Implements IEmployee.LastName

        Get
            IEmployee_LastName = c_sLastName
        End Get
        Set(ByVal Value as String)
            c_sLastName = value
        End Set
    End Property
    Private Function UpdateSalary(ByVal PercentageIncrease as Decimal) _
                    as Decimal Implements IEmployee.ChangeSalary
        Return c_dSalary * (PercentageIncrease / 100)
    End Function
    ' In this example I will not be implementing the event…
    'Although this is required…The syntax is
        ' complex and for brevity will wait for the section on events
End Class
```

The new style is far more flexible. For example, a class can implement more than one interface, and then use a single method to do the implementation of a method in both interfaces. Listings 3.15 and 3.16 show how this had to be implemented in VB 5 or VB 6, whereas Listings 3.17 and 3.20 illustrate how to accomplish this in VB.NET.

Listing 3.15   Implementation of IEmployee **in VB 5 or VB 6**

```
Private Function IEmployee_ChangeSalary() As Decimal
    Return c_dSalary * (PercentageIncrease / 100)
End Function
```

In Listing 3.16 we implement an additional interface in the same class and delegate to the previous interface functionality.

Listing 3.16   Implementation of IEmployee **and** IEmployee2 **in VB 5 or VB 6**

```
Private Function IEmployee_ChangeSalary _
                (ByVal PercentageIncrease as Decimal) As Decimal
    Return c_dSalary * (PercentageIncrease / 100)
End Function
Private Function IEmployee2_ChangeSalary _
                (ByVal PercentageIncrease as Decimal) As Decimal
    Return IEmployee_ChangeSalary(PercentageIncrease)
End Function
```

This isn't the case in VB.NET; you would simply change the existing methods implements clause (see Listing 3.17).

Listing 3.17   Implementation of IEmployee **in VB.NET**

```
Private Function UpdateSalary(ByVal PercentageToChange as Decimal) _
                as Decimal Implements IEmployee.ChangeSalary
    Return c_dSalary * (PercentageToChange / 100)
End Function
```

VB.NET allows us to add just a little bit of extra code to the function declaration to indicate that this function is also the implementation of Iemployee2.ChangeSalary (see Listing 3.18).

Listing 3.18   Implementation of IEmployee **and** IEmployee2 **in VB.NET**

```
Private Function UpdateSalary((ByVal PercentageToChange as Decimal) _
                as Decimal Implements IEmployee.ChangeSalary,
IEmployee2.ChangeSalary
    Return c_dSalary * (PercentageToChange / 100)
End Function
```

Summary

VB.NET has upgraded the VB language to take advantage of every object-oriented feature that has been implemented in the .NET Framework. The single most drastic and time-consuming part of learning how to use VB.NET and the .NET Framework will be to learn how to use the new object-oriented features effectively.

As a VB developer, it will be mandatory to take some time to learn how to use these features in the correct manner. With power comes responsibility, so use the new features wisely and be prepared to spend time changing your first attempts.

This chapter only scratches the surface of the power that object-oriented programming and the .NET Framework provide. The true learning curve of the .NET Framework is learning the portions of the .NET Framework that you will use 80% of the time. In addition, learning how to correctly architect your solutions is paramount.

CHAPTER 4

Methods, Properties, and Events

Classes are made up of methods, properties and events. *Methods* are the actions that the object performs, *properties* provide access to the data of an object, and *events* are notifications that objects provide to users of the object. Although these were all available in previous versions of Visual Basic, they provide a much richer functionality in Visual Basic.NET.

Methods

Methods are the actions that an object performs. There are two types of methods in VB: subs and functions. Although subs and functions in classes are the same as other subs and functions in VB, VB.NET has made quite a few subtle changes.

Changes to Parameters

The default for passing parameters has been changed from `ByRef` to `ByVal`. When converting applications from previous versions, it is very important to explicitly indicate `ByRef` if that is what is needed.

In addition, optional parameters, although they are still supported, must now have default values. Further, because the `IsMissing` function no longer serves any purpose, it has been removed.

In previous versions of VB, changes made to properties that were passed `ByRef` weren't copied out of the procedure. In VB.NET, the property is now passed in and out of the procedure. Listing 4.1 illustrates this change. In this example, the `FirstName` property of the employee will be changed. In VB 6 that wasn't the case.

Listing 4.1 ByRef *Property Parameter*

```
Public Sub ChangeName(ByRef Name as String)
    Name = "Mr. " & Name
End Sub

'Some code that uses the above function
Call ChangeName(oEmployee.FirstName)
```

Calling Procedures

VB.NET now requires that all calls to subs or functions be contained in parenthesis. The following shows two calls: The first one is legal in VB 6, but no longer legal in VB.NET, and the second one shows the legal version in VB.NET.

Legal VB 6, Illegal VB.NET

```
ChangeName sFirstName
```

Legal VB.NET, Illegal VB 6

```
ChangeName(sFirstName)
```

Returning Values

In previous versions of VB, values were returned from functions by assigning them to the name of the function, as shown in Listing 4.2. That syntax is still valid in VB.NET, but the new Return *returnvalue* statement is the preferred syntax. Listing 4.3 shows the syntax of the Return statement.

Figure Listing 4.2   Return a Value in VB6

```
Public Function MyFunction() as String
    MyFunction = "Hello World"
End Function
```

The Return statement returns the value named by the variable, constant, or function that is the parameter (see Listing 4.3). It is extremely important to note that any code following the return statement won't be executed. This is a change from the method in VB 6 where code continues to execute.

Listing 4.3   Return a Value in VB.NET

```
Public Function MyFunction() as String
    Return "ReturnValue"
End Function
```

Listing 4.4 illustrates a technique commonly used in VB 6 that will no longer work if you change it to use the Return statement.

Listing 4.4 *Initialize the Function's Return Value*

```
Public Function MyFunction(byval SomeFlag as Boolean) as String
    MyFunction = "One Value" 'Set the default return value
    If SomeFlag then
        MyFunction = "Another Value" 'Set the return value to a new value
    End If
End Function
```

If you attempt to code the same way in VB.NET using the `Return` statement, you won't get the same results. Listing 4.5 illustrates this problem.

Listing 4.5 `Return` *Statement Will Cease Execution of Function*

```
Public Function MyFunction(byval SomeFlag as Boolean) as String
    Return "One Value" 'This will be the only code in the function that
executes
    If SomeFlag then
        MyFunction = "Another Value" 'Set the return value to a new value
    End If
End Function
```

Static Procedures

`Static` variables maintain their values between calls. In previous versions of VB, declaring a procedure as `Static` would have the effect of declaring all the variables within the procedure as `Static`. This is no longer valid in VB.NET.

Shared Methods

It is now possible to declare a procedure that can be used with or without an instance of the class being created. Declaring the procedure as `Shared` does this. Listing 4.6 illustrates the declaration of a shared method.

Listing 4.6 *Shared Method in VB.NET*

```
Public Class Employee
Public Shared Sub AddEmployee(ByVal FirstName as String, _
                ByVal LastName as String, ByVal Department as String, _
                ByVal SSN as String)
    ' Do some database access to store the new employee
    End Sub
End Class
```

Shared methods can be called from either an instance of the class or without an instance. The following illustrates the use of a shared method through an instance of a class or the use of a shared method simply through the class:

Instance of the Class

```
Dim oEmployee as New Employee()
oEmployee.AddEmployee("Fred","Flinstone","Rock Breaking","111111111")
```

No Instance of the Class

```
Employee.AddEmployee("Fred","Flinstone","Rock Breaking","111111111")
```

Function Overloading

Function overloading allows a developer to define the same function with multiple parameter lists.

The parameter lists might contain the same number of parameters and be of different types or might contain a different number of parameters. The compiler determines at compile time which version of the function should actually be called, based on the parameter list. The data types of the parameter list and the return type if the function returns something make up what is known as the *signature*. Listing 4.7 illustrates two functions with the same signature even though they do different things.

Listing 4.7   Function Signatures

```
Public Function FunctionOne(ByVal companyName as String, _
               ByVal companyID as Integer) as String
End Function
Public Function FunctionTwo(ByVal firstName as String, _
               ByVal employeeID as Integer) as String
End Function
```

Function overloading is a powerful feature that allows a very flexible design when developing code. Listing 4.8 illustrates Function Overloading (notice that the functions have the same name but different signatures). In VB.NET, you need to explicitly declare that the functions are overloads of each other, this is done using the Overloads keyword.

Listing 4.8   Function Overloading

```
Public Overloads Function AddValues(ByVal Value1 as Integer, _
                    ByVal Value2 as Integer) As Integer
    Return Value1 + Value2
End Function
Public Overloads Function AddValues(ByVal Value1 as Integer, _
                    ByVal Value2 as Integer, ByVal Value3 as Integer)_
  As Integer
    Return Value1 + Value2 + Value3
End Function
```

Properties

In VB.NET, there are multiple methods of exposing class data for outside use. The simplest method is to simply create fields that are exposed as Public, as follows:

```
Public FirstName as String
```

Exposing fields as properties by making them public isn't recommended for various reasons. They don't allow you to control the access to the data and to validate the data with code.

At first glance this method seems fine, and in many cases it might be all that is needed. But it does limit the flexibility and encapsulation of the implementation.

For example, say that instead of FirstName we have a field that represents an ItemCount found in a database. To use the field approach for an ItemCount field, a database lookup needs to be done, so more code would be needed in the constructor. This would make the constructor do more work and also do some database access that might never be used.

If ItemCount were to be implemented as a property, it would only retrieve the information from the database when it is required. In addition, values implemented as properties can limit who can change the property value.

The field approach looks as if it might be more efficient for setting and retrieving the information in a simple property (one that has no logic other than storing or retrieving a value). In fact, the Just-In-Time compiler for Windows actually optimizes a simple property so that it is just as fast as a field. This optimization is known as *inlining*.

Properties are nothing new to VB.NET, but the syntax has changed and is now more self-explanatory. In prior versions of VB, properties were defined as shown in Listing 4.9.

Listing 4.9   *Property Procedures in Versions 4–6*

```
Public Property Let FirstName(ByVal Value as String)
    c_sFirstName = Value
End Property

Public Property Get FirstName() as String
    FirstName = c_sFirstName
End Property
```

If the property were an object, a `Property Set` would have been used instead of a `Property Let`. Note that the `Property Get` and the `Property Let` (or `Set`) were treated as two independent blocks of code. Omitting the `Property Let` created read-only properties, and omitting the `Get` created write-only properties.

In VB.NET, the syntax is quite different and more explicit. Listing 4.10 illustrates a VB.NET property.

Listing 4.10   *VB.NET Property*

```
Private c_sFirstName as string
Public Property FirstName() as String
    Get
        Return c_sFirstName
    End Get
```

Listing 4.10   Continued

```
    Set(ByVal Value as string)
        c_sFirstName = Value
    End Set
End Property
```

Note that all the code must stay together and cannot be split by non-related code. To create Read-Only or Write-Only properties, you must explicitly label the property as Read-Only or Write-Only. (No longer available in VB.NET is the capability for the Property Let and Property Get to have different accessibility levels.) Listing 4.11 illustrates a Read-Only property and Listing 4.12 illustrates a Write-Only property.

Listing 4.11   Read-Only Property

```
Private c_sFirstName as string
Public ReadOnly Property FirstName() as String
    Get
        Return c_sFirstName
    End Get
End Property
```

Listing 4.12   Write-Only Property

```
Private c_sFirstName as string
Public WriteOnly Property FirstName() as String
    Set(ByVal Value as String)
        c_sFirstName = Value
    End Set
End Property
```

One other minor modification has been made to properties in VB.NET. In previous versions, default properties were created by using a strange dialog box. Now there is a Default modifier to make a property default, as shown in Listing 4.13. One very important distinction is that a default property in VB.NET must include an index, so only some sort of array or collection can be a default property.

Listing 4.13   Default Property in VB.NET

```
Public Default Property ChildrenNames(ByVal Index as Integer) as String
    Get
    Return c_sChildren(Index)
    End Get
    Set(ByVal Value as String)
    c_sChildren(Index) = Value
    End Set
End Property
```

Shared Properties

Developers occasionally need to create fields and properties that have a single value for all instances of a class. In previous versions of Visual Basic, the only way to accomplish this is to use modules, but this technique frequently has side effects. In VB.NET, this functionality is directly supported in classes by declaring the field or property as Shared. Listing 4.14 is an example of a class with a shared property.

Listing 4.14   Shared *Property Example*

```
Public Class Employee
    Public Shared EmployeeCount as Integer
    Private m_sFirstName as String
    Private m_iEmployeeID as Integer
    Private Sub New(ByVal EmployeeID as Integer)
        ' Get Employee Information from Database and store in member variables
        m_iEmployeeID = EmployeeID
        EmployeeCount = EmployeeCount + 1
    End Sub
    Public Property FirstName() as String
        Get
            FirstName = m_sFirstName
        End Get
        Set(ByVal Value as String)
            m_sFirstName = Value
        End Set
    End Property
    Public ReadOnly Property EmployeeID() as Integer
        Get
            EmployeeID = m_iEmployeeID
        End Get
    End Property

    'Following Sub is from previous example
    Public Shared Sub AddEmployee(ByVal FirstName as String, _
                    ByVal LastName as String, ByVal Department as String, _
                    ByVal SSN as String)
        ' Do some database access to store the new employee
    End Sub
End Class
```

Similar to shared methods, shared properties can be accessed without creating an instance of the class, as shown in Listing 4.15.

Listing 4.15   *Using a Shared Property without a Class Instance*

```
Dim iEmployeeCount as Integer
iEmployeeCount = Employee.EmployeeCount
```

Listing 4.16 illustrates using the shared property with an instance of the class.

Listing 4.16   Using a Shared Property with an Object Instance

```
Dim oEmployee as New Employee(123)
Dim iEmployeeCount as Integer
iEmployeeCount = oEmployee.EmployeeCount
```

Shared properties are a very powerful mechanism. We could have changed the Listing 4.16's implementation to use a shared property rather than a shared field to initially load the EmployeeCount field the first time is required. Listing 4.17 shows this use of a shared property. Every instance of the class will share the same private field to hold the employee count. So if we have 10 instances of Employee and access the Employee count property from any one of those instances, we will get back the same value. We can even get the value by using the class without an instance.

Listing 4.17   Just-In-Time Database Lookup

```
Public Class Employee
    Private Shared c_iEmployeeCount As Integer
    Private c_sFirstName As String
    Private c_iEmployeeID As Integer
    Private Sub New(ByVal EmployeeID As Integer)
        ' Get Employee Information from Database and store in member variables
        c_iEmployeeID = EmployeeID
    End Sub
    Public Property FirstName() As String
        Get
            FirstName = c_sFirstName
        End Get
        Set(ByVal Value As String)
            c_sFirstName = Value
        End Set
    End Property
    Public ReadOnly Property EmployeeID() As Integer
        Get
            EmployeeID = c_iEmployeeID
        End Get
    End Property

    ' Get Employee Count first time that it is needed
    Public Shared ReadOnly Property EmployeeCount() As Integer
        Get
            If c_iEmployeeCount = -1 Then
                'Get Employee Count from database and store in shared field
                c_iEmployeeCount = CountRetreivedFromDatabase
            End If
            Return c_iEmployeeCount
        End Get
    End Property
```

Listing 4.17 *Continued*

```
'Following Sub is from previous example
Public Shared Sub AddEmployee(ByVal FirstName As String, _
                 ByVal LastName As String, ByVal Department As String, _
                 ByVal SSN As String)
    ' Do some database access to store the new employee
    c_iEmployeeCount = c_iEmployeeCount + 1
End Sub
End Class
```

Events

Events are central to building rich applications. They are used when controls on a form are acted upon, such as when a button is clicked, or to notify other code that the state of an object has changed. In a multithreaded environment such as the .NET Framework, events can be used to signal that a task on another thread is complete.

Visual Basic introduced the Windows world to event-driven programming; it's what made VB take off in the first place. But there were some issues with events in earlier versions. For example, they are late bound, and it is difficult to create shared event handlers.

In the .NET Framework, events have been extended to fix some of these issues and to make them even more powerful and provide more control. The key to these improvements is the concept of delegates.

Delegates

The event model in Visual Basic.NET is now based on delegates. A *delegate* is an object that can call object methods. Delegates are often described as type-safe function pointers.

Manually creating delegates in VB.NET is quite easy, as shown in Listing 4.18.

Listing 4.18 *Delegate Example*

```
' Declare the delegate this will define the function
' and the parameters and return type. Any function that has the same signature
' can be called by the delegate.
Delegate Function MyCompareDelegate(ByVal x As Integer, _
                 ByVal y As Integer) As Boolean
' Create code that will use the delegate to invoke _
' the function represented by the delegate
Sub MySub(ByVal MyDelegate as MyCompareDelegate)
    ' Call the function represented by the Delegate
    MyDelegate.Invoke(5,3)
End Sub
' Create Functions that can be represented by the delegate
Function CompareLow(ByVal X as Integer, ByVal Y as Integer) as Boolean
    If X > Y then
        Return True
```

Listing 4.18   Continued

```
    Else
        Return False
    End If
End Function
Function CompareHigh(ByVal X as Integer, ByVal Y as Integer) as Boolean
    If X < Y then
        Return True
    Else
        Return False
    End If
End Function
' Code to call the functions through the Delegate
Sub Main()
    Call MySub(AddressOf Me.CompareLow)
    Call MySub(AddressOf Me.CompareHigh)
End Sub
```

In most cases you won't create your own delegates. Instead, VB.NET will create and handle the delegates on your behalf. The Event statement will implicitly define a delegate class named <EventName>EventHandler. The delegate class will be a nested class in the class containing the Event statement. It will have the same signature as the event.

Event Handlers

In previous versions of VB, there was only one way to create an event handler—by naming the sub in the format shown in Listing 4.19.

Listing 4.19   Event Handler Syntax in VB Prior to VB.NET

```
ObjectName_EventName(Event Parameters)
```

For example, the click event of a button named Button1 would be defined as Button1_Click. In the .NET Framework, events have a new syntax, which is shared by most event handlers, and shown in the following:

```
Sub EventHandlerName(ByVal sender As Object, _
    ByVal e As System.EventArgs) Handles Object.Event
```

In previous versions of VB, parameters for an event were passed explicitly. In the .NET Framework, the parameters are included in the second parameter, which is actually a collection. For example, the Form MouseDown event in a Windows Form application has the event handler depicted in Listing 4.20. What is being done here is that the System.EventArgs class is being subclassed and has added X, Y and Button properties to support the functionality of a mouse.

Listing 4.20 Form `MouseDown` *Event Handler*

```
Public Sub Form1_MouseDown(ByVal sender As Object, _
          ByVal e As System.Windows Forms.MouseEventArgs)
    'Note I added additional code to retrieve the parameters that were used
    'in VB6
    Dim Button As system.Windows Forms.MouseButtons
    Dim X As Integer
    Dim Y As Integer
    Button = e.Button
    X = e.X
    Y = e.Y
End Sub
```

VB.NET has numerous methods for assigning event handlers to events. There is the existing syntax from previous versions of VB. In addition, you can use two new methods for assigning an event handler.

The `Handles` keyword has been added to allow the assignment of event handlers at design time. `Handles` allows multiple events to be handled by one event handler, as shown in Listing 4.21. Note, however, that in order for this to work, all the event handlers must share the same signature.

Listing 4.21 *Common Event Handler*

```
Protected Sub CommonEventHandler(ByVal sender As Object, ByVal e As_
  System.EventArgs) _
              Handles Button1.Click, Button2.Click, Form1.Click
      If sender Is form1 Then
          msgbox("Form Clicked")
      Else
          msgbox(CType(sender, Button).text)
      End If
End Sub
```

The `Handles` keyword allows you to set up event handlers at design time. But sometimes you need to do this at runtime. In VB.NET two new statements, `AddHandler` and `RemoveHandler`, have been added to allow this. As the statements suggest, `AddHandler` assigns an event handler to an event and `RemoveHandler` removes the assignment. The `AddHandler` and `RemoveHandler` syntax and an example are as follows:

AddHandler and RemoveHandler Syntax

```
AddHandler Object.Event, Delegate
RemoveHandler Object.Event, Delegate
```

AddHandler and RemoveHandler Example

```
AddHandler Button1.Click, AddressOf me.EventHandler
RemoveHandler Button1.Click, AddressOf me.EventHandler
```

In Listing 4.20, the AddressOf and the me.EventHandler keywords create a delegate on-the-fly. AddressOf was introduced in VB 5 to allow developers to use API calls that used required callbacks, but they could only be used in modules. In VB.Net, AddressOf can be used to create a delegate for any function, sub, or property method.

Creating Events

It has been possible to create events in Visual Basic since version 5.0. The feature has always been very simple to implement, and this hasn't changed in VB.NET. In fact, the syntax hasn't changed.

To declare an event in a class, you simply use the Event keyword to describe the name and the parameters that the event passes to the event handler, as shown in the following:

```
Public Event EventName(event parameters)
```

One thing to keep in mind is that you might want your event parameters to be defined the same way as the events in the .NET Framework. With that in mind, you would define your events as follows:

```
Public Event EventName(ByVal sender as Object, ByVal e as System.EventArgs)
```

Events follow nearly the same rules as subs and functions when you define the event parameters. They can be ByVal or ByRef, but they cannot have any named or optional parameters. Also, events cannot have a return value.

Raising Events

As simple as it is to create an event, it might be even easier to raise an event. VB.NET uses the same syntax that VB 5 and 6 does, as shown in the following:

```
RaiseEvent EventName(eventparameters)
```

Using EventArgs

System.EventArgs is a very simple class that defines the base class for event arguments (parameters). System.EventArgs doesn't do much itself, but it does provide a class from which to derive your specific event parameters. An example of this is shown in Listing 4.22.

Listing 4.22 Inherit from System.EventArgs to Create Event Handler Parameters

```
Public Class MyMouseEventArgs
    Inherits System.EventArgs
    Public ReadOnly Property XPosition() As Integer
        Get
            Return cursor.Position.X
        End Get
    End Property
```

Listing 4.22 Continued

```
Public ReadOnly Property YPosition() As Integer
    Get
        Return Cursor.Position.Y
    End Get
End Property
End Class
```

Listing 4.23 shows an example of an event using the custom `EventArgs` class.

Listing 4.23 Using a Custom EventArgs Class

```
Public Event MouseOver(ByVal Sender as Object, ByVal e as System.EventArgs)
' Define a test subroutine to Raise the event
Public Sub TestRaiseEvent()
    RaiseEvent Ctype(MouseOver(Me,New MyMouseEventArgs),System.EventArgs)
End Sub
' In a form class define a variable as the test event raiser
Private WithEvents MyEventObject as MyEventObjectTester
' In the form class define the event handler to handle the
' event raised from MyEventObject and the Form Click
Private Sub MyEventHandler(ByVal Sender as Object, _
            ByVal e as System.EventArgs) Handles MyEventObject.MouseDown,_
            Form1.Click
    Dim oMyMouseEventArgs as MyMouseEventArgs
    If Not Sender is Form1 Then
        oMyMouseEventArgs = Ctype(e, MyMouseEventArgs)
        Console.WriteLine(e.XPosition.ToString())
        Console.WriteLine(e.YPosition.ToString())
    Else
        Console.WriteLine("Form Raised Click Event")
    End If
End Sub
```

Attributes

One of the most powerful innovations in the .NET Framework is the new attribute-based programming model. *Attributes* are tags that are placed in code and can be applied to assemblies, classes, fields, methods, or properties.

Attributes add a declarative functionality to the .NET Framework and the code that you create. The functionality that attributes provide to the .NET Framework normally would require a great deal of custom code.

In VB.NET, the syntax for adding attributes is simple but there are a few rules. Let's start with the basic syntax, which is shown in the following:

```
<AttributeClass(AttributeParameter,AttributeParameter,…)>
```

An example attribute is WebMethod, which can be placed at the method level, as shown in Listing 4.24.

Listing 4.24 WebMethod ***Attribute***

```
<WebMethod()> _
Public Function GetEmployees() as DataSet
    Dim oDataSet as New DataSet
    'Code to create a dataset
    Return oDataSet
End Function
```

Because WebMethod doesn't have any required parameters, it is simply stated as Listing 4.33.

To declare attributes at the assembly level, the attribute tags must be the first code found in the source file and a modifier must be placed in the tag. The syntax is illustrated as follows:

```
<Assembly: AttributeClass(AttributeParameter,AttributeParameter,...)>
```

To declare attributes at class, method, field, or property levels, the attribute tags must be placed inline in the class, method, field, or property declaration before the name. Listing 4.25 uses the WebMethod attribute to illustrate this.

Listing 4.25 ***Declaring a Function as*** WebMethod

```
<WebMethod()> _
Public  Function GetClientName(ByVal ClientID as Integer) as String
End Function
```

The WebMethod attribute exposes a method as a Web Service. When a method is exposed as a Web Service through the use of the WebMethod attribute, the *Common Language Runtime (CLR)* marshals information as XML.

Integration with Visual Studio.NET for designer support and other integration features is also partially done through the use of attributes. Listing 4.26 uses attributes to indicate how properties of an ASP.NET Server control should appear in the property page in Visual Studio.NET.

Listing 4.26 ***Properties in the Property Page Window***

```
<Bindable(True), Category("Dates"), DefaultValue("")>Property EndDate() As Date
    Get
        Return CType(State("EndDate"), Date)
    End Get
    Set
        c_dteEndDate = Value
        State("EndDate") = Value
        If c_dteStartDate < c_dteEndDate Then
            CreateTimeTable()
```

Listing 4.26 *Continued*

```
        End If
    End Set
End Property
```

In Listing 4.26, the property `EndDate` is decorated with a number of attributes. `Bindable` indicates that the property can be bound. `Category` indicates what category the property should be included in the property browser, in this case `"Dates"`. `DefaultValue` sets the default value of the property.

Finally, attributes are very important to interoperability in the .NET Framework. Listing 4.27 illustrates using attributes to effect COM Interop marshalling.

Listing 4.27 *Using Attributes to Effect COM Interop Marshalling*

```
Declare Auto Sub CopyFile Lib "Kernel32" _
                (ByVal <MarshalAs(UnmanagedType.LPTStr)> existingfile As_
                String, _
                ByVal <MarshalAs(UnmanagedType.LPTStr)> newfile As String, _
                ByVal failifexists As Boolean)
```

Summary

The .NET Framework has forced the addition of many new features to the event and object-oriented programming model of VB. The more I work with .NET, the more I feel that the single feature that puts .NET above all other development platforms is the addition of attributes. The VB.NET method supports attributes for properties, methods, and events and make VB as easy or easier than ever to develop with.

CHAPTER 5

Creating and Destroying Objects

A great improvement to Visual Basic is the addition of constructors to the language. *Constructors* provide the ability to initialize an object when it is first created. They provide the ability to pass in parameters to the object when it is constructed. VB.NET allows constructors for both classes and intrinsic types such as integers and strings.

Constructors

Constructors for intrinsic types are referred to as *initializers*. Listing 5.1 shows the method used to initialize an integer in previous versions of VB. In previous versions of VB, you had to declare the variable and initialize it in two steps.

Listing 5.1   Initializing an Integer Pre-VB.NET

```
Dim I as integer
I = 5
```

In the .NET Framework, VB has been enhanced to allow you to initialize the variable when you declare it. Listing 5.2 illustrates this in VB.NET.

Listing 5.2   Initializing an Integer in VB.NET

```
Dim I as integer = 5
```

Visual Basic has supported a `Class_Initialize` event since version 4. The `Class_Initialize` event was executed when an object was created, but there was no way to pass any information to it. If a parameter-driven initialization was required, it was necessary to add an initialize method to the class, as shown in Listing 5.3.

Listing 5.3   Initializing an Object in VB4–VB6

```
Set oEmployee = New CEmployee
oEmployee.Init iEmployeeID
'Elsewhere in project is a Cemployee.cls file with the following code
Public Sub Init(ByVal employeeID as Integer)
    Dim oDBConnection as ADODB.Connection
    Dim oDBCommand as ADODB.Command
    Dim oDBRecordSet as ADODB.RecordSet
    '.....Do Database Access code to retrieve the
    'Employee from the database and fill properties
End Sub
```

In VB.NET, the Class_Initialize event has been replaced by class constructors. Constructors are defined by creating a sub called New. By using function overloading, a class might have multiple constructors. Listing 5.4 illustrates a class in VB.NET using overloading and multiple constructors.

Listing 5.4   VB.NET Overloaded Constructors

```
Public Class Employee
    Private c_sFirstName as string
    Private c_sLastName as String
    Public Overloads Sub New()
        MyBase.New() ' Call the Base Class Constructor
    End Sub
    Public Overloads Sub New(ByVal FirstName as String,ByVal LastName as
String)
        MyBase.New()' Call the Base Class Constructor
        Me.FirstName = FirstName
        Me.LastName = LastName
    End Sub
    Public Property FirstName() as String
        Get
            FirstName = c_sFirstName
        End Get
        Set(ByVal Value as String)
            c_sFirstName = value
        End Set
    End Property
    Public Property LastName() as String
        Get
            LastName = c_sLastName
        End Get
        Set(ByVal Value as String)
            c_sLastName = value
        End Set
    End Property
End Class
```

The first line of code in a class constructor must be a call to `MyBase.New`. `MyBase` is a special variable that refers to the base class from which a class inherits. (Remember that at the very least, all classes inherit from `System.Object`.) If you don't create a constructor, the compiler will automatically create one and call `MyBase.New` for you.

Destructors

Similar to the `Class_Initialize` event, Visual Basic has supported a `Class_Terminate` event since version 4. The `Class_Terminate` event would fire after the last reference to an object instance was released. This functionality was based on reference counting, which was the COM method of resource management.

Because the .Net Framework doesn't use reference counting, as we'll see in Chapter 10, "ADO.NET," the `Class_Terminate` event is no longer part of the language. If there is any explicit cleanup of resources that a class must complete, you must code a `Finalize` method, as shown in Listing 5.5.

Listing 5.5 `Finalize` *Method*

```
Protected Sub Finalize()
    'Close Database Connection
    oDBConnection.Close
End Sub
```

When a class has a `Finalize` method, the compiler marks that it requires finalization. When the .Net Framework garbage collector encounters an instance of a class that has a `Finalize` method, the garbage collector will move the class instance into a queue of objects in need of finalization. After the garbage collection process completes collecting, it will then call the `Finalize` method of the objects in the Finalization queue.

An important point to understand is that the `Finalize` method will be called sometime after the last reference to an instance of the class has been released, but not immediately after. You should design your components to avoid using Finalizers. They slow down the garbage collection process.

When an object must be cleaned up as soon as it is released, such as when the object holds scarce resources such as database connections, file handles, and so on; you should use the Dispose design pattern (See the following sidebar) rather than the `Finalize` method.

WHAT IS A DESIGN PATTERN?

A design pattern is a description of a recurring problem with a pattern to solve the problem. Not only does a design pattern describe the problem but it also describes the solution.

The pattern is quite simple. All you need to do is implement the `System.IDisposable` interface. `System.IDisposable` has one method you need to implement called `Dispose`, and have users of the class call the method after an object is no longer in use.

The pattern does harm the encapsulation of the object to a small extent because it requires that objects must be explicitly disposed. If a developer fails to call the Dispose method, the required clean up won't be performed until the Finalize method. (Classes that implement System.IDisposable should also implement a Finalize method in case the Dispose method wasn't called.)

Another potential problem can arise with the Dispose design pattern if the Finalize method is called from within the Dispose method and then again at a latter time. To fix this, the SuppressFinalize method should be called from within any Dispose method if the class has a Finalize method. The syntax of the SuppressFinalize method is shown in Listing 5.6.

Listing 5.6   Suppress Finalization

```
System.GC.SuppressFinalize()
```

The Dispose pattern is used throughout the .NET Framework itself. For example, when you create a Windows form, the form designer inserts calls to Dispose methods. Listing 5.7 shows some of the code generated by the Windows Form designer.

Listing 5.7   Dispose in a Windows Form

```
'Form overrides dispose to clean up the component list.
    Public Overrides Sub Dispose()
        MyBase.Dispose()
        If Not (components Is Nothing) Then
            components.Dispose()
        End If
    End Sub
```

Accessibility Modifiers

Accessibility modifiers control the visibility of classes, methods, properties, and events. In VB 6, accessibility was controlled by a property of a class and accessibility modifiers on the methods, properties, and events.

Modifiers for Classes

Table 5.1 illustrates the accessibility in VB 6 (In VB 6 this was called *instancing* and was a combination of accessibility and creation rules).

Table 5.1   VB6 Class Instancing

Instancing	Description
Private	Class is only available in the project it was created in.
PublicNotCreatable	Class is available outside of the project it was created in but must be created by code internal to the project.
SingleUse	Class is available and creatable by code outside of the project it was created in.

Table 5.1   Continued

Instancing	Description
GlobalSingleUse	Class is available and creatable by code outside of the project it was created in. This instancing property isn't available in VB.NET.
MultiUse	Class is available and creatable by code outside of the project it was created in.
GlobalMultiUse	Class is available and creatable by code outside of the project it was created in. This instancing property isn't available in VB.NET.

In VB.NET, there are a number of changes in class Accessibility levels. Table 5.2 illustrates the VB.NET accessibility levels.

Table 5.2   VB.NET Class Accessibility Levels

Accessibility levels	Description
Public	Class is available with no restrictions
Private	Class is available to only code within the current namespace. This includes nested classes.
Protected	Class is available to derived types.
Friend	Class is available to other types in the same Namespace.
Protected Friend	Class is accessible as a combination of the Protected and Friend.

Table 5.3 cross references the VB 6 Class instancing properties with how you achieve them in VB.NET (if possible).

Table 5.3   VB6—VB.NET Instancing Cross Reference

Visual Basic 6	Visual Basic.NET
Private	Class marked as Private
PublicNotCreatable	Class marked as Private, Constructor marked as Friend
SingleUse	Not supported
GlobalSingleUse	Not supported
MultiUse	Class marked as Public, Constructor marked as Public
GlobalMultiUse	Not supported

Modifiers for Methods and Properties

Modifiers aren't limited to classes. VB.NET also has a set of modifiers that affect the accessibility of methods and properties. In Table 5.4, you can see the modifiers in VB 6.

Table 5.4   VB 6 Method and Property Accessibility

Accessibility Levels	Description
Private	Method or property is only available in the class it was created in.
Public	Method or property is available outside of the class.
Friend	Method or property is available by code inside the same project but private to outside code.

Similar to class accessibility, the accessibility levels for methods and properties have changed a great deal in VB.NET. Table 5.5 shows the modifiers in VB.NET.

Table 5.5   VB.NET Method and Property Accessibility Levels

Accessibility Levels	Description
Public	Method or property is available with no restrictions.
Private	Method or property is available only in class that it was created in.
Protected	Method or property is available in class that it was created in or any classes that derive from the class it was created in.
Friend	Method or property is available to code in the same Namespace.
Protected Friend	Method or property is accessible as a combination of the Protected and Friend.

Summary

VB is now a 100% object-oriented programming language. This is required because of the .NET Framework being a 100% object-oriented programming environment. VB is the most self-documenting language currently available for the .NET Framework. The self-documenting nature is shown full force with the object-oriented languages features introduced in VB.NET.

CHAPTER 6

Creating VB.NET Projects

VB.NET supports all the project types available in the .NET Framework, including Windows Services and Console applications. At the same time, VB.NET has removed a few project types that were available in earlier versions. This chapter gives you a brief tour of each of the project types available in VB.NET. Figure 6.1 shows the parts of the .NET Framework covered in this chapter.

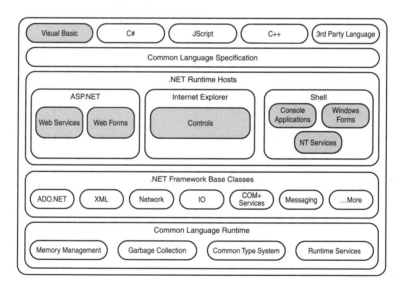

Figure 6.1

Coverage of the .NET Framework.

Unsupported Project Types

The .NET Framework doesn't support all the project types that were available in previous versions of VB.

VB 6 supported a number of Web application models that are no longer available in the .NET Framework, including WebClasses, DHTML Applications, and ActiveX Documents. The migration tool will convert WebClasses to Web Forms, which will then require changes, but won't convert DHTML applications or ActiveX documents.

Finally Microsoft removed support for the Data Report project in the .NET Framework.

Class Libraries

VB 5 and 6 allowed developers to create ActiveX DLL and ActiveX EXE projects. The corresponding project type VB.NET is the Class Library project.

Class libraries aren't quite the same as ActiveX EXEs or DLLs, but they do provide the ability to create re-usable components. The majority of other reasons for using VB ActiveX EXEs have been replaced with the new capabilities of the .NET Framework. For example, the .Net Framework supports true multithreading, creating applications that can be automated is supported in Windows Form applications, and DCOM applications are built using the new remoting features of the .NET Framework.

Class library projects provide a designer that integrates with the Server Explorer and the Toolbox to provide a mechanism to do Rapid Application Development of components.

Let's walk through the process of creating a class library. Figures 6.2–6.8 illustrate the complete process for creating a class library. When this process is complete, the resulting code is illustrated in Listing 6.1.

Figure 6.2 shows the first step in the process. From the Visual Studio.NET Start Page, click New Project.

This brings up the New Project window as illustrated in Figure 6.3. From this window, select Class Library and name it `ClassLibraryProject`.

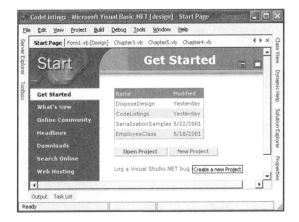

Figure 6.2

Create a New Project.

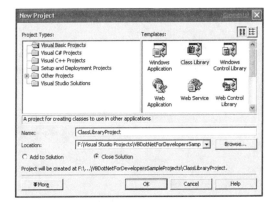

Figure 6.3

Create a Class Library project.

Next, right-click the class1.vb file in the Solution Explorer and delete it from the project. This is illustrated in Figure 6.4.

After you have deleted the class1.vb file from the project, choose Add Component from the Project menu, which brings up the dialog in Figure 6.5. Name the component class Chapter6.

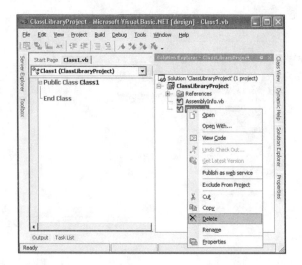

Figure 6.4

Delete class1.vb from the project.

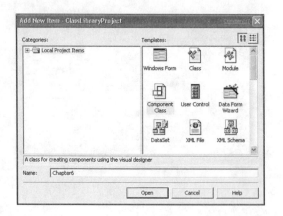

Figure 6.5

Add a new component class to the project.

After Visual Studio has completed creating the new component, it will open it up in the Design window as illustrated in Figure 6.6.

After adding the component to the project, we want to change the root namespace of the project. The way to do that is to bring up the Project Properties dialog by right-clicking the project in the Solution Explorer and choosing Properties. This brings up the dialog box in Figure 6.7. Enter a root namespace that is meaningful to you.

Figure 6.6

Visual Studio.NET open to the component designer.

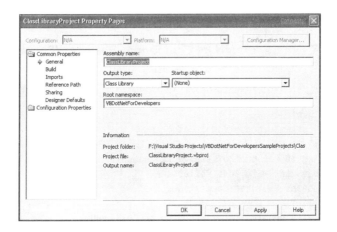

Figure 6.7

Project Properties page.

The last thing we are going to do with this sample is add one method to the class. To do this, double-click the designer and add the code in Figure 6.8.

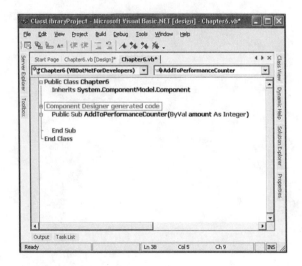

Figure 6.8

Add a method to the component.

All this work resulted in the source code in Listing 6.1.

Listing 6.1 Code Generated by Component Designer (Comments Added for Clarity)

```
'Visual Studio.NET adds the Inherits System.ComponentModel.Component
    ' so that it can provide designer support
Public Class Chapter6
    Inherits System.ComponentModel.Component

'The #Region Tag is not part of the VB language it is a
'Editor tag to assist with Code Collapsing
#Region " Component Designer generated code "

    'The following constructor is used by the designer
    Public Overloads Sub New(Container As System.ComponentModel.IContainer)
        'Call the Base Class Constructor
        MyClass.New()

        'Required for Windows.Forms Class Composition Designer support
        Container.Add(me)
    End Sub

    'The following constructor is used by your applications
    Public Overloads Sub New()
        MyBase.New()
```

Listing 6.1 Continued

```
        'This call is required by the Component Designer.
        InitializeComponent()

        'Add any initialization after the InitializeComponent() call

    End Sub

    'Required by the Component Designer
    Private components As System.ComponentModel.Container

    'NOTE: The following procedure is required by the Component Designer
    'It can be modified using the Component Designer.
    'Do not modify it using the code editor.
    <System.Diagnostics.DebuggerStepThrough()> Private Sub
InitializeComponent()
        '
        'Chapter6
        '

    End Sub

#End Region
    'Add all of your methods after the #End Region tag, which is
    'used by the editor for collapsing code
    Public Sub AddToPerformanceCounter(ByVal amount As Integer)

    End Sub
End Class
```

The code in Listing 6.1 illustrates a number of things. First of all, it shows how inheritance is used by the .NET Framework to provide services, in this case designer (through inheritance) and debugger services (through attributes). It also illustrates how integration between simple source code and the designers in Visual Studio.NET is accomplished through inheritance.

The class inherits from System.ComponentModel.Component, which provides methods that allow the .NET Framework to control the component, and also allows Visual Studio.NET to provide a drag-and-drop metaphor for building components that is similar to the one used for building forms.

Web Form Applications

One of the design goals of the .NET Framework was to make the production of HTML-based Web applications as easy as developing form-based Windows applications in Visual Basic.

Prior to the release of *Active Server Pages (ASP)* by Microsoft in 1996, most Web application development was done using *Common Gateway Interface (CGI)* in the form of executables that did extensive string handling to create dynamic HTML. ASP introduced the ability to mix static HTML with ASP script.

Unfortunately, this architecture required presentation and code to be intermingled on a single page, which caused problems for both implementation and maintenance. WebClasses, introduced in Visual Basic 6.0, attempted to address this problem, but they had problems of their own, mostly having to do with poor documentation, which led to poor scalability. (WebClasses could scale, but documentation and reference applications showed poor design decisions.)

The .Net Framework includes a new version of ASP called ASP.NET. One of the technologies in ASP.NET is the new project type called Web Forms. Web Forms bring the drag-and-drop model of building form-based Windows applications to the dynamically built nature of Web applications.

Web forms are built around server-side controls. The properties, methods, and events execute on the server rather than the client.

Developers can write code to respond to events, set properties, and call methods rather than using procedural logic and string manipulation to build applications. The difference between Web Forms and Windows Forms is basically that Windows Forms controls have a user interface associated with them and Web Forms emit HTML to build an interface in a browser.

Creating a Web Form Application

When you start up a new Web Form application with Visual Studio.NET, the development environment will do a number of things for you. First, it will create an ASP.NET application for you in *Internet Information Server (IIS)*, creating all the required IIS metabase entries and all the folders for the application. Then it will create a default Web Form and open it in the Web Form designer.

Select New Project from the Visual Studio.NET Start Page. This brings up the New Project dialog box. Select ASP.NET Web Application and name it as illustrated in Figure 6.9.

After selecting OK, Visual Studio.NET interfaces with IIS makes the IIS Metabase entries, and creates all the files required for a Web Form application. Figure 6.10 shows the status window that Visual Studio.NET displays while this process is completing.

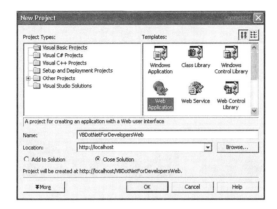

Figure 6.9

Create a Web Form application.

Figure 6.10

IIS and Visual Studio.NET creating the project.

After Visual Studio.NET is done creating the project, it will open to the initial WebForm that was created. This is illustrated in Figure 6.11.

Select from the toolbox and drag a Label control to the Web Form. Figure 6.12 shows the Label control selected in the toolbox.

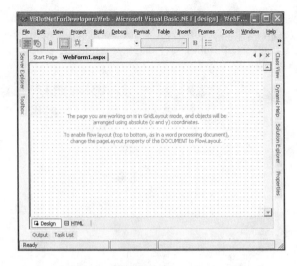

Figure 6.11

A created WebForm project in the HTML designer.

Figure 6.12

Add a label to a WebForm.

Figure 6.13 shows the WebForm after the label has been dropped on it.

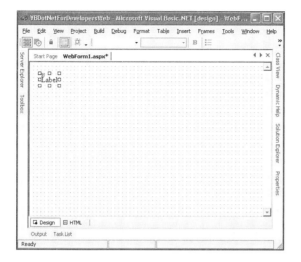

Figure 6.13

A label on the WebForm.

After creating the form and adding the label, double-click the page to go into the Page_Load event of the form and add the code in Figure 6.14.

Figure 6.14

Add code to put Hello World!!!! *into the label.*

After adding the code, the complete code for the Web Form is depicted in Listing 6.2.

Listing 6.2   Resulting Source Code for the WebForm

```
Public Class WebForm1
    Inherits System.Web.UI.Page
    Protected WithEvents Label1 As System.Web.UI.WebControls.Label

#Region " Web Form Designer Generated Code "

    'This call is required by the Web Form Designer.
    <System.Diagnostics.DebuggerStepThrough()> Private Sub
InitializeComponent()

    End Sub

    Protected Sub Page_Init(ByVal Sender As System.Object, _
                    ByVal e As System.EventArgs) Handles MyBase.Init
        'CODEGEN: This method call is required by the Web Form Designer
        'Do not modify it using the code editor.
        InitializeComponent()
    End Sub

#End Region

    Private Sub Page_Load(ByVal sender As System.Object, ByVal e As_
    System.EventArgs) Handles MyBase.Load
        'Put user code to initialize the page here
        Label1.Text = "Hello World!!!!"
    End Sub

End Class
```

After walking through Figures 6.9–6.14, you should have a working Web Form Hello World application. You'll notice that we didn't have to touch any HTML or do any string manipulation to create the page.

When you run the application, the page will resemble Figure 6.15.

Figure 6.15

`Hello World!!!!` *Web page in the browser.*

The HTML generated by the application is depicted in Listing 6.3.

Listing 6.3 `Hello World!!!!` *Output*

```
<HTML>
    <HEAD>
        <meta name="GENERATOR" content="Microsoft Visual Studio.NET 7.0">
        <meta name="CODE_LANGUAGE" content="Visual Basic 7.0">
        <meta name=vs_defaultClientScript content="JavaScript">
        <meta name=vs_targetSchema content="Internet Explorer 5.0">
        </HEAD>
        <body MS_POSITIONING="GridLayout">
        <TABLE height=73 cellSpacing=0
                cellPadding=0 width=64 border=0 ms_2d_layout="TRUE">
                <TR vAlign=top>
                    <TD width=64 height=73>
                <form name="WebForm1" method="post" action="WebForm1.aspx"
                    id="WebForm1">
                            <input type="hidden" name="__VIEWSTATE"
                                value="Viewstateommitted" />
                            <TABLE height=47 cellSpacing=0 cellPadding=0
width=61 border=0 ms_2d_layout="TRUE">
                                <TR vAlign=top>
                                    <TD width=25 height=27>
                </TD>
                <TD width=36>
                </TD>
                </TR>
                                <TR vAlign=top>
                    <TD height=20>
                </TD>
                <TD>
                    <span id="Label1">Hello World!!!!</span>
                </TD>
                </TR>
            </TABLE>
            </form>
        </TD>
        </TR>
    </TABLE>
    </body>
</HTML>
```

The Web Form has an HTML view to see the HTML designed by the designer.
Listing 6.4 is the HTML designed by Visual Studio.NET.

Listing 6.4 *Hello World ASP.NET Web Form HTML Design*

```
<%@ Page Language="vb" AutoEventWireup="false" Codebehind="WebForm1.aspx.vb"
Inherits="VBDotNetForDevelopersWeb.WebForm1"%>
```

Listing 6.4   Continued

```html
<HTML>
    <HEAD>
        <meta name="GENERATOR" content="Microsoft Visual Studio.NET 7.0">
        <meta name="CODE_LANGUAGE" content="Visual Basic 7.0">
        <meta name=vs_defaultClientScript content="JavaScript">
        <meta name=vs_targetSchema content="Internet Explorer 5.0">
    </HEAD>
    <body MS_POSITIONING="GridLayout">
        <TABLE height=73 cellSpacing=0 cellPadding=0
            width=64 border=0 ms_2d_layout="TRUE">
            <TR vAlign=top>
                <TD width=64 height=73>
                    <form id="WebForm1" method="post" runat="server">
                        <TABLE height=47 cellSpacing=0 cellPadding=0
                            width=61 border=0 ms_2d_layout="TRUE">
                            <TR vAlign=top>
                                <TD width=25 height=27>
                                </TD>
                                <TD width=36>
                                </TD>
                            </TR>
                            <TR vAlign=top>
                                <TD height=20>
                                </TD>
                                <TD>
                                    <asp:Label id=Label1 runat="server">Label
                                    </asp:Label>
                                </TD>
                            </TR>
                        </TABLE>
                    </form>
                </TD>
            </TR>
        </TABLE>
    </body>
</HTML>
```

All this adds up to a much easier and incredibly more productive method of creating browser-based applications.

Web Form Controls

Sticking to the .NET Framework method of building components, the creators of ASP.NET Web Forms make extending the set of ASP.NET Server controls follow the same pattern as any other component. ASP.NET Web Form Controls allow developers to create their own controls that emit HTML. The HTML can be browser-specific, least common denominator, or both. This is all done through inheritance.

In Figures 6.16 and 6.17, I will walk you through creating a simple "Hello World" Web Form control. You will notice that this project type takes only two steps to get the initial project started. In addition, there is no designer support for Web Form Controls—they are built with code.

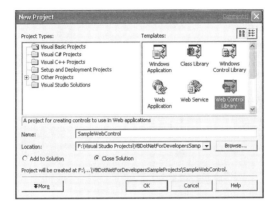

Figure 6.16
Create a Web Form Control project.

Visual Studio.NET will open in the Code editor for a Web Form Control.

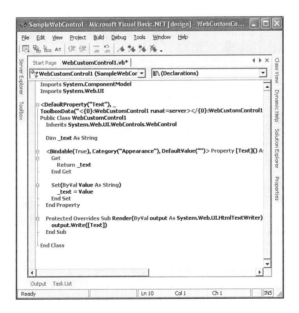

Figure 6.17
Web Control in Code editor.

After you have created the Web Form Control, it is time to create code. First I will clear out the code that I won't need. Listing 6.5 is the code that will be in my "HelloWorld" Web Form Control.

Listing 6.5 HelloWorld ***Web Form Control Implementation***

```
Imports System.ComponentModel
Imports System.Web.UI
Imports System.Web.UI.WebControls
Public Class HelloWorldWebControl
    Inherits System.Web.UI.WebControls.WebControl
    Protected Overrides Sub Render(ByVal output As
System.Web.UI.HtmlTextWriter)
        Dim oTable As New Table()
        Dim oRow As New TableRow()
        Dim oCell As New TableCell()

        oCell.Text = "Hello World"
        oCell.BorderColor = system.Drawing.Color.Firebrick
        ocell.BorderStyle = BorderStyle.Solid

        oRow.Cells.Add(oCell)
        oTable.Rows.Add(oRow)

        oTable.RenderControl(output)
    End Sub
End Class
```

We now need to test the Web Control library. Choose File, Add Project, Existing Project from Web. This is depicted in Figure 6.18.

Making the selection shown in Figure 6.18 brings up the dialog in Figure 6.19.

The Windows Open File Dialog shows you the project on the Web server you chose in Figure 6.19. Choose the project created in the previous section, "Creating a Web Form Application." Then in the Solution Explorer, right-click on the newly added project and set it as the startup project.

Now you need to add a reference to the Web Control library you created. In the Solution Explorer, right-click on references of the Web Form project and choose Add Reference. The Add References dialog box (see Figure 6.20) will come up; select the project tab, and then select the Web Control Library that we just created.

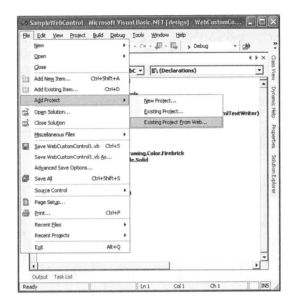

Figure 6.18

The File, Add Project, Existing Project from Web menu selection.

Figure 6.19

Select the Web server.

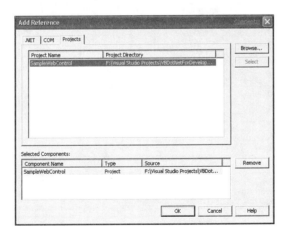

Figure 6.20

The Add Reference dialog box.

Now we need to add the control to the Toolbox. Right-click on the ToolBox and choose Customize. The dialog box in Figure 6.21 comes up; select the .NET Framework Components tab, and on choose browse. Then browse to the control library, find the DLL, and select it. Then back in the .NET Framework Components tab, find the name in the list, select it, and click OK. By default, you will find the DLL in a subdirectory, called BIN, of the Web Control library you created.

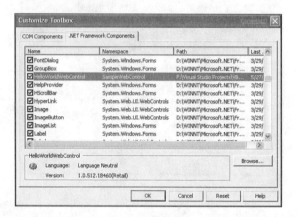

Figure 6.21

Customize Toolbox.

Now drag the control to the WebForm, and it should resemble Figure 6.22.

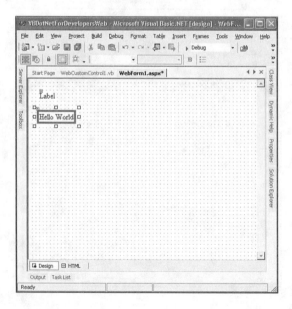

Figure 6.22

WebForm with a custom Web Control.

The HTML in the designer, after adding the form to a Web Form, is depicted in Listing 6.6.

Listing 6.6   *Web Form Designer HTML Using Web Form Control*

```
<%@ Page Language="vb" AutoEventWireup="false" Codebehind="WebForm1.aspx.vb"
Inherits="VBDotNetForDevelopersWeb.WebForm1"%>
<%@ Register TagPrefix="cc1" Namespace="SampleWebControl"
       Assembly="SampleWebControl" %>
<HTML>
    <HEAD>
        <meta name="GENERATOR" content="Microsoft Visual Studio.NET 7.0">
        <meta name="CODE_LANGUAGE" content="Visual Basic 7.0">
        <meta name=vs_defaultClientScript content="JavaScript">
        <meta name=vs_targetSchema content="Internet Explorer 5.0">
    </HEAD>
    <body MS_POSITIONING="GridLayout">
        <form id="WebForm1" method="post" runat="server">
            <asp:Label id=Label1 runat="server"
                style="Z-INDEX: 100; LEFT: 25px; POSITION: absolute; TOP:_
            27px">Label</asp:Label>
            <cc1:HelloWorldWebControl id=HelloWorldWebControl1
            style="Z-INDEX: 101; LEFT: 17px; POSITION: absolute; TOP: 65px"
            runat="server">
            </cc1:HelloWorldWebControl>
        </form>
    </body>
</HTML
```

When you run the project, the browser will be displayed with the Web page as shown in Figure 6.23. The code is depicted in Listing 6.7.

Figure 6.23

The Web Form Control in the browser.

Listing 6.7   HTML Emitted from Web Form

```
<HTML>
    <HEAD>
        <meta content="Microsoft Visual Studio.NET 7.0" name=GENERATOR>
        <meta content="Visual Basic 7.0" name=CODE_LANGUAGE>
        <meta content=JavaScript name=vs_defaultClientScript>
        <meta content="Internet Explorer 5.0" name=vs_targetSchema>
    </HEAD>
    <body MS_POSITIONING="GridLayout">
        <form name="WebForm1" method="post" action="WebForm1.aspx"_
        id="WebForm1">
            <input type="hidden" name="__VIEWSTATE"
value="dDwtNjIwMTE4MTE1O3Q8O2w8aTwxPjs+O2w8dDw7bDxpPDE+Oz47bDx0PHA8cDxsPFRle_
HQ7PjtsPEhlbGxvIFdvcmxkISEhITs+Pjs+Ozs+Oz4+Oz4+Oz4=" />
            <span id="Label1" style="Z-INDEX: 100; LEFT: 141px; POSITION:_
            absolute; TOP: 65px">Hello World!!!!</span>
            <table border="0">
                <tr>
                    <td style="border-color:Firebrick;border-style:Solid;">
                        Hello World
                    </td>
                </tr>
            </table>
        </form>
    </body>
</HTML>
```

Web Form controls are a very powerful mechanism to encapsulate HTML user interface. In the download for this book (www.samspublishing.com), I have included a Web Form application, which utilizes a more advanced Web Form control for time reporting.

Web Service Projects

Web Services allow you to expose programmatic functionality to your intranet or the Internet. These services are invoked via HTTP Get, HTTP Post, or, most commonly, SOAP.

VB.NET fully supports the creation of Web Service projects. In Figures 6.24–6.27, I will step you through the creation of a simple "Hello World" Web Service.

This little sample Web Service returns an object. This is one of the capabilities of the .NET Framework Web Services that can return objects serialized as XML. A client on the other side can simply use the XML or rebuild an object. If the client is another .NET Framework application, the XML will be used to rebuild the object. In this example, I return a simple object. Later in this chapter, I will show a simple Windows Form application that uses this Web Service.

First, we need to create a Web Service project. From the Visual Studio.NET Start Page, select New Project. Figure 6.24 illustrates the New Project dialog box with ASP.NET Web Service selected.

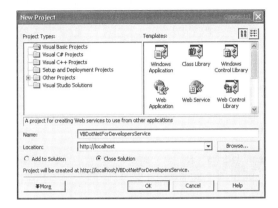

Figure 6.24

Create a Web Service project.

Similar to most projects in Visual Studio.NET, a Web Service will open into a designer. Because a Web Service is basically a class library that can be called via XML, treat the designer as you would the Component Designer. In this example, we won't be using the designer, so simply double-click the designer to go into code view.

To get started, add a new class to the bottom of the editor. The code for the class is in Listing 6.9.

Listing 6.9 HelloWorld *Class*

```
Public Class HelloWorld
    Public Hello As String = "Hello"
    Public World As String = "World"
End Class
```

Now we need to add the WebService method. Add the code in Listing 6.10 to the Service1 Class to replace the commented out HelloWorld method.

Listing 6.10 SayHelloWorld *Web Method*

```
<WebMethod()> Public Function SayHelloWorld() As HelloWorld
    Return New HelloWorld()
End Function
```

The complete Web Service code is illustrated in Listing 6.11.

Listing 6.11   Source Code for Web Service

```
Imports System.Web.Services

Public Class Service1
    Inherits System.Web.Services.WebService

#Region " Web Services Designer Generated Code "

    Public Sub New()
        MyBase.New()

        'This call is required by the Web Services Designer.
        InitializeComponent()

        'Add your own initialization code after the InitializeComponent() call

    End Sub

    'Required by the Web Services Designer
    Private components As System.ComponentModel.Container

    'NOTE: The following procedure is required by the Web Services Designer
    'It can be modified using the Web Services Designer.
    'Do not modify it using the code editor.
    <System.Diagnostics.DebuggerStepThrough()> Private Sub
InitializeComponent()
        components = New System.ComponentModel.Container()
    End Sub

    Overrides Sub Dispose()
        'CODEGEN: This procedure is required by the Web Services Designer
        'Do not modify it using the code editor.
    End Sub

#End Region

    ' WEB SERVICE EXAMPLE
    ' The HelloWorld() example service returns the string Hello World.
    ' To build, uncomment the following lines then save and build the project.
    ' To test this web service, ensure that the .asmx file is the start page
    ' and press F5.
    '
    <WebMethod()> Public Function SayHelloWorld() As HelloWorld
        Return New HelloWorld()
    End Function

End Class
```

Listing 6.11   Continued

```
Public Class HelloWorld
    Public Hello As String = "Hello"
    Public World As String = "World"
End Class
```

Now we want to test the WebService. The .NET Framework makes this extremely easy. If you go into a browser and type the URL of the service or simply run the service from Visual Studio.NET, the test page shown in Figure 6.25 will be displayed in the browser.

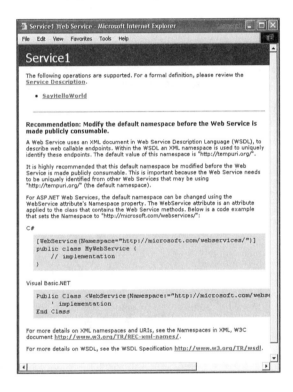

Figure 6.25

Web Service test page.

Clicking on the SayHelloWorld link will bring you to a page to test the individual method. The SayHelloWorld test page is partially shown in Figure 6.26.

Click the Invoke button to execute the method. The output of the method is shown in Figure 6.27. You will notice that the class returned from the method was serialized into XML. This is a fantastic feature of the .NET Framework that you get XML serialization from types in the .NET Framework without any code.

Figure 6.26

SayHelloWorld test page.

Figure 6.27

SayHelloWorld XML Output.

Windows Applications

A great deal of press and discussion has gone on about the new Internet development features of the .NET Framework. But Microsoft is still committed to delivering Rich Client applications.

If you are a VB developer, you should be familiar with Windows applications and how you create them with VB. This hasn't changed in VB.NET and the .NET Framework.

Windows Forms take the ideas based on Visual Basic forms, extending and improving them. Any .NET language can use Windows Forms. They provide a tremendous amount of new functionality and capability to Rich Client applications. Coupled with the new Security, Deployment, and Versioning features of the .NET Framework, it has never been easier to deliver Rich Client applications.

Windows Forms take advantage of all the new features of the .NET framework. Similar to everything else in the framework, forms and controls are classes that can be inherited and extended by developers. Through the use of delegates, the event model has been significantly improved. Multiple controls and events can now be controlled through a single event handler. Developers can use Visual Inheritance of forms to insure that all forms in an application or in an organization's applications have a similar look and feel.

In the example depicted in Figures 6.28–6.40, I will build a small Windows Form application that uses the Web Service from the previous example. Once again, we will start from the Visual Studio.NET Start page and select New Project. From the New Project dialog box, select Windows Application and name it as shown in Figure 6.28.

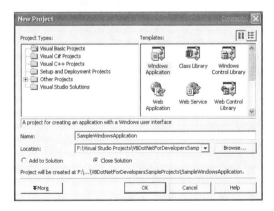

Figure 6.28

Create the Windows application.

After we create the project, Visual Studio.NET will open into the Windows Form designer as shown in Figure 6.29.

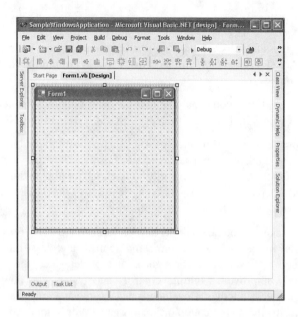

Figure 6.29

Windows application open in Forms Designer.

Now we need to add a Web Reference. Figure 6.30 shows adding a Web Reference from the Solution Explorer.

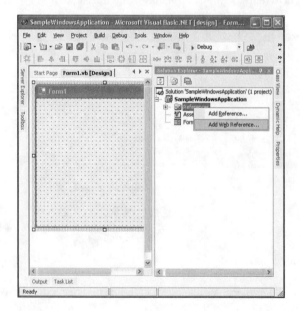

Figure 6.30

Add Web Reference.

The Web Reference dialog box allows you to search the UDDI directory (for more information, go to www.uddi.org) or any Web server you choose through the URL at the top, or you can simply search the local Web server by clicking the link. Figure 6.31 depicts the search of the local Web server.

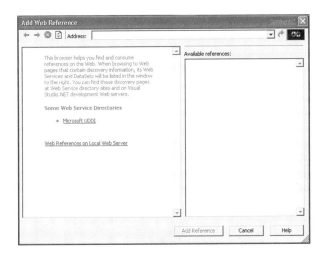

Figure 6.31

Web Reference dialog box (click Web references on local Web server).

After Visual Studio.NET interrogates the Local Web Server, it will present a list of services on the local machine. Now select the Web Service we created earlier. Figure 6.32 depicts the Web Service reference dialog box after selecting the previously created Web Service.

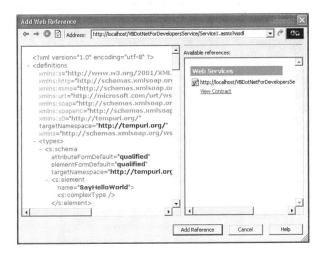

Figure 6.32

After choosing the Web Service created earlier.

Click the Add Reference button to return to the project with a Web Reference. Figure 6.33 illustrates Visual Studio.NET with the Web Reference made.

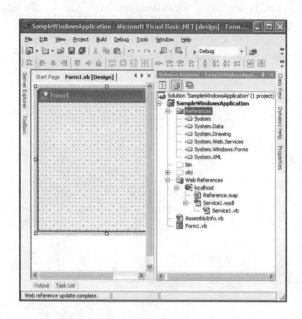

Figure 6.33

Visual Studio.NET after adding a reference.

Now add two text boxes and a button to the form as shown in Figure 6.34.

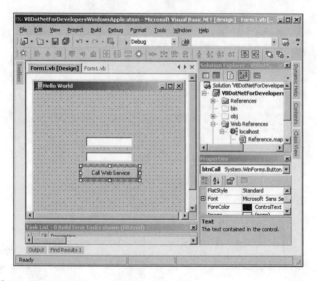

Figure 6.34

After adding two text boxes and a button.

Double-click the button and add the code shown in Listing 6.12.

Listing 6.12 `BtnClick_Event` *Code*

```
Dim oHelloWorldWebService As New localhost.Service1()
Dim oHelloWorld As localhost.HelloWorld
oHelloWorld = oHelloWorldWebService.SayHelloWorld
txtHello.Text = oHelloWorld.Hello
txtWorld.Text = oHelloWorld.World
```

The resulting code is shown in Listing 6.13.

Listing 6.13 *Code after Adding Code in the* `BtnCall` *Click Event (to Call Web Service)*

```
Public Class Form1
    Inherits System.Windows.Forms.Form

#Region " Windows Form Designer generated code "

    Public Sub New()
        MyBase.New()

        'This call is required by the Windows Form Designer.
        InitializeComponent()

        'Add any initialization after the InitializeComponent() call

    End Sub

    'Form overrides dispose to clean up the component list.
    Public Overrides Sub Dispose()
        MyBase.Dispose()
        If Not (components Is Nothing) Then
            components.Dispose()
        End If
    End Sub
    Private WithEvents txtHello As System.Windows.Forms.TextBox
    Private WithEvents txtWorld As System.Windows.Forms.TextBox
    Private WithEvents btnCall As System.Windows.Forms.Button

    'Required by the Windows Form Designer
    Private components As System.ComponentModel.Container

    'NOTE: The following procedure is required by the Windows Form Designer
    'It can be modified using the Windows Form Designer.
    'Do not modify it using the code editor.
    <System.Diagnostics.DebuggerStepThrough()> Private Sub
```

Listing 6.13   Continued

```
InitializeComponent()
Me.txtHello = New System.Windows.Forms.TextBox
Me.txtWorld = New System.Windows.Forms.TextBox
Me.btnCall = New System.Windows.Forms.Button
Me.SuspendLayout
'
'txtHello
'
Me.txtHello.Location = New System.Drawing.Point(96, 80)
Me.txtHello.Name = "txtHello"
Me.txtHello.TabIndex = 0
Me.txtHello.Text = ""
'
'txtWorld
'
Me.txtWorld.Location = New System.Drawing.Point(96, 112)
Me.txtWorld.Name = "txtWorld"
Me.txtWorld.TabIndex = 1
Me.txtWorld.Text = ""
'
'btnCall
'
Me.btnCall.Location = New System.Drawing.Point(96, 144)
Me.btnCall.Name = "btnCall"
Me.btnCall.Size = New System.Drawing.Size(100, 23)
Me.btnCall.TabIndex = 2
Me.btnCall.Text = "Call Web Service"
'
'Form1
'
Me.AutoScaleBaseSize = New System.Drawing.Size(5, 13)
Me.ClientSize = New System.Drawing.Size(294, 267)
Me.Controls.AddRange(New System.Windows.Forms.Control() _
   {Me.btnCall, Me.txtWorld, Me.txtHello})
Me.Name = "Form1"
Me.Text = "Hello World"
Me.ResumeLayout(false)

    End Sub

#End Region

    Private Sub btnCall_Click(ByVal sender As System.Object, ByVal e As
System.EventArgs) _
      Handles btnCall.Click
        Dim oHelloWorldWebService As New localhost.Service1()
        Dim oHelloWorld As localhost.HelloWorld
```

Listing 6.13   Continued
```
        oHelloWorld = oHelloWorldWebService.SayHelloWorld
        txtHello.Text = oHelloWorld.Hello
        txtWorld.Text = oHelloWorld.World

    End Sub
End Class
```

Run the application and click the Call Web Service button to invoke the Web Service. The form should now resemble Figure 6.35.

Figure 6.35

Running Windows Form Application after pressing the button.

From this sample, you should have an idea of how to build a user interface with Windows Forms. In addition, you should also see how Visual Studio.NET and the .NET Framework make using Web Services almost trivial.

Windows Controls

Developers have been able to create their own custom controls in Visual Basic since version 5.0. VB.NET has enhanced this capability to support all elements of the .Net Framework.

In Figures 6.41–6.46, I will introduce you to the "Hello World" Windows Controls. First, select New Project from the Visual Studio.NET Start Page, and the New Project dialog box opens. Figure 6.36 shows the New Project dialog box with Windows Control Library selected.

A Windows Control Library starts in the Windows Control Designer illustrated in Figure 6.37.

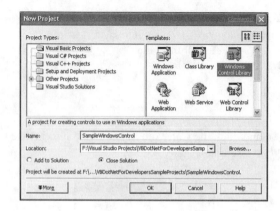

Figure 6.36

Create a Hello World *Windows Control.*

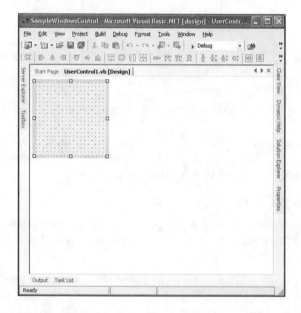

Figure 6.37

Windows Control Designer.

Now as in VB 6, we build the control through composition. Add two buttons to the control. Figure 6.38 depicts the control.

Switch to Code view by double-clicking one of the buttons and add the code illustrated in Figure 6.39. You need to add two event handlers and one event.

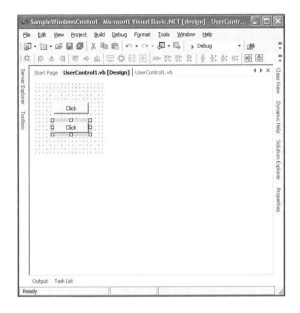

Figure 6.38

Add a couple buttons to the control.

Figure 6.39

Code view of custom control.

After you are done, the code for the control should resemble the code in Listing 6.14.

Listing 6.14 Control Code

```
Public Class UserControl1
    Inherits System.Windows.Forms.UserControl

    Public Event HelloWorldDisplayed()

#Region " Windows Form Designer generated code "

    Public Sub New()
        MyBase.New()

        'This call is required by the Windows Form Designer.
        InitializeComponent()

        'Add any initialization after the InitializeComponent() call

    End Sub

    'UserControl1 overrides dispose to clean up the component list.
    Public Overrides Sub Dispose()
        MyBase.Dispose()
        If Not (components Is Nothing) Then
            components.Dispose()
        End If
    End Sub
    Private WithEvents btnHello As System.Windows.Forms.Button
    Private WithEvents btnWorld As System.Windows.Forms.Button

    'Required by the Windows Form Designer
    Private components As System.ComponentModel.Container

    'NOTE: The following procedure is required by the Windows Form Designer
    'It can be modified using the Windows Form Designer.
    'Do not modify it using the code editor.
    <System.Diagnostics.DebuggerStepThrough()> Private Sub
InitializeComponent()
        Me.btnWorld = New System.Windows.Forms.Button()
        Me.btnHello = New System.Windows.Forms.Button()
        Me.SuspendLayout()
        '
        'btnWorld
        '
        Me.btnWorld.Location = New System.Drawing.Point(40, 80)
        Me.btnWorld.Name = "btnWorld"
        Me.btnWorld.TabIndex = 1
        Me.btnWorld.Text = "Click"
```

Listing 6.14 *Continued*

```
        '
        'btnHello
        '
        Me.btnHello.Location = New System.Drawing.Point(40, 40)
        Me.btnHello.Name = "btnHello"
        Me.btnHello.TabIndex = 0
        Me.btnHello.Text = "Click"
        '
        'UserControl1
        '
        Me.Controls.AddRange(New System.Windows.Forms.Control() _
            {Me.btnWorld, Me.btnHello})
        Me.Name = "UserControl1"
        Me.ResumeLayout(False)

    End Sub

#End Region

    Private Sub btnHello_Click(ByVal sender As System.Object, _
            ByVal e As System.EventArgs) Handles btnHello.Click
        btnHello.Enabled = False
        btnHello.Text = "Hello"
        If btnWorld.Enabled = False Then
            Me.BackColor = System.Drawing.Color.Yellow
            RaiseEvent HelloWorldDisplayed()
        End If
    End Sub

    Private Sub btnWorld_Click_
            (ByVal sender As System.Object, ByVal e As System.EventArgs)_
            Handles btnWorld.Click
        btnWorld.Enabled = False
        btnWorld.Text = "World"
        If btnHello.Enabled = False Then
            Me.BackColor = System.Drawing.Color.DarkMagenta
            RaiseEvent HelloWorldDisplayed()
        End If
    End Sub
End Class
```

Now to test the control, you need to go through the same process that you did when you used the Web Control earlier. After you have done that, drag the sample control from the toolbox to a form in a Windows Application. (I added a new form to the previous Windows Application and set that form as the startup form.) Figure 6.40 illustrates the form with the control on the form.

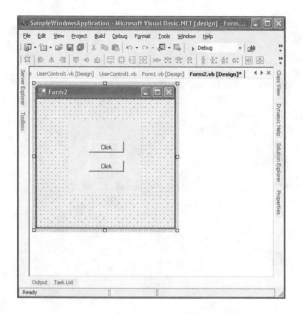

Figure 6.40

Control on a Windows Form before clicking buttons.

Now run the application and click both buttons. Figure 6.41 depicts the application after you have clicked the buttons.

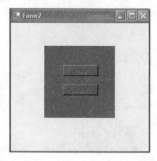

Figure 6.41

Control on a Windows Form after clicking buttons.

Although the example is rather trivial, it gives you the same sort of capabilities and the same method of building controls through containment. Containment isn't the only method of building Windows controls with VB.NET.

Windows Services

New to Visual Basic is the much-requested ability to create a Windows Service. In Figure 6.42 and Listing 6.15, I built a Windows Service that will simply write to the Event Log when it starts and again when it ends.

Start a new project by clicking New Project from the Visual Studio.NET Start Page. Select Windows Service from the New Project dialog box as depicted in Figure 6.42.

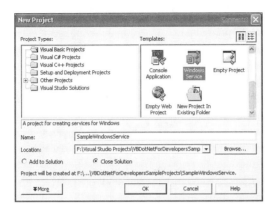

Figure 6.42

Create Windows Service.

Add a reference to `System.Configuration.Install`. Paste the code from Listing 6.15 into the Code view of the application.

Listing 6.15   Base Code for Windows Service

```
Imports System.ServiceProcess
Imports System.ComponentModel
Imports System.Configuration.Install

Public Class Service1
    Inherits System.ServiceProcess.ServiceBase

#Region " Component Designer generated code "

    Public Sub New()
        MyBase.New()

        ' This call is required by the Component Designer.
        InitializeComponent()

        ' Add any initialization after the InitializeComponent() call

    End Sub

    ' The main entry point for the process
    Shared Sub Main()
        Dim ServicesToRun() As System.ServiceProcess.ServiceBase
```

Listing 6.15   Continued

```
        ' More than one NT Service may run within the same process. To add
        ' another service to this process, change the following line to
        ' create a second service object. For example,
        '
        '   ServicesToRun = New System.ServiceProcess.ServiceBase () _
              {New Service1, New MySecondUserService}
        '
        ServicesToRun = New System.ServiceProcess.ServiceBase () {New Service1}

        System.ServiceProcess.ServiceBase.Run(ServicesToRun)
    End Sub


    'Required by the Component Designer
    Private components As System.ComponentModel.Container

    ' NOTE: The following procedure is required by the Component Designer
    ' It can be modified using the Component Designer.
    ' Do not modify it using the code editor.
    <System.Diagnostics.DebuggerStepThrough()> Private Sub
InitializeComponent()
        components = New System.ComponentModel.Container()
        Me.ServiceName = "Service1"
    End Sub

#End Region

    Protected Overrides Sub OnStart(ByVal args() As String)
        ' Add code here to start your service. This method should set things
        ' in motion so your service can do its work.
        Dim oEventLog As New EventLog("Application", "red-leader", _
                "HelloWorldService")
        oEventLog.WriteEntry("Hello World Windows Server Started")
    End Sub

    Protected Overrides Sub OnStop()
        ' Add code here to perform any tear-down necessary to stop your
service.
        Dim oEventLog As New EventLog("Application", "red-leader", _
            "HelloWorldService")
        oEventLog.WriteEntry("Hello World Windows Server Stopped")
    End Sub
```

Listing 6.15   *Continued*

```
End Class
<RunInstaller(True)> Public Class HelloWorldServiceInstaller
    Inherits Installer
    Private oServiceInstaller As ServiceInstaller
    Private oProcessInstaller As ServiceProcessInstaller

    Public Sub New()
        MyBase.New()
        oServiceInstaller = New ServiceInstaller()
        oProcessInstaller = New ServiceProcessInstaller()

        oProcessInstaller.Account = ServiceAccount.LocalSystem

        With oServiceInstaller
            .StartType = ServiceStartMode.Manual
            .ServiceName = "HelloWorldWindowsService"
        End With

        Installers.Add(oProcessInstaller)
        Installers.Add(oServiceInstaller)
    End Sub
End Class
```

NOTE

Notice that an installer class is used in Listing 6.15. This is required to install the service into Windows. After adding this class and compiling the service, you need to use the InstallUtil.exe command-line tool to install the service.

Console Applications

VB also now has the capability to create true Console applications. Console applications run from the command window, also known as the DOS Window. Typically, console applications are used for utility programs.

In Figure 6.43 and Listing 6.16, I walked through the creation of a "Hello World" Console application. This little sample will read a number from the console, which will determine how many times "Hello World" is displayed.

Select New Project from the Visual Studio.NET Start Page to invoke the New Project dialog box and select Console Application as shown in Figure 6.43.

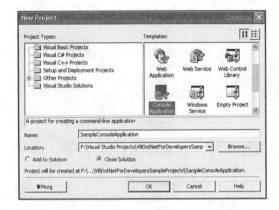

Figure 6.43

Create a Console Application.

Paste the code from Listing 6.16 into the Code view of the application.

Listing 6.16   Console Application Code

```
Imports System.Console
Module HelloWorldConsoleApplications

    Sub Main()
        Dim iNumberOfTimes As Integer
        Dim i As Integer

        iNumberOfTimes = System.Convert.ToInt32(Read())
        For i = 1 To iNumberOfTimes
            WriteLine("Hello World")
        Next
    End Sub
End Module
```

Summary

VB.NET is now fully capable of building every type of application that the .NET Framework is capable of. More importantly, every type of application that could be needed for a scalable, flexible, enterprise application is capable of being built with VB.

Later in the appendixes of this book, I will showcase a number of samples that move beyond the simple examples in this chapter.

CHAPTER 7

Data and Object Types

Every application uses some sort of data. Holding on to data
languages and platforms have made it possible to store the data
internal to the application to allow for structured manipulation
of the data. The .NET Framework and VB.NET are no different. Because the .NET Framework is an object-oriented framework, the types are objects. This is unlike previous versions of
VB, which were a mix of objects and memory.

In order to ensure cross language integration in the .NET
Framework, the *Common Language Specification (CLS)*
dictates how languages can extend themselves and create new
data types. In addition, each language might have a set of
intrinsic types that map directly to types in the framework. For
instance, the VB.NET String type maps to the `System.String`
class, whereas Integer maps to the `System.Int32` class.

Types in the .NET Framework

The .NET Framework supports a wide variety of types for data
manipulation and for the creation of user-defined data types.
All data types in the .NET Framework are now objects, derived
from the `System.Object` class.

In the .NET Framework, data types are broken up into two categories: value types and reference types.

Value Types

In previous versions of Visual Basic, there were objects and
intrinsic variables. Intrinsic variables were memory locations,
and the language provided functions that would act on the contents of these locations. Objects were memory locations that
were controlled through COM and vTables.

The manipulation of variables and objects was handled differently. The following shows an assignment to a variable in VB 6.

```
sName = sFirstName
```

This code causes the value from sFirstName to be copied to sName. But similar code that is used for assignments of objects resulted in both oSalariedEmployee and oEmployee referring to the same object. If either one of the objects was used to change a property value (oSalariedEmployee.FirstName = "NewValue" or oEmployee. FirstName = "NewValue"), both objects would reflect the change. The following shows an assignment to an object variable in VB 6:

```
Set oSalariedEmployee = oEmployee
```

In the .NET Framework, everything is an object. So this required a change to objects or, more specifically, how some objects work; otherwise simple assignments would begin to work like object assignments.

To rectify this situation, the .NET Framework introduces the concept of value types. *Value types* are a special form of object that inherits from the System.ValueType that provides value assignments.

Value types allow value assignment like the intrinsic types in previous versions of Visual Basic, but they have additional capabilities. Because they are objects, they have properties, methods, and events to manipulate the object.

Boolean Values

Boolean variables are a very basic data type that can have one of two values: true or false. In the .NET Framework, a Boolean data type is now an object and has methods to manipulate the type. Most of these are conversion methods to translate Boolean values into strings, integers, and other data types.

In VB 5 or VB 6, if you wanted to convert a Boolean value to a string, you would use the CSTR function, as shown in the following:

```
sFlag = CSTR(bFlag)
```

In VB.NET, you can continue to use the old syntax or use the more object-oriented version:

```
sFlag = bFlag.ToString()
```

Integer Types

One of the most commonly used variable types is the integer. Integers in previous versions were capable of holding values from -32,768 to 32,767. In VB.NET, an Integer type can hold values from -2,147,483,648 to 2,147,483,647. There are a number of variants of the Integer type, which are also Value types. These are as follows: Short, Long, and Byte.

Similar to the Boolean, the Integer types have methods to manipulate the value. In addition, the Integer has a `Format` method that can be used to replace the `Format` function used in previous versions of Visual Basic. The Format functions of VB 6 and VB.NET are as follows:

VB 6

```
sFormatedNumber = Format(iNumber,"$##,###")
```

VB.NET

```
sFormatedNumber = iNumber.Format("$##,###")
```

High Precision Math Types

Highly precise mathematical operations in VB.NET are performed with the Floating Point types and the Decimal, which are also value types. In VB.NET, these types are the Single and Double Floating Point types and the Decimal type, which replaces the Currency type.

Similar to the Boolean and Integer types, these types have methods to manipulate the value.

Conversion Between Types

All the value types have a `ToString` method to convert the value from their type to a string. But for other conversions (string to integer, string to date, integer to Boolean, and so on), you can use the functions that VB has always had such as `CSTR`, `CINT`, `CLNG`, and so on, or you can use the `System.Convert` class, which has many methods to do conversion (much more than what VB supplies intrinsically).

One other conversion function you need to become very familiar with is the new `CTYPE` function. **CTYPE** casts an object from one type to another. Throughout the rest of the book, you will see numerous examples of `CTYPE`. The syntax of `CTYPE` is as follows:

```
CTYPE(ObjectToCase,TypeToCastTo)
```

User-Defined Types

Previous versions of Visual Basic had the capability to create user-defined types that consisted of a collection of different data types combined to represent a type of data. Listing 7.1 shows a User-Defined Type in VB 6.

Listing 7.1   Person User-Defined Type in VB6

```
Public Type Person
    FirstName as String
    LastName as String
    ID as Integer
End Type
```

VB.NET also has this capability, although the keywords have changed from `Type` to `Structure`. It is important to remember that `Structures` are value types. Listing 7.2 shows a User-Defined Type in VB.NET.

Listing 7.2   Person Structure in VB.NET

```
Public Structure Person
    Public FirstName as String
    Public LastName as String
    Public ID as Integer
End Structure
```

Reference Types

Unlike value types, a reference type doesn't contain any data. Instead, a reference type points to an object in memory. When you assign a reference type to another variable, the only thing that gets copied is the reference to the object, so that both variables point to the same object. This is how object variables worked in previous versions of VB.

The vast majority of types in the .NET Framework are reference types. The following list summarizes the basic reference types:

- The Object type
- The String type
- Delegates
- Arrays
- Interfaces
- The Class type

The Object Type

Object is the base type that all reference types inherit from. This means that any other type can be assigned to object. For a VB developer, this functionality makes the Object type the equivalent to the Variant data type found in previous versions.

To create a user-defined reference type, developers use a Class.

Delegates

A delegate is a very special reference type that provides a type safe pointer to a function. Delegates are key to the event model and multithreading model for the .NET Framework.

String Handling

Since the Internet became popular, one of the features that VB didn't keep up with was string handling. VB supplied a library of string handling functions—but not the complete set that is required by the demands of HTML based Internet applications. Experienced developers developed methods to get around this limitation, but it was often a great deal of code that was needed simply to make the code perform better. Listing 7.3 illustrates code that efficiently builds an HTML table from an ADO RecordSet in VB 6.

Listing 7.3   Efficient String Handling to Build an HTML Table in VB 6

```
Private Function BuildHTMLTable(ByVal statsRecordset As ADODB.Recordset) _
                As String
    Dim sHTMLTable As String
    Dim lMaxLength As Long
    Dim iFields As Integer
    Dim iRecordCount As Integer
    Dim lCurrentPos As Long
    Dim sFieldValue As String
    'Determine max size of string
    lMaxLength = Len("<TABLE></TABLE>")
    iRecordCount = statsRecordset.RecordCount

    For iFields = 0 To statsRecordset.Fields.Count - 1
        iMaxLength = iMaxLength + _
            (statsRecordset.Fields(iFields).DefinedSize * iRecordCount)
    Next

    sHTMLTable = Space(iMaxLength)

    Mid(sHTMLTable, 0, 7) = "<TABLE>"
    lCurrentPost = 6

    Do Until statsRecordset.EOF
        Mid(sHTMLTable, lCurrentPos, 8) = "<TR><TD>"
        lCurrentPos = lCurrentPos + 8

        sFieldValue = Trim(statsRecordset.Fields("PlayerName").Value)
        iFieldLength = Len(sFieldValue)
        Mid(sHTMLTable, lCurrentPos, iFieldLength) = sFieldValue
        lCurrentPos = lCurrentPos + iFieldLength

        Mid(sHTMLTable, lCurrentPost, 9) = "</TD><TD>"
        lCurrentPos = lCurrentPos + 9

        sFieldValue = Trim(statsRecordset.Fields("PlayerAverage").Value)
        iFieldLength = Len(sFieldValue)
        Mid(sHTMLTable, lCurrentPos, iFieldLength) = sFieldValue
        lCurrentPos = lCurrentPos + iFieldLength

        Mid(sHTMLTable, lCurrentPost, 10) = "</TD></TR>"
        lCurrentPos = lCurrentPos + 10
        statsRecordset.MoveNext
    Loop

    Mid(sHTMLTable, lCurrentPos, 8) = "</TABLE>"
    'Get rid of blank space at end
    sHTMLTable = Trim(sHTMLTable)
End Function
```

The .NET Framework Base Class library supplies a wealth of string handling functionality within the System.String (equivalent to the VB.NET intrinsic String) and the System.Text.StringBuilder class.

System.String Class

In the .NET Framework, the String intrinsic is actually a synonym for the System.String class. (I'll use String from now on.) This class provides a great deal more functionality than the String intrinsic did in VB 6. The String class adds methods to manipulate the object beyond what VB 6 provided.

An important concept to understand about the .NET Framework String class is that it is an immutable object. (VB 6 was this way also.) Immutable with regard to the String class means that the actual string inside of the class cannot be changed. Immediately developers start asking, "If the string can't be changed why does the code in Listing 7.4 work?" This is actually simple to explain, and it also explains why the code is slow in VB 6, VB.NET, and C#. When you concatenate the string, the CLR is actually behind the scenes creating new string buffers to hold the strings concatenated together. Figure 7.1 illustrates this process, the list following Figure 7.1 describes the process.

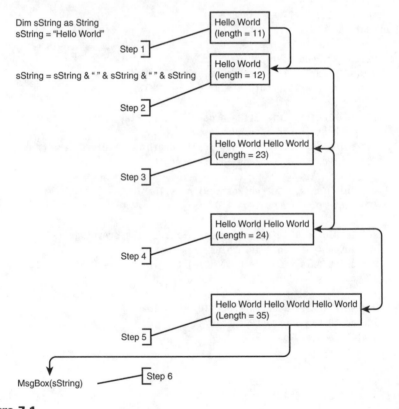

Figure 7.1

How the CLR concatenates the string.

1. CLR creates a String buffer large enough to hold `"Hello World"`. String object is pointed to this buffer.
2. CLR creates a String buffer large enough to hold `"Hello World"` and the first one-character empty string. String value and the one-character empty string are copied to the new buffer and the reference is changed to point to the new buffer.
3. CLR creates a String buffer large enough to hold the previous string and the `"Hello World"` string. The old string and the `"Hello World"` string are copied to the new buffer. The reference is changed to point to the new buffer.
4. CLR creates a String buffer large enough to hold the previous string and the second one-character empty string. String value and the one-character empty string are copied to the new buffer and the reference is changed to point to the new buffer.
5. CLR creates a String buffer large enough to hold the previous string and the `"Hello World"` string. The old string and the `"Hello World"` string are copied to the new buffer. The reference is changed to point to the new buffer.
6. `MsgBox` displays the string in the buffer.

Listing 7.4   Concatenate a String
```
Dim sString as sString
sString = "Hello World"
sString = sString & " " & sString & " " & sString
MsgBox(sString) 'Displays "Hello World Hello World Hello World"
```

As you can see in Figure 7.1, the CLR does a great deal of work so that you can perform simple string manipulation. This is how the VB Runtime worked in VB 6; unfortunately, not everyone realized this. So to start the `String` class has added a method to make string concatenation easier (for a simple scenario). The method provided by the `String` class is the `ConCat` method. Listing 7.5 illustrates the `ConCat` method doing the same as the code in Listing 7.4.

Listing 7.5   `String ConCat` Method
```
Public Sub UseConcat()
    Dim sString as String
    sString = "Hello World"
    sString = System.String.ConCat(sString," ", sString, " ", sString)
    MsgBox(sString)
End Sub
```

The code in Listing 7.10 is far more efficient because using the `ConCat` method indicated to the CLR that it should first figure out the total length that the buffer needs to be. Then the CLR will copy all the characters into the buffer.

The String class also has numerous other methods that allow you to manipulate the string. Some of the new functionality provided is as follows:

- The capability to iterate through the characters of the string through the use of the Chars property.
- The StartsWith and the EndsWith methods allow you to check whether a string starts or ends with a given string.
- The Remove method removes a specific number of characters at a given position.
- The PadLeft and PadRight pads characters to either the left or the right of the string.

For a moment, go back to the string concatenation problem solved in Listing 7.5. This solves some simple string concatenation scenarios, but to fix the problem in Listing 7.3, a different class in the .NET Framework is used.

System.Text.StringBuilder Class

The .NET Framework Base Class library has added functionality to make creating long strings more efficient. The System.Text.StringBuilder provides this functionality. Listing 7.6 is the code that replaces the code in Listing 7.3 to build that same HTML table using an ADO RecordSet and the System.Text.StringBuilder class.

Listing 7.6   Use the StringBuilder Class to Build a String

```
Private Function BuildHTMLTable(ByRef statsRecordset As ADODB.Recordset) _
                    As String
    Dim sHTMLTable As New System.Text.StringBuilder()
    sHTMLTable.Append("<TABLE>")

    Do Until statsRecordset.EOF
        sHTMLTable.Append("<TR><TD>")
        sHTMLTable.Append( _
        statsRecordset.Fields("PlayerName").Value.ToString.Trim)
        sHTMLTable.Append("</TD><TD>")
        sHTMLTable.Append( _
        statsRecordset.Fields("PlayerAverage").Value.ToString.Trim)
        sHTMLTable.Append("</TD></TR>")
        statsRecordset.MoveNext()
    Loop

    sHTMLTable.Append("<TABLE>")
    Return sHTMLTable.ToString
End Function
```

Boxing and Unboxing

Sometimes it is useful to treat a value type as a reference type and vice versa. This can be accomplished using the techniques known as boxing and unboxing. *Boxing* allows you to take a value type and create a reference type from it. *Unboxing* allows you to take a reference type and create a value type from it.

The Common Type Specification defines a corresponding reference type for every value type. These types are called `Boxed Types`. Creating a `Boxed Type` in VB.NET is very easy, as shown in Listing 7.7.

Listing 7.7   Boxing

```
Dim iIntegerValue as Integer
Dim iBoxedInteger as Object
iIntegerValue = 5
iBoxedInteger = iIntegerValue
```

Unboxing is the reverse of boxing. Not all reference types have a corresponding value types, and it isn't possible to unbox these types.

The syntax for unboxing a reference type in VB.NET is shown in Listing 7.8. It is nearly as easy as boxing.

Listing 7.8   Unboxing

```
Dim iIntegerValue as Integer
Dim iBoxedInteger as Object
Dim iUnBoxedValue as Integer

iIntegerValue = 5
iBoxedValue = iIntegerValue
iUnBoxedVale = Ctype(iBoxedValue,Integer)
```

It is important to note that the preceding code will fail with a type mismatch if the `CType` attempted to convert the type into anything other than `Integer`.

Intrinsic Data Types in VB.NET

All the languages that support the .NET Framework are free to support a set of primitive or intrinsic data types that map to types in the .NET Framework. The set supported by VB.NET is shown in Table 7.1.

Table 7.1   VB.NET Intrinsic Data Types

Type	Size in Bytes	.NET Framework Class	VB 6 Type
Boolean	4	System.Boolean	Boolean
Byte	1	System.Byte	Byte
Char	2	System.Char	N/A
Date	8	System.DateTime	Date
Decimal	12	System.Decimal	Currency
Double	8	System.Double	Double
Integer	4	System.Int32	Long
Long	8	System.Int64	N/A
Object	4	System.Object (class)	Object

Table 7.1   Continued

Type	Size in Bytes	.NET Framework Class	VB 6 Type
Short	2	`System.Int16`	Integer
Single	4	`System.Single`	Single
String	10 +(2* String Length)	`System.String`	String
User Defined Type (Structure)	Sum of the sizes of its members	`System.ValueType` (Inherits from)	Type

VB wants to be the easiest language to produce cross-language integration. This is why some types have been deliberately left unsupported in VB.NET. In some other .NET languages, it is possible to create types that won't be supported by other .NET languages if they expose publicly types that aren't part of the Common Type Specification. VB.NET doesn't allow you to expose these types.

VB.NET has been architected to only supply intrinsic data types for types that are supported in the Common Type Specification. This means that VB doesn't support the following:

- Unsigned Types (Internal variables can be types as unsigned but cannot be exposed)
- Operator Overloading

Date

In VB 6, the Date type was stored in four bytes. This was actually the same as the Double data type. In VB.NET, a Date type uses the .NET Framework `DateTime` data type. `DateTime` is an eight-byte integer value. Because of this change, there is no automatic conversion between the Date and Double data types in VB.NET, but the `System.Convert.ToDouble` and `System.Convert.ToDateTime` methods are available to translate `DateTime` values to Doubles, and vice versa.

Decimal

Previous versions of VB had a currency data type that is no longer supported. The Decimal data type provides all the functionality that the currency type provided and more. The Decimal data type supports more precision on either side of the decimal.

Short, Integer, and Long

Perhaps the change to data types in VB.NET with the most impact will be the change to the Integer and Long data types from VB 6 to VB.NET. In VB 6, the Integer data type was a 16-bit integer and the Long data type was a 32-bit integer. In VB.NET, the new Short data type is a 16-bit integer, Integer is now a 32-bit integer, and the Long is a 64-bit integer.

This might cause problems when code is migrated from VB 6 to VB.NET, particularly when dealing with traditional Win32 API calls.

Object

The Variant data type, which was able to hold any type of data, no longer exists in VB.NET. Because everything is an object in the .NET Framework, the Object type serves the purpose of the Variant, and it no longer has the restriction that it can't be used to reference simple data types such as Integers.

String

One of the most important data types in VB has always been the String. Unfortunately, it was also the type most likely to create performance problems when developers concatenate strings.

In VB.NET, the String data type no longer supports fixed length strings. In the .NET Framework, all strings are variable length. The length of a string is determined by the value placed into it.

String concatenation has always been a very expensive piece of code in VB. This has been addressed in VB.NET.

Char

VB.NET has added a new intrinsic data type to handle Unicode strings. The Char type is a 16-bit numeric value used to store a single Unicode character. Char variables can only be converted to numeric types via explicit conversion.

Classes

The key type in creating object-oriented systems is the Class. VB has had the capability to build classes since VB 4. VB.NET builds on the capabilities that previous versions introduced to the language.

Classes are reference types and include three types of members: data members, function members, and nested types. Data members are available directly through data types, or through properties. Function members act on data held by data members (in most cases). New to VB.NET is the ability to create a child class directly in a class. This is called a *nested type*.

In previous versions of VB, each class was held in a separate .CLS file. In VB.NET, you can organize Classes as you best see fit. They can all be placed in separate files, all in the same file, or any combination.

To create an object hierarchy in previous versions of VB, classes were created with no explicit relationship. Take a look at Listings 7.9, 7.10, and 7.11 to compare and contrast the class hierarchy between VB 6 and VB.NET.

Listing 7.9 shows a VB 6 Class called COrder that has a couple of properties; one of which is typed as ClineItem.

Listing 7.9 COrder.CLS *File*

```
Private m_lOrderNumber as long
Private m_oLineItem as ClineItem

Public Property Get LineItem() as ClineItem
    Set LineItem = m_oLineItem
End Property

Public Property Get OrderNumber() as Long
    OrderNumber = m_lOrderNumber
End Property

Public Property Let OrderNumber(ByVal RHS as Long)
    m_lOrderNumber = RHS
End Property
```

Listing 7.10 shows the VB 6 CLineItem class that also has a few properties. What these classes don't imply is any specific relationship.

Listing 7.10 ClineItem.CLS *File*

```
Private m_lProductCode as Long
Private m_sProductDescription as String

Public Property Get ProductCode() as Long
    ProductCode = m_lProductCode
End Property

Public Property Let ProductCode (ByVal RHS as Long)
    m_lProductCode = RHS
End Property

Public Property Get ProductDescription() as Long
    ProductDescription = m_sProductDescription
End Property

Public Property Let ProductDescription (ByVal RHS as Long)
    m_sProductDescription = RHS
End Property
```

Now in VB.NET, we can build the relationship directly into the class structure. Listing 7.11 shows a VB.NET Class COrder, which has a nested type ClineItem. In the VB 6 versions, someone could create a Line item without an Order. (This could be minimized if the ClineItem was defined as PublicNotCreatable.) In the VB.NET versions, this isn't possible.

Listing 7.11   Subclass in VB.NET

```
Public Class COrder

    Private c_lOrderNumber as long
    Private c_oLineItem as New ClineItem()
    Public ReadOnly Property LineItem() As ClineItem
        Get
            Return c_oLineItem
        End Get
    End Property
    Public Property OrderNumber as long
        Get
            OrderNumber = c_lOrderNumber
        End Get

        Set(ByVal  Value as Long)
            c_lOrderNumber = value
        End Set

    End Property
    Public Class ClineItem

        Private c_lProductCode as Long
        Private c_sProductDescription as String

        Friend Sub New()
            MyBase.New()
        End Sub

        Public Property ProductCode as Long
            Get
                ProductCode = c_lProductCode
            End Get
            Set(ByVal Value as Long)
                c_lProductCode = value
            End Set
        End Property

        Public Property ProductDescription as String
            Get
                ProductDescription = c_sProductDescription
            End Get
            Set(ByVal Value as String)
                c_sProductDescription = value
            End Set
        End Property

    End Class
End Class
```

Structures

VB has had the capability to create *User Defined Data Types (UDT)* in previous versions via the Type statement. A UDT is a concatenation of various data types into one type, as shown in Listing 7.12.

Listing 7.12   Employee Type in VB6

```
Public Type Employee
    FirstName as String
    LastName as String
    SocialSecurityNumber as String
    BirthDate as Date
    Dependents as Integer
End Type
```

In VB.NET, the Type statement has been replaced with the Structure statement, as shown in Listing 7.13.

Listing 7.13   Employee Structure in VB.NET

```
Public Structure Employee
    Public FirstName as String
    Public LastName as String
    Public SocialSecurityNumber as String
    Public PirthDate as Date
    Public Dependents as Integer
End Structure
```

The Structure statement actually creates a value type. In effect, Structures are a type of value class.

A Structure in VB.NET not only can contain data types, but also can contain properties and methods.

In Listing 7.14, the individual data types have public access modifiers except the *SocialSecurityNumber* field. In VB.NET, all members in a structure must have an access modifier. The capability to limit the scope of access for some members is new in VB.NET. This wasn't possible with a UDT in previous versions of VB. Listing 7.14 also illustrates the capability for structures to have properties and methods.

At first glance, it appears that a Structure really is the same as a class. In many ways this is true, but Structures have a few key differences.

Listing 7.14   Example Structure

```
Public Structure TEmployee

    Public FirstName as String
    Public LastName as String
    Private SocialSecurityNumber as String
```

Listing 7.14   Continued

```
    Public BirthDate as Date
    Public Dependents as Integer

    ReadOnly Property FullName
        Get
            Return FirstName & " " & LastName
        End Get
    End Property

    Public Function CalculateExemptionAmount(ByVal AmountPerDependent as
Decimal) _
                    as Decimal
        Return AmountPerDependent * Dependents
    End Function
End Structure
```

Structures are allocated as value types (intrinsic data types such as Integer, Boolean, and so on are value types) in memory not as objects, so the runtime manages them in a more efficient manner with less overhead for garbage collection, and so on. Because of this, structures are much faster in performance. Structures can't inherit from a class or structure, nor can another structure or class inherit from a structure.

Structures also behave differently with regard to constructors and destructors. An instance of a class is created when the New operator is applied to a class, as shown in the following:

```
Dim oEmployee as New CEmployee
```

This isn't the case with a structure. Similar to any other value type, a structure doesn't need to be explicitly created. This is demonstrated in the following:

```
Dim tEmployee as TEemployee
```

When a structure is created, all its members are initialized to the default values dictated by the .NET Framework. (Numeric types default to 0, strings to an empty string, and Booleans to False).

Structures are allowed to have constructors, but aren't allowed to have a default constructor because the .NET Framework implicitly creates one for the structure.

Nor are structures allowed to have destructors. In order to maintain the performance of structures, the CLR will just clean the memory allocated to the structure as soon as the variable drops out of scope or is set to nothing.

Structures, similar to Types in VB 6, are a very valuable type for simple data structures and should be used in that fashion. Structures should *not* be used to represent a complex object, but rather just a piece of data with some as simple functions.

Summary

The .NET Framework and therefore VB.NET provides a multitude of new features for the usage and creation of data types. VB.NET has been developed not only to create applications easily, but also to very easily create components that are capable of being used by other languages that support the .NET Framework

The new object-oriented features in VB.NET provide an incredible amount of power to classes in VB. Not only do these features add to the power of classes, but also add an incredible amount of power to simple User Defined Types. Not only has the power of VB object-oriented features been increased, but also the ease of creating robust object hierarchies has increased.

CHAPTER 8

Controlling the Flow of Logic

Among the core set of language statements that all modern programming languages have is the flow of control statements. Visual Basic has always had a rich set of structured programming statements that control the flow of logic, along with a few that aren't so structured.

VB.NET has taken steps to clean up the core language and remove or modify some of the legacy, non-structured statements.

Flow of control statements can be categorized into three types: selection, iteration, and legacy constructs.

Short-Circuited Expressions

Before moving into the different types of flow of control statements in VB.NET, an extremely important new feature of VB.NET needs to be introduced. Up until VB.NET, short-circuited expressions weren't supported in the VB language.

Short-circuited expressions are a new feature that could potentially enhance performance. When a conditional expression is evaluated, the outcome of the expression can be determined without evaluating all the portions of the expression and then the statement would short-circuit and complete without all code being executed. An example will help out. Listing 8.1 is a bit of VB.NET code that doesn't support short-circuited expressions.

Listing 8.1   Introduction to Short-Circuited Expressions

```
Private Function EligibleForDependentBenefits(ByVal bEmployee as Boolean, _
    Byval SSN as String) as Boolean
    Dim bDependentBenefits as Boolean
    bDependentBenefits = bEmployee And EmployeeHasDependents(SSN)
    Return bDependentBenefits
End Function
Private Function EmployeeHasDependents(ByVal SSN as String) as Boolean
    'Call a StoredProcedure that determines if employee has benefits
    'Return true if employee has dependents and false if they dont
End Function
```

What happens in this example? In the first function, a conditional expression is evaluated. The conditional expression gets the value of a Boolean variable and compares it against a Boolean value returned from a function. If they are both true, the Boolean variable is set to True. If the Boolean variable is false, the function will still be called. In my example, the function calls a stored procedure (this is an expensive operation). There was no need for the function to ever be called. Short-circuiting fixes this problem. What it does is evaluate the expression from left to right. In an expression using the And logical operator, if the item being checked is false, the remaining expressions won't be executed. If it is true, the next portion of the expression will be checked.

To achieve short-circuited expression in VB.NET, you need to make use of the short-circuited versions of the And and Or logical operators: AndAlso and OrElse. Listing 8.2 is the short-circuited version of the function in Listing 8.1 that could be short-circuited.

Listing 8.2   Short-Circuited Expression

```
Private Function EligibleForDependentBenefits(ByVal bEmployee as Boolean, _
    Byval SSN as String) as Boolean
    Dim bDependentBenefits as Boolean
    bDependentBenefits = bEmployee AndAlso EmployeeHasDependents(SSN)
    Return bDependentBenefits
End Function
```

The stored procedure will only be called if the bEmployee flag is true.

Now that I have introduced short-circuited expressions, let's move on to the language structures that make the most use of expressions.

Selection

The purpose of a selection statement is to determine which path of execution should be taken. In VB.NET, there are two types of selection statements: IF statements and Select Case statements.

IF Statements

The first and probably most important flow of control statement in both structured programming and object-oriented programming is the simple decision branch. In Visual Basic, this is represented by the IF statement, shown in Figure 8.1.

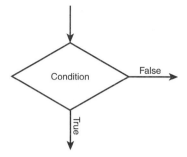

Figure 8.1

The IF *statement.*

The structure of an IF statement in VB.NET is shown in Listing 8.3. ELSEIF is shown in Listing 8.4.

Listing 8.3 IF *Statement*

```
IF Boolean expression THEN
    Statements to execute if Boolean expression is true
ELSE
    Statements to execute if Boolean expression is false
END IF
```

Listing 8.4 *Extended* ELSEIF *Syntax*

```
IF Boolean expression THEN
    Statements to execute if Boolean expression is true
ELSEIF Boolean expression THEN
    Statements to execute Boolean expression is true
ELSE
    Statements to execute if Boolean expression is false
END IF
```

Although the IF Statement in VB.NET appears to be exactly the same as the IF Statement in VB 6, there are some changes. One very minor change is that the THEN portion of the statement is no longer required.

Also, VB.NET is a strictly typed language by default. This means that the Boolean expression portion of the code must, in fact, be a Boolean expression. Previous versions of VB would convert the value on-the-fly, so the following code would be valid:

```
IF 5 THEN
```

This isn't the case in VB.NET. The preceding code would actually create the compile time error shown in Figure 8.2.

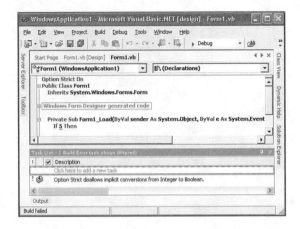

Figure 8.2

Option Strict disallows implicit conversions from System.Integer to System.Boolean.

The syntax of the IF statement allows a group of conditions to be tested in single IF statement. This is done through the ELSEIF variation. This can be used to have multiple conditions tested in one IF and each one has different code executed if true, as shown in Listing 8.5.

Listing 8.5 *ELSEIF IF Variant*

```
IF sEmployeeType = "E" THEN
    Call HandleExemptEmployee(lEmployeeID)
ELSEIF HasOverTime(lEmployeeID) THEN
    Call ReportOverTime(lEmployeeID)
ELSEIF WorkedNightShift(lEmployeeID)
    Call ReportNightShiftWorker(lEmployeeID)
END IF
```

The IF and all the ELSEIFs test different conditions. If the conditions were to check the same variable for different values, a Select Case statement, described next, would be the better choice.

Select Case

The Select Case statement (see Figure 8.3) was designed to make it easy to test multiple values in a single expression.

Select Case doesn't allow the expression being evaluated on each level to change like the IF..ELSEIF..END IF construct does. The structure of the Select Case statement is illustrated in Listing 8.6.

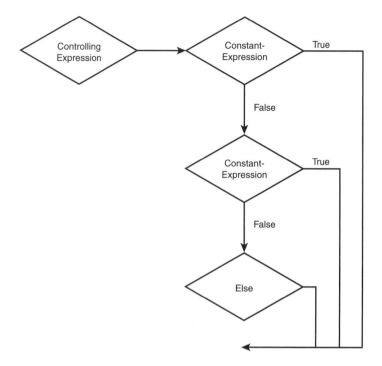

Figure 8.3

Select Case *statement.*

Listing 8.6 Select Case *Syntax*

```
Select Case test expression
    Case expression list
        'Statements to Execute
    Case expression list
        'Statements to Execute
    Case Else
        'Statements to Execute
End Select
```

The syntax is simple, but there are a few options and subtle choices that developers should take into account when they are coding.

First, the test expression should have more than two outcomes; otherwise, an IF statement would be a better choice. It wouldn't be wise then for the test expression to evaluate to a Boolean.

Second, every Case will be evaluated until a true condition has been met or the Case Else is executed. With this in mind, you should place the Case statements in order of probability. For example, if the test expression was an Employee object and the Cases were for each type of employee within an organization, the first Case should be the

Employee type that is most common, and the last Case should be the Employee type that is least common.

Expression lists in Select Case statements can be complex and have a number of variations, as illustrated in the following:

Simple expression:

```
Case 5
```

Multiple items in an expression list:

```
Case 5,10,15
```

Range in an expression list:

```
Case 5 To 15
```

Comparison expression:

```
Case Is > 10
```

Compound expression:

```
Case 5,8, 11 To 15, IS > 30
```

Iteration

The purpose of iteration statements is to execute a given set of statements numerous times. VB.NET has three core iteration statements. For Next is used to iterate code based on a set of bounds. For Each is used to iterate through a data type that support enumeration. Do...Loop allows for looping based on a Boolean expression.

For Next

There are cases in which you have to iterate through a set of statements a certain number of times. The most efficient method of doing this is through the use of the For Next statement, shown in Figure 8.4.

The For Next statement consists of a bounds expression, an optional increment expression, and a terminator, as shown in Listing 8.7.

Listing 8.7   Syntax of For Next

```
FOR variable = expression TO expression STEP expression
    Statements to execute
NEXT
```

For Next has a very simple syntax. The most complex part of the statement is the assignment and test. The syntax consists of an initializer, a test, and an increment value.

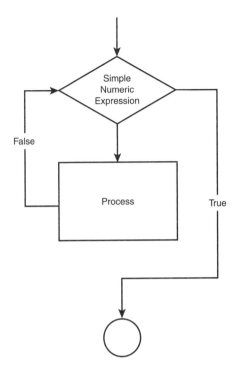

Figure 8.4

For Next *statement.*

The following three For Next examples illustrate different uses of the initializer and test (Note that in the third example, the increment is a negative value.):

```
For I = 5 to 10
For I = 5 to 10 Step 2
For I = 100 to 10 Step -1
```

Another item to note is the value of the variable after the For Next has completed execution. In the second line, for example, the value of I will be 12 when the For Next statement has completed execution.

The For Next statement allows the use of an Exit For statement to prematurely exit the For Next iteration and execute the next line of code following the Next. This is illustrated by the example in Listing 8.8.

*Listing 8.8 **Prematurely Exiting** For Next*

```
For I = 1 to 100
    If sEmployeeType(I) = "Salaried" Then
        Exit For
    End If
Next
Call ProducePayCheck(oEmployee(I))
```

For Each

The For Each statement iterates through a collection of items that support enumeration, as shown in Figure 8.5.

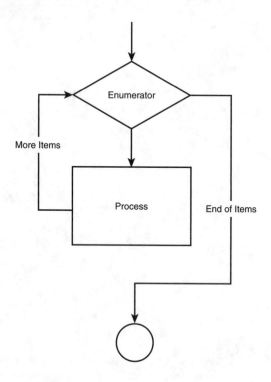

Figure 8.5

For Each *statement.*

The For Each Statement is deceptively simple, as shown in Listing 8.9. The key is not the syntax of the statement, but the implementation of the items that you are trying to enumerate.

Listing 8.9   For Each **Example**

```
For Each element In group
    Statements to execute
Next
```

The *element* in the For Each statement can be the System.Object type or it can be a specific object interface that all the items in the group implement. The For Each statement, similar to the For Next statement, supports the use of Exit For to prematurely jump out of the enumeration to the next line of code following the Next.

The *group* must have a GetEnumerator method. The GetEnumerator method returns an Enumerator object.

The syntax of the For Each statement hasn't changed in VB.NET, but the implementation details of objects you want to use for enumeration has. Most collections and arrays of objects in the .NET Framework support enumeration on data structures in VB.NET. One nice change is that arrays in the .NET Framework can be enumerated with For Each.

In Listings 8.10–8.13, I will be building a Stack that supports enumeration. It uses three classes: a Node class, a Stack class, and a Stack Enumerator class.

Listing 8.10 is the Node class, which holds a string value and points to the next node in the list.

Listing 8.10   Node Class

```
'Node class for implementing a linked list
Class Node
    Public Value As String
    Public NextNode As Node

    ' Constructor for Node Class takes a String and a
    ' Node that represents the next node in the list
    Sub New(ByVal val As String, ByVal nnode As
Node)
        MyBase.New()
        Value = val
        NextNode = nnode
    End Sub
End Class
```

The Stack class in Listing 8.11 is the class that will be enumerated in the For Each statement. The Stack class contains the required GetEnumerator function that For Each uses to retrieve the enumerator.

In order for the For Each statement to use the Stack class, the class must provide a GetEnumerator method. GetEnumerator will return a new instance of the StackEnumerator class that is initialized to start at the top of the list. The important thing to note about this is that it allows multiple For Each statements to be enumerating the same Stack class simultaneously.

Listing 8.11   Stack Class

```
'Stack class that stores a stack of strings using a linked list of node
instances
Class Stack

    Private Top As Node = Nothing    'points to the top of the stack
```

Listing 8.11 Continued

```
'Push adds a new string to the stack
Sub Push(ByVal s As String)
    Top = New Node(s, Top)
End Sub

'Pop pops the top string off the stack
Function Pop() As String
    If Top is Nothing Then
        Throw New Exception("Stack Empty")
    End If
    Pop = Top.Value
    Top = Top.NextNode
End Function

'GetEnumerator returns an instance of the StackEnumerator class
'Every collection must have a GetEnumerator method that returns
'a class supporting a MoveNext() method and a Current property
Function GetEnumerator() As StackEnumerator
    Return New StackEnumerator(Top)
End Function
End Class
```

The StackEnumerator class shown in Listing 8.12 is the class that is used by For Each to enumerate through the linked list. The StackEnumerator class is the workhorse used by the For Each statement to retrieve items. To support enumeration, this class must support a MoveNext method and a Current property. The MoveNext method simply repositions the item that is the current node to be the next node in the list. The Current property returns the current node. You will also notice that in the constructor, the current node is set to an empty node placed at the top of the list. This handles the case in which the linked list is empty.

Listing 8.12 StackEnumerator *Class*

```
'StackEnumerator enumerates items in the Stack
Class StackEnumerator
    'CurrentNode maintains a reference to the node currently being
enumerated
    Private CurrentNode As Node

    'MoveNext is called to move the enumerator through the items it is
    'enumerating.  It returns False when there are no more items
    Function MoveNext() As Boolean
        CurrentNode = CurrentNode.NextNode
        Return Not IsNothing(CurrentNode)
    End Function
```

Listing 8.12   Continued

```
'Current returns the currently enumerated item
ReadOnly Property Current() As String
    Get
        Return CurrentNode.Value
    End Get
End Property

'Constructs a StackEnumerator instance given the top of the stack
Sub New(ByVal top As Node)
    'Add an extra node on the front because MoveNext is called before
    'the first item is retrieved.
    'This is in order to handle an empty collection
    CurrentNode = New Node(Nothing, top)
End Sub

End Class
```

Listing 8.13 shows the VB.NET code to enumerate the Stack class. The client code simply places some items in the list and then uses For Each to write the items to the console. It then removes a few items from the list, puts a couple of new items on the list, and again uses For Each to write the items to the console.

Listing 8.13   Enumerate Stack Class

```
'Sample code
Module Module1

    Sub Main()
        Dim Stk As New Stack()
        Dim Str As String

        Stk.Push("time")
        Stk.Push("the")
        Stk.Push("is")
        Stk.Push("Now")
        For Each Str In Stk
            Console.Write(Str + " ")
        Next
        Console.WriteLine()

        Stk.Pop()
        Stk.Pop()
        Stk.Push("isn't")
        Stk.Push("Now")

        For Each Str In Stk
            Console.Write(Str + " ")
```

Listing 8.13 Continued

```
      Next
      Console.WriteLine()
      Console.WriteLine()
      Console.WriteLine("Hit <Enter> when done")
      Console.ReadLine()
   End Sub

End Module
```

Do Loop

Whereas For Next uses numeric values to control how many times that a loop should be executed and For Each uses an enumerator to control the number of times a loop should be executed, Do While Loop and Do Loop Until are controlled by Boolean expressions more like an IF Statement. The Boolean expressions can be complex and include multiple conditions. Figure 8.6 illustrates the Do While Loop, and Figure 8.7 illustrates the Do Loop Until.

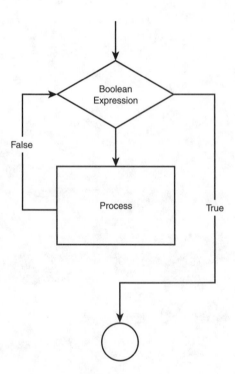

Figure 8.6

Do While Loop.

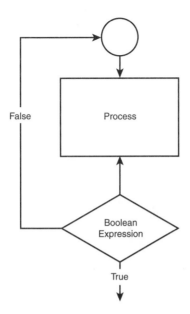

Figure 8.7
Do Loop Until.

The Do Loop statement provides a very powerful construct for controlling a loop. Do While Loop is a top-driven loop. The code contained within the loop can be executed from zero to many times. Do Loop Until is a bottom-driven loop that will ensure that a process is executed at least once. It is important to note that both Do Loop statements allow the use of an Exit Do statement to exit out of the loop prematurely. Listing 8.14 shows the syntax for Do While Loop and Listing 8.15 shows the syntax for Do Loop Until.

Listing 8.14   Do While Loop

```
Do While Condition
    Statements to execute
Loop
```

Listing 8.15   Do Loop Until

```
Do
    Statements to execute
Loop Until Condition
Change
```

The change to short-circuited operations in VB.NET has an effect on Do Loops. In previous versions of Visual Basic, if the Do Loop condition had multiple conditions using Boolean operators, all conditions functions would be executed. In VB.NET, if the first condition satisfies the overall condition, the subsequent conditions won't be executed.

Similar to the IF statement, this can improve performance but also cause subtle problems in legacy systems if part of the condition was a function that you always needed executed.

While Loop

Microsoft has changed the syntax of the While Wend statement to While End While. While Wend was the first attempt to add a structured loop construct to Basic.

Many developers find the syntax a little ugly, but its functionality is nearly equivalent to the Do Loop construct. One difference is that the Do Loop statement has the Exit Do statement to prematurely exit the loop.

Again, similar to IF statements and Do Loop statements, the short-circuited operations affect the While End While statement.

Statements Removed

The VB language contains a variety of legacy flow of logic statements. Some of these have been removed in VB.NET and some have been changed.

In an effort to clean up the language, Microsoft has removed a few language elements from Visual Basic, including a number of flow of control statements. VB.NET doesn't support the GoSub statement, the On x Goto, or On x GoSub statements. These statements are rarely used and generally result in unstructured code. VB developers really don't need them any longer.

Note that On Error Goto has not been removed, nor has GoTo, although in my opinion it should have been.

Summary

Basic has evolved from a language with few structured programming constructs to a great structured programming language in VB.

VB.NET really only makes minor changes to the structured programming constructs of previous versions while also adding short-circuited operations, which can improve performance simply because code that doesn't need to execute, won't. Code that took advantage of the lack of short-circuited operations might need revisiting.

Finally, Microsoft has chosen to clean up some legacy constructs and remove some constructs that don't fit in with the way developers build solutions today. This might require some changes to existing code, but in the long run will help developers build more maintainable systems.

CHAPTER 9

Error Handling

Error handling is a process for handling situations when something goes wrong. The kinds of problems that need to be handled can be categorized into environmental problems and developer-created problems.

Environmental problems deal with issues such as a floppy not being is a drive, the network being down, or a database being shutdown. These are problems that should be handled, but cannot be predicted easily.

A developer-created problem is quite often something that can be avoided if proper precautions are taken. (And this is preferred over trapping an error.) Examples of developer-created problems include code that attempts to do something invalid such as dividing an integer by zero, trying to access an item in an array with a index that is out of range, and attempting to use an object variable that hasn't been initialized.

Error handling might be the most important aspect of robust applications. One of the worst things that a developer can do is to allow an error to make its way back to the user. Proper error handling fixes errors that can be fixed and logs unfixable errors and returns a friendly message to the user.

Error handling falls into two kinds: business rule exceptions tied to the business requirements and exception handling tied to problems that occur with computer systems. The second kind is sometimes neglected because it isn't directly tied to the business requirements.

In previous versions of Visual Basic, the primary method of error handling was the On Error statement, although other objects and statements were often used alongside the On Error statement to record when errors occur, to handle errors produced by API calls, and to resume processing after an error has been handled.

There are a number of problems with this method of error handling. In many situations, it was difficult to determine which error handler was currently in control. Different components handled errors in different ways: dealing with COM components that raised errors one way, dealing with API calls that returned an error code, dealing with API calls that set the LastError, and dealing with Database exceptions.

This has all changed in the .NET Framework. Error handling has been integrated into the .NET Framework so that it is consistent throughout all languages. The method chosen is known as *structured exception handling*, a well-established method used by many other languages. Structured exception handling is a much more elegant solution than the On Error method.

The .NET Framework specifies that all error handling be implemented using structured exception handling. In fact, structured exception handling is deeply embedded in the .NET Framework itself. Even though VB.NET still supports the On Error method of error handling, under the hood VB.NET implements On Error and the associated commands using structured exception handling.

Because exception handling is so deeply embedded in the CLR, it works across component, language, and even machine boundaries without the problems that error handling had in VB prior to .NET. The exception handling mechanism is more stable, faster, and portable across languages.

The System.Exception Class

Structured exception handling is an object-oriented approach to handling exceptions. In fact, when an exception is encountered, the actual exception information is an object.

All exceptions in the .NET Framework inherit from the System.Exception class, and it is important to understand the type of information that all exceptions will provide. Table 9.1 lists the properties of the base exception class and the information that is provided.

Table 9.1 System.Exception *Properties*

Property	Description
HelpLink	The HelpLink property of the System.Exception class provides a method for a developer to provide detailed help information in the form of a *Uniform Resource Locator (URL)* or a *Uniform Resource Name (URN)*.
InnerException	The InnerException property provides a method to embed exceptions within exceptions. This allows developers to include the original exception with any additional exceptions that they throw.
Message	The Message property provides a localized description of the exception that has occurred.
StackTrace	The StackTrace property provides a complete trace of the call stack, including line number and source code filename.

Try...Catch...Finally Statement

In VB.NET the exception-handling construct is the Try...Catch...Finally statement. The Try...Catch...Finally statement wraps a portion of code that will be checked for exceptions. Try...Catch...Finally statements can be nested.

If an exception does occur, a Catch clause will trap the exception and apply some sort of exception handling logic. (Assuming that one is available for the exception that occurred. More on this later.) The Finally clause, if used, will handle cleanup code and is guaranteed to run no matter what the code outcome is in the Try and Catch clauses. Listing 9.1 illustrates the use of the Try...Catch...Finally statement.

Listing 9.1   Try...Catch...Finally *Statement*

```
Try
    ' Some code that could cause an exception
Catch oException as SomeSortOfException When OptionalExpression
    ' Some code that will execute if exception is encountered
Finally
    ' Some code that will always execute exception or no exception
End Try
```

Try Clause

The Try clause contains the code that could cause an exception. Code encased in a Try clause will be executed until an exception occurs or the code is complete. If an exception does occur then the CLR will immediately look for the first Catch clause that handles the exception or that handles an exception that is part of the inheritance hierarchy of the class of the exception that occurred. Exceptions are objects themselves and they all ultimately derive from the System.Exception class. When you build your handlers your Catch clauses can use very explicit exception types or a more generic type. When an exception occurs the first Catch clause that specifies a type that the exception that was thrown is a derivative of is encountered. This Catch clause will handle the exception. That is quite a mouthful: A later example in this chapter will clarify this.

Exit Try Statement

The Exit Try statement lets you explicitly jump out of a Try block. This is similar to the use that Exit For or Exit Do statements provide in For and Do loops, respectively.

Catch Clause

The Catch clause consists of two parts, one of which is required. The *exception declaration* is an object parameter that must be of a type that has ultimately inherited from System.Exception. The optional When clause allows further filtering to be done on the actual reason the exception occurred.

A Try...Catch...Finally statement must have at least one, but might have many Catch clauses. If a Catch clause that matches the exception thrown is not present, the Finally clause will be executed and the exception will be passed up the call chain

Exceptions should be caught in Catch clauses from a most specific to least specific order. The first Catch clause that is found that matches the exception thrown will be the only one executed for the exception. If you aren't careful and you place a more general Catch clause before a more specific Catch clause, the specific Catch clause will never be executed.

Finally Clause

The Finally clause is used for any code that must run whether the code in the Try clause threw an exception or not. This is important for resources such as files and database connections that must be closed no matter how the routine is exited. This was much more difficult to do in previous versions of VB 6.

Throw Statement

There are times when code itself needs to create an exception, for example if the code has detected an invalid condition or if a Catch clause needs to push the exception up the call chain. This is done using the following Throw statement:

```
Throw exceptionobject
```

The *exceptionobject* must be a type that has ultimately inherited from System.Exception.

In VB.NET, an exception will also be thrown if the Err.Raise syntax from previous versions of VB is used. This is not encouraged for new development, but if you are reusing existing code then the code will still have the expected behavior.

Implementing Structured Exception Handling

The code in Listing 9.2 uses one of the .NET methods to access the file system. The code opens a log file and writes to the contents to the console. One exception handler is being used to handle all possible *System.IO.IOException*.

Listing 9.2   VB.NET File Not Open Exception

```
Private Sub DumpFileToConsole(ByVal FileName As String)
    Dim oFileStream As New FileStream(FileName, FileMode.Open, FileAccess.Read)
    Dim oStreamReader As New StreamReader(oFileStream)

    Do While oStreamReader.Peek() > -1
        System.Console.WriteLine(oStreamReader.ReadLine)
    Loop
End Sub
Public Sub DumpDebugLogFile()
    Try
        Call DumpFileToConsole(txtFile.Text)
    Catch e As IOException
        MsgBox("The File was not found")
    End Try
End Sub
```

Notice that `Try...Catch...Finally` doesn't allow you to resume execution with the line that caused the exception. (This would make a nice addition in a future version of VB.NET.) Also notice that the exception handled was `System.IO.IOException` rather than the more general `System.Exception`.

DETECTING THE EXCEPTION TYPE

The code in Listing 9.2 doesn't use the VB Err object Number property (`Err.Number`). This is one of the major benefits of .NET exception handling. Error handling in previous versions of VB has been inconsistent. There are special commands for getting errors that occur when a DLL is called using `Err.LastDLLError`. COM errors are based on Hresults, which are long unexplainable numbers. Some API calls simply return the error code as a return value of the call or as a parameter of the API.

In the .NET Framework, exceptions are objects of a given type and if you need to throw your own exceptions, you inherit from an exception type rather than defining a number.

Now I have developed more of the application and realized that I should have more explicit exception handling. Listing 9.3 illustrates the code changes. I changed the `Try...Catch...Block` to catch both a `System.IO.FileNotFoundException` and a `System.IO.DirectoryNotFoundException`. In addition, I have included a `Catch` for `System.Exception` and will simply throw that back to the higher level in the call chain.

Listing 9.3 `Try...Catch...Finally` **with Two** `Catch` **Clauses**

```
Private Sub DumpFileToConsole(ByVal FileName As String)
    Dim oFileStream As New FileStream(FileName, FileMode.Open, FileAccess.Read)
    Dim oStreamReader As New StreamReader(oFileStream)

    Do While oStreamReader.Peek() > -1
        System.Console.WriteLine(oStreamReader.ReadLine)
    Loop
End Sub
Public Sub DumpDebugLogFile()
    Try
        Call DumpFileToConsole(txtFile.Text)
    Catch e As FileNotFoundException
        MsgBox("The File was not found")
    Catch e As DirectoryNotFoundException
        MsgBox("The directory was not found")
    Catch e as Exception
    Throw e
    End Try
End Sub
```

Throwing Exceptions

To throw an exception in VB.NET, you use the `Throw` statement. `Throw` has one mandatory parameter, which is an object that derives from `System.Exception`. (Listing 9.3 uses the exception that was thrown in the `Try` block.)

If I need to throw an exception anywhere, I can generate an exception with any of the methods in Listing 9.4.

Listing 9.4   Throwing Exceptions

```
'Create and throw an exception in one statement
Throw New System.Exception() ' Throws the base exception

'Create an exception and throw separately
Dim oIOException As System.IO.EndOfStreamException
oIOException = new System.IO.EndOfStreamException( _
            "Sample End of Stream Exception")
Throw oIOException
```

Ensuring That Clean Up Code Is Executed

Suppose that we have a routine to write log file records, and that the routine needs to open the file and write out a record.

Keep in mind that object termination works differently in the .NET Framework than in previous versions of Visual Basic. In VB 6 a developer could create a File object, open it, write a record, and then let the object go out of scope, effectively closing the file.

In VB.NET this could cause a problem because even though the object goes out of scope, the garbage collector might not collect the object for quite some time. Because of this, it is imperative that the file is always closed. Listing 9.5 uses the `Finally` clause to ensure that the file is closed whether or not an exception occurs.

Listing 9.5   Try...Catch...Finally *with the* Finally *Clause Closing the File*

```
Private Sub DumpFileToConsole(ByVal FileName As String)

    Dim oFileStream As FileStream

    Try
        oFileStream = New FileStream(FileName, FileMode.Open, FileAccess.Read)
        Dim oStreamReader As New StreamReader(oFileStream)

        Do While oStreamReader.Peek() > -1
            System.Console.WriteLine(oStreamReader.ReadLine)
        Loop
    Finally
        Try
            oFileStream.Close()
```

Listing 9.5   Continued

```
        Catch
        End Try
    End Try

End Sub
```

Creating Custom Exception Types

In previous versions of VB, a developer would raise an error and give pertinent information in the parameters of raise error. For complex problems, this would evolve into groups of constants or Enums defined to provide error information. This is unnecessary in the .Net Framework.

As we have seen, many exception types are already defined in the .NET Framework, and it is possible to throw an exception of any of these types and to supply custom information along with the exception. But the .NET Framework also provides a mechanism for creating custom exceptions.

Similar to nearly every other process, you use inheritance to create a custom exception type when creating types in VB. Listing 9.6 creates a new exception type called LogFileException, which inherits from System.IO.IOException. The class is rather simple; I extended the base class to include a ReadOnly filename property. This also involved changing the constructors.

One item to note is that when you create your own custom exception, you should always provide a constructor that allows the propagation of an exception in the InnerException property.

Listing 9.6   LogFileException

```
Public Class LogFileException
    Inherits System.IO.IOException
    Private c_sFileName As String
    Public Sub New(ByVal message As String, ByVal fileName As String)
        MyBase.New(message)
        c_sFileName = fileName
    End Sub
    Public Sub New(ByVal message As String, ByVal fileName As String, _
                ByVal e As System.IO.IOException)
        MyBase.New(message, e)
        c_sFileName = fileName
    End Sub
    ReadOnly Property FileName() As String
        Get
            Return c_sFileName
        End Get
    End Property
End Class
```

This exception class has an additional property and two new constructors. One constructor takes a message and a filename, and the other also includes an exception typed as System.IO.IOException. Throw a LogFileException with the code in Listing 9.7.

Listing 9.7 Using LogFileException

```
Private Sub DumpFileToConsole(ByVal FileName As String)

    Dim oFileStream As FileStream
    Dim oStreamReader As StreamReader

    Try
        Try
            oFileStream = New FileStream(FileName, FileMode.Open, _
                FileAccess.Read)
            oStreamReader = New StreamReader(oFileStream)
        Catch e As IOException
            Throw New LogFileException("File not found", FileName, e)
        End Try

        Do While oStreamReader.Peek() > -1
            System.Console.WriteLine(oStreamReader.ReadLine)
        Loop
    Finally
        Try
            oFileStream.Close()
        Catch
        End Try
    End Try

End Sub
```

Elsewhere in the application, a Try...Catch...Finally statement like the one in Listing 9.8 would catch the LogFileException.

Listing 9.8 Catching LogFileException

```
Public Sub TryCustomeLogException()
    Try
        Call DumpFileToConsole(txtFile.Text)
    Catch e As LogFileException
        MsgBox("Encountered " & e.message & " with " & e.filename)
    Catch e As Exception
        Throw e
    End Try
End Sub
```

Global Exception Handlers

For many years, VB developers have been asking for a method to attach a global error handler that would be activated at any point in which an error was encountered with no error handler on the stack. This is now possible in the .NET Framework.

In the .NET Framework, an application runs inside of what is known as an *application domain*. An application domain can be thought of as a process (although multiple application domains can run inside of one process). Through the use of delegates and events, a developer can supply an event that will be executed if an unhandled exception occurs. This is done by using the System.AppDomain class, as shown in Listing 9.9.

Listing 9.9   Global Exception Handler in a Console Application

```
Module Module1
    Sub Main()
        AddHandler AppDomain.CurrentDomain.UnhandledException, _
             AddressOf GlobalExceptionHandlerr
        Throw New ArgumentException()
        Console.ReadLine()
    End Sub
    Sub GlobalExceptionHandlerr(ByVal sender As Object,_
      ByVal e As UnhandledExceptionEventArgs)
        Console.WriteLine("In CatchExceptions")
        Console.WriteLine("{0} threw a {1}", sender, e.ExceptionObject)
        Console.WriteLine("Leaving CatchExceptions")
    End Sub
End Module
```

Using Structured Exception Handling Effectively

Structured exception handling, like many of the other new capabilities of VB.NET, requires that developers put more effort into design.

DESIGN, DESIGN, DESIGN

In the .NET Framework, it is more important than ever to design and research your applications. It has never been more important to make sure that you are doing things the correct way. The .NET Framework supplies so much new functionality that it is easy to overlook the best way to do something. It is also very easy to misuse a capability, which in the end can result in application problems.

The bar has been raised, and an application developer's role is changing. More and more development time will be spent doing research and less time will be spent coding. In many situations, management might not believe that developers are being productive unless they are coding heads down. This is a mistake. Design is meant to shorten the actual amount of code that is needed and to make the test phase shorter because the code is of better quality.

It will be very easy for developers to misuse structured exception handling. Some of the things to beware of are the following:

- Creating custom exception types arbitrarily
- Wrapping everything in exception handlers
- Replacing condition testing with exception handlers
- Throwing all exceptions back to the caller

Creating Custom Exception Types Arbitrarily

When you have decided that you need to throw an exception, it is extremely important that you explore the exceptions already defined in the .NET Framework before you decide to create your own.

After you are certain that you need to create your own custom exceptions, here are a few guidelines you should follow:

- End the name of your custom exception class with the word Exception.
- Don't derive your exception class from System.Exception. Choose from one of the exception classes that are more specific to the problem you're trying to report. In most cases, this will be System.ApplicationException.
- Make sure that your exception handler has a constructor that allows the innerexception to be set. The most common constructors in a custom exception class have the structure shown in Listing 9.10.

Listing 9.10   Custom Exception Constructor

```
Public Sub New() 'Constructor with no parameters
End Sub
Public Sub New(ByVal Message as String) ' Constructor with message parameter
End Sub
Public Sub New(ByVal Message as String, _
            ByVal Inner as Exception) ' Constructor with InnerException
End Sub
```

Wrapping Everything in Exception Handlers

A common error that occurs when developers first start using exception handlers is over using the functionality, as shown in Listing 9.11.

Listing 9.11   Write an Array of Object to a Database

```
Public Sub InsertEmployees(ByVal Employees() as Employee)
    Dim oEmployee as Employee
    For Each oEmployee in Employees
        Try
            Call InsertEmployeeRow(oEmployee)
        Catch e as Exception
            System.Console.WriteLine(e.Message)
        End Try
    Next
End Sub
```

The code in Listing 9.11 can be made much more efficient by restructuring the exception handling as shown in Listing 9.12.

Listing 9.12   Listing 9.11 Adds far too Much Overhead to the Code, but Can Become More Efficient

```
Public Sub InsertEmployees(ByVal Employees() as Employee)
    Dim oEmployee as Employee
    Try
        For Each oEmployee in Employees
            Call InsertEmployeeRow(oEmployee)
        Next
    Catch e as Exception
        System.Console.WriteLine(e.Message)
    End Try
End Sub
```

You may even see something similar to the code in Listing 9.13.

Listing 9.13   Wrap Each Line of Code in Its Own Try...Catch...Finally **Block**

```
Try
    I = I + 1
Catch e as System.Exception
    System.Console.WriteLine(e.Message)
End Try
Try
    If I = 5 then
        Try
            Call DoSomethingWhenIEqualsFive
        Catch e as System.Exception
            System.Console.WriteLine(e.message)
        End Try
    Else
        Try
            Call DoSomethingWhenINotEqualToFive
        Catch e as System.Exception
            System.Console.WriteLine(e.Message)
        End Try
Catch e as Exception
    System.Console.Writelin(e.Message)
End Try
```

That is a mess and should've been written with one Try...Catch...Finally statement. Listing 9.14 is a rewritten version of Listing 9.13.

Listing 9.14   Restructured with Effective Exception Handling

```
Try
    I = I + 1
    If I = 5 Then
        Call DoSomethingWhenIEqualsFive
    Else
        Call DoSomethingWhenINotEqualToFive
    End If
Catch e as System.Exception
    System.Console.WriteLine(e.Message)
End Try
```

As you can see, the structure of your exception handling can have a great deal of impact on the amount of code you write. It also can greatly decrease performance, if not design correctly.

Replacing Condition Testing with Exception Handlers

Substituting exception handling for condition testing is poor design. By testing variables before using them, semi-excepted exceptions can be avoided. This provides numerous benefits, including clarity and performance. You don't want exceptions to be raised simply as a design pattern.

The proper use of VB.NET error handling is illustrated in Listing 9.15.

Listing 9.15   Correct Use of Exception Handling in VB.NET

```
Private Sub DumpFileToConsole(ByVal FileName As String)

    Dim oFileStream As FileStream
    Dim oStreamReader As StreamReader

    Try
        oFileStream = New FileStream(FileName, FileMode.Open, _
            FileAccess.Read)
        oStreamReader = New StreamReader(oFileStream)

        Do While oStreamReader.Peek() > -1
            System.Console.WriteLine(oStreamReader.ReadLine)
        Loop
    Finally
        Try
            oFileStream.Close()
        Catch
        End Try
    End Try

End Sub
```

Listing 9.15   Continued

```
Public Sub DumpToConsole(ByVal sFile As String)
    If File.Exists(sFile) Then
        Try
            Call DumpFileToConsole(sFile)
        Catch e As Exception
            Throw e
        End Try
    Else
        MsgBox(sFile & " does not exist.")
    End If
End Sub
Private Sub Button1_Click_1(ByVal sender As System.Object, _
            ByVal e As System.EventArgs) Handles Button1.Click
    Call DumpToConsole(txtFile.Text)
End Sub
```

Throwing All Exceptions Back to the Caller

Exception handlers that simply pass the exceptions back to the code that called them are a sign of lazy developers. A properly designed and developed component should deal with as many exceptions as it can, and anything else should be recorded before being thrown back to the caller.

Sample Windows Form Application Using Exception Handling

Finally in Listing 9.16 I have included a small application to view a text file.

Listing 9.16   Log File Viewer

```
Imports System.IO
Public Class frmLogViewer
    Inherits System.Windows.Forms.Form
    Private c_sFileName As String
    Private c_oFileStream As FileStream
    Private c_oStream As StreamReader
#Region " Windows Form Designer generated code "

    Public Sub New()
        MyBase.New()

        'This call is required by the Windows Form Designer.
        InitializeComponent()

        'Add any initialization after the InitializeComponent() call

    End Sub
```

Listing 9.16 *Continued*

```
'Form overrides dispose to clean up the component list.
Protected Overloads Overrides Sub Dispose(ByVal disposing As Boolean)
    If disposing Then
        If Not (components Is Nothing) Then
            components.Dispose()
        End If
    End If
    MyBase.Dispose(disposing)
End Sub
Friend WithEvents btnSelect As System.Windows.Forms.Button
Friend WithEvents btnOpen As System.Windows.Forms.Button
Friend WithEvents btnView As System.Windows.Forms.Button
Friend WithEvents opnDialog As System.Windows.Forms.OpenFileDialog
Friend WithEvents lstLog As System.Windows.Forms.ListBox


'Required by the Windows Form Designer
Private components As System.ComponentModel.Container

'NOTE: The following procedure is required by the Windows Form Designer
'It can be modified using the Windows Form Designer.
'Do not modify it using the code editor.
<System.Diagnostics.DebuggerStepThrough()> Private Sub
InitializeComponent()
    Me.lstLog = New System.Windows.Forms.ListBox()
    Me.btnSelect = New System.Windows.Forms.Button()
    Me.btnOpen = New System.Windows.Forms.Button()
    Me.btnView = New System.Windows.Forms.Button()
    Me.opnDialog = New System.Windows.Forms.OpenFileDialog()
    Me.SuspendLayout()
    '
    'lstLog
    '
    Me.lstLog.Location = New System.Drawing.Point(16, 8)
    Me.lstLog.Name = "lstLog"
    Me.lstLog.Size = New System.Drawing.Size(536, 199)
    Me.lstLog.TabIndex = 0
    '
    'btnSelect
    '
    Me.btnSelect.Location = New System.Drawing.Point(16, 216)
    Me.btnSelect.Name = "btnSelect"
    Me.btnSelect.TabIndex = 1
    Me.btnSelect.Text = "Select"
    '
    'btnOpen
    '
    Me.btnOpen.Location = New System.Drawing.Point(104, 216)
    Me.btnOpen.Name = "btnOpen"
```

Listing 9.16   Continued

```
        Me.btnOpen.TabIndex = 2
        Me.btnOpen.Text = "Open"
        '
        'btnView
        '
        Me.btnView.Location = New System.Drawing.Point(192, 216)
        Me.btnView.Name = "btnView"
        Me.btnView.TabIndex = 3
        Me.btnView.Text = "View"
        '
        'frmLogViewer
        '
        Me.AutoScaleBaseSize = New System.Drawing.Size(5, 13)
        Me.ClientSize = New System.Drawing.Size(562, 295)
        Me.Controls.AddRange(New System.Windows.Forms.Control() _
                {Me.btnView, Me.btnOpen, Me.btnSelect, Me.lstLog})
        Me.Name = "frmLogViewer"
        Me.Text = "frmLogViewer"
        Me.ResumeLayout(False)

    End Sub

#End Region

    Private Sub btnSelect_Click(ByVal sender As System.Object, _
            ByVal e As System.EventArgs) Handles btnSelect.Click
        Try
            opnDialog.ShowDialog()
            c_sFileName = opnDialog.FileName
        Catch exp As Exception
            lstLog.Items.Clear()
            lstLog.Items.Add(exp.Message)
        End Try
    End Sub

    Private Sub btnOpen_Click( _
        ByVal sender As Object, ByVal e As System.EventArgs)_
        Handles btnOpen.Click
        Try
            c_oFileStream = New FileStream(c_sFileName, FileMode.Open,
FileAccess.Read)
            c_oStream = New StreamReader(c_oFileStream)
        Catch exp As Exception
            lstLog.Items.Clear()
            lstLog.Items.Add("You must select a file before opening")
        End Try
    End Sub
```

Listing 9.16   Continued

```
    Private Sub btnView_Click(ByVal sender As Object, _
            ByVal e As System.EventArgs) Handles btnView.Click
        Dim sLog() As String
        Dim i As Integer
        Try
            lstLog.Items.Clear()
            Do While c_oStream.Peek() > -1
                ReDim Preserve sLog(i)

                sLog(i) = c_oStream.ReadLine
                i = i + 1
            Loop
            lstLog.DataSource = sLog
        Catch exp As Exception
            MsgBox(exp.Message)
            lstLog.Items.Add("You must select and open the file first")
        End Try

    End Sub
End Class
```

Summary

The .NET Framework and VB.NET have brought exception handling to new levels for VB developers. The more robust nature of exception handling and the more structure of object-oriented techniques should result in better more maintainable applications.

For the interim, you will be able to move existing VB code to the .NET Framework or use it through interop and still use the existing VB error handling syntax.

Similar to many changes in the .NET Framework, exception handling requires you to be diligent in your design. Design simply shortens the development of the application, but not the fun part of the development. Design reduces the tedious debugging and troubleshooting part of the development cycle.

CHAPTER 10

ADO.NET

Fundamental to nearly every business application is the ability
to access data from some sort of database. Combine this with
the need for business components or applications to interact
with each other through the use of straight XML and XML-
based services over the Internet, and you end up with
ADO.NET.

"Another database access model" is a phrase that has been said
more than once by developers who have used VB. Many people reading this are probably saying that yet again with
VB.NET. In my opinion, ADO.NET isn't just another database
access method. It is a totally new model that in its first version
is built strictly for disconnected access scenarios and scalability.

From DAO to ADO.NET

Microsoft has made several attempts at providing high-level
APIs for accessing databases. When Microsoft was designing
Access, it built an object-based method of talking to the Jet
database engine. This data access method is known as *Data
Access Objects*, or more commonly as just *DAO*. DAO was primarily intended to provide a method for accessing Microsoft
Jet databases although you could also use DAO to access
ODBC-based data sources. But the performance was optimized for Access, not ODBC. DAO was the primary data
access method in Access up until Access 2000. Figure 10.1
illustrates the object model for DAO 3.6.

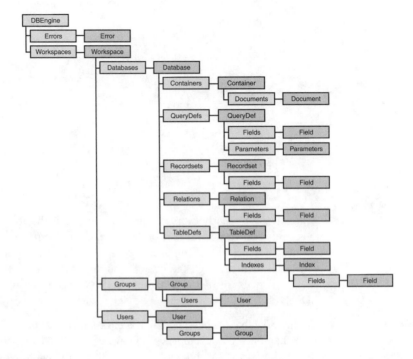

Figure 10.1

The DAO object model.

DAO was designed for database access using a permanent connection and doesn't provide methods for using data while not connected to a database. DAO allowed the use of client-side and server-side cursors. To use these cursors, you can never completely disconnect from the database. This model worked very well with Access applications, but could be a problem with SQL Server and Oracle databases in many situations.

Remote Data Objects

In order to deal with server-based databases more efficiently, Microsoft built a thin wrapper on top of ODBC called *Remote Data Objects (RDO)*.

RDO provided for high performance ODBC-based access to data in SQL databases. It provided an object model that was similar to DAO (although it wasn't as large). Figure 10.2 shows the RDO object model.

RDO was an improvement over DAO for SQL Server and other server-based DBMSs, but it was still primarily designed to model cursors and provide connected data access. RDO did introduce a method to disconnect from a database and reconnect at some later point to update data. Unfortunately, this was limited because the objects wouldn't marshal across a network.

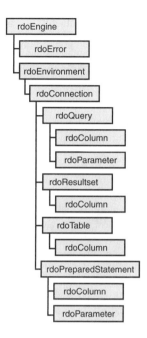

Figure 10.2

The RDO object model.

If a developer were to create an rdoResultSet in a server process in MTS or COM+ on one machine, and then use that rdoResultSet on a client, many network roundtrips would be required. This severely limited scalability.

OleDB and Active Data Objects

DAO and RDO were both based on an API approach to accessing data. Although VB developers were isolated from the APIs used to access the data sources, the developers responsible for providing data through ODBC to DAO (for datasources other then Jet) or RDO weren't. Microsoft was in the midst of using COM to build object models. Data access was one of the technologies in which Microsoft wanted to use a COM-based approach to Data Access. DAO and RDO were also deeply tied to relational databases, and Microsoft felt that it was extremely important to also provide an access model for non-relational database data.

At this time, Microsoft began building a data access specification that would use COM and be geared toward any structured data source. The result was OleDB and ADO. ADO is the OLE Automation implementation built on top of OleDB. It provides methods to access data that can be presented in a tabular format.

ADO was introduced with the first version of ASP in 1996. It is the database access method used in ASP and is highly scalable (if used correctly). ADO did follow the guide of DAO and RDO and has a similar object model. When you initially look at the object models, you might have a different opinion. But all three primarily used a few objects. Table 10.1 compares the main objects used.

Table 10.1   ADO, RDO, and DAO for Relational Database Access

Purpose	ADO	RDO	DAO
Connection to the database	Connection	rdoConnection	Database
Stored Procedure or SQL Statement	Command	rdoQuery	QueryDef
Resultset returned from database	Recordset	rdoResultset	Recordset
Database column	Field	rdoColumn	Field

ADO isn't optimized for any particular method of data access. It works with both connected and disconnected scenarios. But because it was modeled after DAO and RDO, it fit better in connected scenarios. Figure 10.3 illustrates the ADO object model.

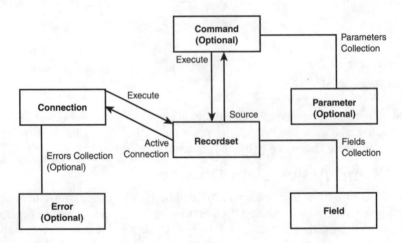

Figure 10.3

The ADO object model.

The primary advantage of ADO was improved support for disconnected data and the ability for a disconnected recordset to marshal across a network. This became one of the models used to move data over the network in distributed applications. This also became the basis for ADO.NET.

ADO.NET

Microsoft decided to create a database access method for the .NET Framework that is highly focused on a few key goals:

- XML integration
- Disconnected data model
- Scalability

The result is ADO.NET. Before going further into the object model of ADO.NET and how to use it, a core design choice has to be pointed out. For reasons of scalability, ADO.NET only supports ReadOnly ForwardOnly cursors. ReadOnly ForwardOnly are the fastest way to get data out of a relational database with the least amount of stress to the database. This doesn't mean that ADO.NET isn't powerful. This takes a great deal of confusion out of the database access method. Some developers might feel that this limits their choices, but that is one of the solutions to the scalability issues. It takes away what could amount to be bad choices.

The ADO.NET Object Model

ADO.NET is broken down into three namespaces in the .NET Framework listed in Table 10.2.

Table 10.2 ADO.NET Namespaces

NameSpace	Description
System.Data	The non provider specific (non database aware classes) are located in System.Data.
System.Data.SQLClient	Managed Provider for SQL Server. This gives the best performance for SQL Server running directly over the SQL Server Tabular Data Stream (TDS) protocol.
System.Data.OleDB	Managed Provider for OleDB Providers. This provides access to any OleDB Provider.

This is different from previous data access methods in which the attempt was to create the method as generic as possible. In the past with ODBC and OleDB, Microsoft pushed the idea that all you needed to do (theoretically) was to change the OleDB Provider or ODBC driver and you wouldn't need to change your code. This isn't the case with ADO.NET: If you built an application against SQL Server with the System.Data.SQLClient and then needed to talk to Oracle or DB2, you would need to change your code to the System.Data.OleDB namespace. Microsoft has put the generic classes in System.Data, and supplied two data providers: one that can access any data source and a second one that is optimized for SQL Server. In the future, Microsoft or a third party can create providers that are optimized for other database products.

I will use the OleDB Managed provider for the examples in this chapter. The objects provided by the SQL Managed provider are the same, just prefixed with SQL rather than OleDB. Figure 10.4 illustrates the ADO.NET Object Model.

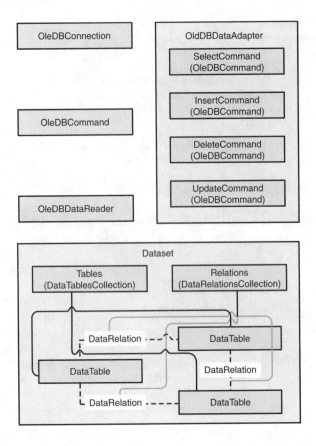

Figure 10.4

The ADO.NET object model.

Although the ADO.NET object model is quite a bit different from earlier models, it does have some similarities. The OleDBConnection and OleDBCommand objects are basically the same as the ADO Connection and Command objects. Similar to ADO, the ADO.NET object model is largely a set of objects that interact with each other rather than an object hierarchy such as DAO or RDO. Now let's look at the objects in the model.

OleDBConnection

This object is analogous to the connection object from ADO and provides the actual connection to the database server. This object provides all the functionality to execute commands.

OleDBCommand

Similar to the OleDBConnection object, the OleDBCommand object is analogous to an ADO object, in this case the Command object. The OleDBCommand object is used to set up stored procedures or a SQL command string to be executed at the server.

Please only use SQL strings in test scenarios. Stored procedures are far better for performance and scalability. They contain additional objects for parameters and methods to execute queries that return resultsets, scalar values, or simply return code.

OleDBDataReader

The `OleDBDataReader` object is used to get resultsets from the database server. The `OleDBDataReader` provides a ReadOnly, ForwardOnly means of retrieving data.

Listing 10.1 shows the code to iterate through an ADO Recordset and Listing 10.2 depicts the code to iterate through an `OleDBDataReader` object.

Listing 10.1 Iterate Through the ADO Recordset

```
Do Until oPublishersRecordset.EOF
    Console.WriteLine(oPublishersRecordset.Fields("pub_name").Value.ToString)
    oPublishersRecordset.MoveNext()
Loop
```

Note that the `Read` method in Listing 10.2 positions the reader to the next record. This eliminates the need for a `MoveNext` method, which is often accidentally omitted during development. In fact, when the reader is first opened, it isn't positioned on a record.

Also note that the `Read` method returns a Boolean indicating whether the read was successful.

Listing 10.2 Iterate Through the ADO.NET `OleDbDataReader`

```
Do Until oPublishersDataReader.Read()
    Console.WriteLine(oPublishersDataReader.GetValue(0).ToString)
Loop
```

OleDbDataAdapter

The `OleDBDataAdapter` is new in ADO.NET. It is a container that controls and contains four `OleDBCommand` objects. The objects are contained in four properties described in Table 10.3.

Table 10.3 Four Command Objects of `DataAdapter`

`OleDBDataAdapter` Command Properties	Description
SelectCommand	Used to retrieve data from a database
InsertCommand	Used to insert data into a database
UpdateCommand	Used to update data in the database
DeleteCommand	Used to delete data from the database

The OleDBDataAdapter is used along with the DataSet object for the functionality of ADO.NET that is described in the rest of this chapter. The OleDBDataAdapter is the object that is used to fill an ADO.NET DataSet. The OleDBDataAdapter is also the mechanism for batch updating a database.

OleDbException

In ADO.NET when a database exception is encountered, an exception of type OleDbException is thrown. This is unlike ADO, where error information was a member of the Connection class. The exception information from the database is contained in a member of the OleDbException class. The member is the Errors property, which returns a class called OleDbErrorCollection that holds a collection of OleDbError objects.

Batch Updates

RDO and ADO supplied a method for retrieving data from a database and then dropping the database connection. You could change the data in the Recordset by adding records, deleting records, or changing records, and then reconnect the Recordset to the database and push the changes to the database. Under the covers, RDO and ADO would create stored procedures on-the-fly, one each for inserts, updates, and deletes. This often had quirky little problems.

In ADO.NET, this functionality has been greatly improved. A developer can still choose to have ADO.NET generate the commands on-the-fly for you, or you now have the ability to provide the commands yourself. Through the use of the InsertCommand, UpdateCommand, and UpdateCommand properties, you can supply the stored procedures to handle the manipulation of data. This will result in far fewer errors and will improve performance because stored procedures won't need to be created and recreated constantly. Using your own stored procedures will increase the performance of your application because your stored procedures will be pre-compiled and cached on the server.

DataSet

The DataSet is the true power object of ADO.NET. Unlike other objects in ADO.NET, the DataSet isn't typed as an OleDB or SQL DataSet. This is because the DataSet isn't tied to any database. The DataSet is an in-memory data store that is filled from a DataAdapter, XML, or by code. The DataSet object provides methods to sort, filter, and query data contained within the DataSet.

The DataSet is the closest thing to a Recordset in ADO.NET, but it is much more. A Recordset could contain only one resultset from the database. A DataSet, on the other hand, can contain many DataTables, and each DataTable can come from a different data source. Not only can a DataSet contain many tables, but also you can create relationships between tables through the DataRelationsCollection.

DataTable

A `DataSet` contains a collection of tables of data known as a `DataTable`. A `DataTable` is where the actual data from a database (or other source) is stored after you fill a `DataSet`. You can think of a `DataTable` as roughly equivalent to a Recordset.

DataRelation

A `DataSet` contains a collection of `DataRelation` objects in the `DataRelationCollection` property. When you establish a relationship between two `DataTables`, the tables will be controlled much the same way that they are in a database.

For example, if you create a relationship between two tables via a foreign key and then attempt to add a record to the child table with a foreign key value that doesn't exist in the parent, an exception will be thrown.

The `DataRelation` also assists with movement through records in a `DataTable` using the `DataRow.GetChildRows` method.

ADO.NET Support in Visual Studio.NET

Now I will show you an example that puts all the objects together. I will use the Northwind Sample Database that is included with SQL Server 2000. Figure 10.5 is a database diagram of the customers, orders, and order_details tables of the Northwind database.

Figure 10.5

Database Diagram of Northwind.

Create a new Windows application, which opens to a new form in the designer. I will be using three tables in this example. Figure 10.5 depicts the three tables involved in a DataBase diagram built in VS.NET from the Server Explorer. Figures 10.9–10.15 illustrate the Data Adapter Configuration Wizard, which is invoked when you drag an OleDBDataAdapter from the toolbox to the form designer.

1. Drag an OleDBDataAdapter from the toolbox to the form. Figure 10.6 shows the OleDBDataAdapter in the toolbox. The dialog box illustrated in Figure 10.7 will be shown.

Figure 10.6

The OleDBDataAdapter in the Visual Studio.NET toolbox.

Figure 10.7

The Data Adapter Configuration Wizard.

2. Click the Next button to bring up the dialog box illustrated in Figure 10.8.

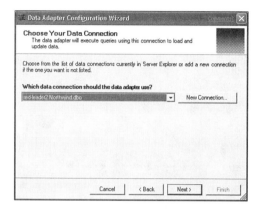

Figure 10.8

Select the database connection.

3. Create a new connection to the Northwind database, choose it from the drop-down list, and click Next to bring up the dialog box shown in Figure 10.9.

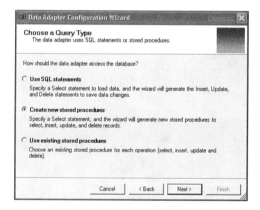

Figure 10.9

Choose to create new stored procedures.

4. Figure 10.9 allows you to choose one of three options: Use SQL Statements, Create New Stored Procedures, or Use Existing Stored Procedures. In this example, choose Create New Stored Procedures and click Next to bring up the dialog box shown in Figure 10.10.

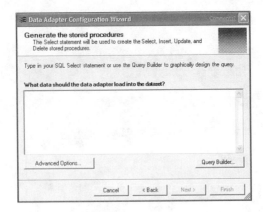

Figure 10.10

Empty Query to use in a stored procedure.

5. Figure 10.10 is used to illustrate the query that will be used to create the stored procedures. To make this easier, click the Query Builder button to bring up the Query Builder dialog box shown in Figure 10.11.

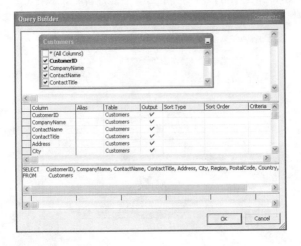

Figure 10.11

Query Builder selecting all columns from Customers table.

6. Select all the columns in the Customers table (Choose each column individually) and click OK (see Figure 10.12).

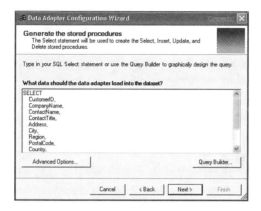

Figure 10.12

Returned query from the Query Builder.

7. Figure 10.12 is the same dialog box as shown in Figure 10.10, but the query is filled in. Click the Advanced Options button to bring up the dialog box shown in Figure 10.13.

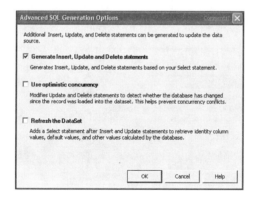

Figure 10.13

The Advanced SQL Generation Options dialog box.

8. Check the option to create Insert, Update, and Delete stored procedures, uncheck the other options, and click OK to return to the dialog box shown in Figure 10.12. Click Next to proceed to the dialog box shown in Figure 10.14 to name the stored procedures that will be created.

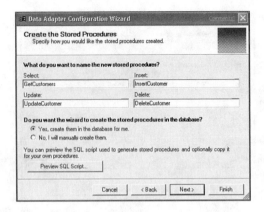

Figure 10.14

Name the stored procedures.

9. After you name the stored procedures, click the Next button to complete the wizard, which will bring up the dialog box shown in Figure 10.15.

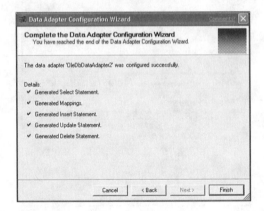

Figure 10.15

Wizard is complete.

Now it is your task to create two more OleDBDataAdapters for the Orders and Order Details tables. Now Add a DataGrid and two buttons to the form. Size and move the controls so that the form looks similar to the form in Figure 10.16.

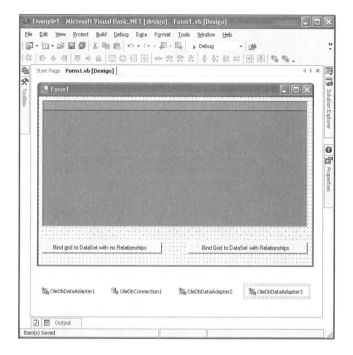

Figure 10.16

A form with controls.

Listing 10.3   Code to Create and Test Datasets

```vb
Private Sub BindGridToDataSetWithRelationShip()
    Me.Text = "Grid is Bound to a DataSet with defined relationships"
    Dim oDS As New DataSet()
    oleDbConnection1().Open()
    oleDbDataAdapter1().Fill(oDS, "Customers")
    oleDbDataAdapter2().Fill(oDS, "Orders")
    oleDbDataAdapter3().Fill(oDS, "OrderDetails")
    oleDbConnection1().Close()

    oDS.Relations.Add("CustomerOrders", _
            oDS.Tables("Customers").Columns("CustomerID"), _
        oDS.Tables("Orders").Columns("CustomerID"))
    oDS.Relations.Add("OrderOrderDetails", _
            oDS.Tables("Orders").Columns("OrderID"), _
        oDS.Tables("OrderDetails").Columns("OrderID"))

    dataGrid1().DataSource = oDS
    dataGrid1().DataMember = "Customers"
End Sub
```

Listing 10.3   Continued

```
Private Sub BindGridToDataSetNoRelationShip()
    Me.Text = "Grid is Bound to a DataSet with no defined relationships"
    Dim oDS As New DataSet()
    oleDbConnection1().Open()
    oleDbDataAdapter1().Fill(oDS, "Customers")
    oleDbDataAdapter2().Fill(oDS, "Orders")
    oleDbDataAdapter3().Fill(oDS, "OrderDetails")
    oleDbConnection1().Close()

    dataGrid1().DataSource = oDS
    dataGrid1().DataMember = "Customers"
End Sub

Private Sub button1_Click(ByVal sender As System.Object, _
            ByVal e As System.EventArgs) Handles button1.Click
    Call BindGridToDataSetNoRelationShip()
End Sub

Private Sub button2_Click(ByVal sender As System.Object, _
            ByVal e As System.EventArgs) Handles button2.Click
    Call BindGridToDataSetWithRelationShip()
End Sub
```

Now run the application and press the Bind Grid to DataSet with No Relationships button: This will show the form as it is in Figure 10.17.

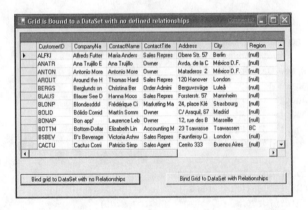

Figure 10.17

DataSet *with no relationships bound to grid.*

Now press the Bind Grid to DataSet with Relationships button. This will change the form as shown in Figure 10.18. (I also clicked the first plus sign on the left.)

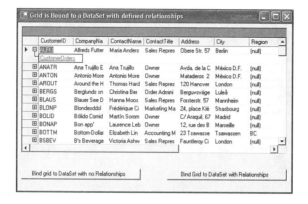

Figure 10.18

DataSet *with relationships bound to grid.*

The example illustrates how relationships defined on a dataset affect how a data-aware control such as the datagrid acts differently. This is just one function of relationships.

Listing 10.4 is a changed version of the BindGridToDataSetNoRelationShip method to bind the grid to the Orders table rather than the Customers table.

Listing 10.4 BindGridToDataSetNoRelationShip *Changed*

```
Private Sub BindGridToDataSetNoRelationShip()
    Me.Text = "Grid is Bound to a DataSet with no defined relationships"
    Dim oDS As New DataSet()
    oleDbConnection1().Open()
    oleDbDataAdapter1().Fill(oDS, "Customers")
    oleDbDataAdapter2().Fill(oDS, "Orders")
    oleDbDataAdapter3().Fill(oDS, "OrderDetails")
    oleDbConnection1().Close()

    dataGrid1().DataSource = oDS
    dataGrid1().DataMember = "Orders"
End Sub
```

Now run the application again and click the Bind Grid to DataSet with No Relationships, as shown in Figure 10.19.

When the form comes up, it will display the Orders table, similar to what's shown in Figure 10.20.

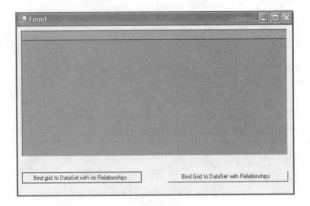

Figure 10.19

Click the Bind Grid to DataSet with No Relationships button.

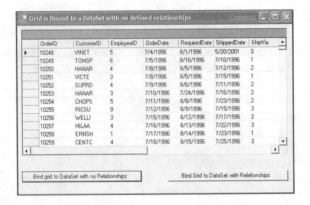

Figure 10.20

Grid filled with data from the Orders table.

Change the CustomerID column and move to a different row. The grid will allow this.

Now press button2 and drill-down in the grid to the Order table. Figure 10.21 depicts the form with the CustomerOrders link exposed.

This will change the grid to show the orders, as illustrated in Figure 10.22.

Then change the CustomerID and move to another row. The value will be changed back. This illustrates how the relationship is preserving the parent/child relationship.

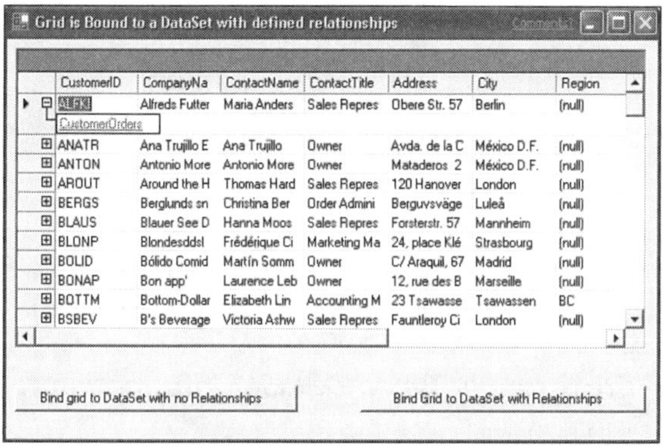

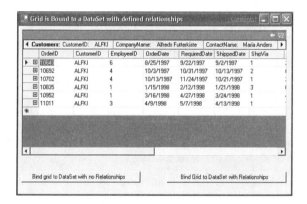

Figure 10.21

Click the CustomerOrders link.

Figure 10.22

Grid drilled down to the Orders table.

Strongly Typed `DataSets`

A fantastic new feature of ADO.NET is the concept of a strongly typed `DataSet`. An example will illustrate this better than words can. Listing 10.5 illustrates the code to write out information from a `DataSet` to the console.

Listing 10.5 **Write** DataSet *Information to the Console*

```
Private Sub DumpDataSetToConsole()
    Dim oDS As New DataSet()
    Dim oDataRow As DataRow
    oleDbConnection1().Open()
    oleDbDataAdapter1().Fill(oDS, "Customers")
    oleDbConnection1().Close()
```

Listing 10.5   Continued

```
    For Each oDataRow In oDS.Tables(0).Rows
        Console.WriteLine(oDataRow.Item("CustomerID").ToString & " " & _
            oDataRow.Item("CompanyName").ToString)
    Next
End Sub
```

Now let's dump the same data to the console using a Strongly Typed DataSet. Listing 10.6 is the code that dumps a Strongly Typed DataSet to the console.

Listing 10.6   Write Strongly Typed DataSet Information to the Console

```
Private Sub DumpStronglyTypedDataSetToConsole()
    Dim oCustomers As New CustomersOrdersAndOrderDetails()
    Dim oCustomerRow As CustomersOrdersAndOrderDetails.CustomersRow
    oleDbConnection1().Open()
    oleDbDataAdapter1().Fill(oCustomers, "Customers")
    oleDbConnection1().Close()
    For Each oCustomerRow In oCustomers.Customers.Rows
        Console.WriteLine(oCustomerRow.CustomerID.ToString & _
                          " " & oCustomerRow.CompanyName)
    Next
End Sub
```

The examples in Listing 10.5 and Listing 10.6 illustrate the use of a Strongly Typed DataSet. Where you previously had an Item property of a DataRow that you passed in an indexed parameter, you now have a property of the DataRow called the Field name. This makes the code easier to create and debug.

Previously you would need to refer back to the database schema to figure out exactly the name of the field. Now IntelliSense will tell you the names of the fields. In addition, before all fields were of type object. You could set a field called *CompanyName* to a numeric value and the error wouldn't be caught. With a Strongly Typed DataSet, the following code would not only be caught, but also it would be caught at compile time.

```
oCustomerRow.CustomerName = 5
```

Strongly Typed DataSets are created using Visual Studio.Net. After creating your dataadapters, choose Generate Dataset from the Data menu, as shown in Figure 10.23.

This will open the Generate DataSet dialog box shown in Figure 10.24.

Figure 10.23

Invoke the Create DataSet dialog box.

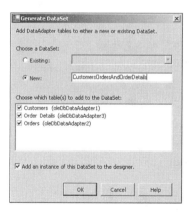

Figure 10.24

Choose the DataSet options.

After making your selections, an XSD Schema will be added to your project with a VB code behind the file hidden. This file contains classes that inherit from ADO.NET base classes and use the XSD schema to create a Strongly Typed DataSet. Recall that in Listing 10.3, the code to create relationships can be done at design time with the

VS.NET XSD schema designer. Double-click the XSD file, and the designer in Figure 10.25 will be displayed.

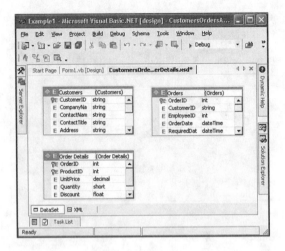

Figure 10.25

XSD Schema designer.

From the toolbox, drag a Relation from to one of the tables depicted in Figure 10.25 and drop it on the table to open the dialog box shown in Figure 10.26. When the project is compiled, the Strongly Typed DataSet will have a relationship set up through the designer.

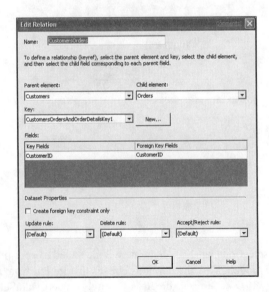

Figure 10.26

Data Relation editor.

After creating the relationships through the designer, the XSD Schema designer will resemble Figure 10.27.

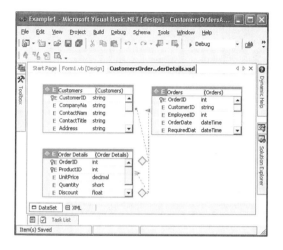

Figure 10.27

XSD Schema designer after creating relationships.

Summary

The data access story in the .NET Framework is a huge advance for applications that can use disconnected data. Through the tools included in VS.NET, you can create highly scalable and flexible methods of retrieving and moving data within your applications.

There are many features of ADO.NET for you to explore that I have not covered here. (Don't worry; there will be many books on ADO.NET to help you out.) Some of the features I didn't explore are the extensive XML integration, the rich programmatic features to manipulate your datasets, and the powerful and scalable data binding features of the .NET Framework. You did see data binding put to use, but there is much more to the binding story.

If you are in a situation in which you will need connected access to your databases, ADO.NET isn't for you. The solution is to continue using ADO through COM Interop for those circumstances and use ADO.NET for disconnected scenarios.

CHAPTER 11

.NET Application Development Design, Architecture, and Implementation

To some people, .NET will create a great deal of confusion with regard to how Microsoft has told them how to design, architect, and implement systems. In this chapter, you will find some guidelines that illustrate features of the .NET Framework that you should be familiar with. You will find information that should relieve architectural confusion. Finally, this chapter should help you separate what Microsoft marketing has stated and what as developers you need to understand. Figure 11.1 illustrates what portions of the .NET Framework this chapter covers.

Security

In the age of the Internet, security models for applications are more complex than they have ever been. Different models have been built into and on top of various platforms. Microsoft built ActiveX on top of the COM platform and, in ActiveX, built a trust-based security mechanism. Sun built a sandbox based security mechanism into the Java platform.

The mechanism added to COM involves the use of digital certificates and trusting the developer of the software. This mechanism evolved into giving users and administrators the ability to give specific sites and categories of sites permissions.

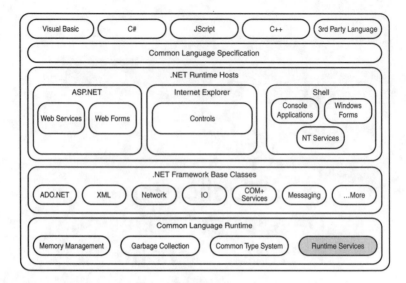

Figure 11.1

Coverage of the .NET Framework.

But this model simply trusted or didn't trust software; it did not limit what it could do. So a user could go to a site they trusted and install an ActiveX component. But if that component could be used in a malicious way, another site could access it and do harm to the users' machine.

The Java method of security was to have the applet run inside what is referred to as a *sandbox* and no activities outside the sandbox were allowed. So, for example, actions such as using files or other resources were off limits. This severely limited what applets could do.

In the .NET Framework, Microsoft has built a highly dynamic and robust security subsystem. The Security systems extend from simple sandbox based security to highly dynamic and deep security that will potentially allow a .NET assembly access to low-level functionality for one user of the assembly while denying access by another user of the assembly.

To the user, the .NET Framework security model is similar to the Java sandbox model. A user is no longer required to respond to a dialog box asking whether she trusts code from a given vendor. But unlike Java, a .NET Framework application can access protected resources if the proper security policy and clearances have been set. This allows a .NET Framework control to access the file system in a trusted deployment, but denies access in a untrusted deployment.

Code Identity

The basis for the .NET Security model is the *identity* of the code. Some of the information provided by the identity is the publisher, Internet site or zone from which the code originated, and its shared name. The identity of code is used in other security processes in the .NET Framework.

After identity has been established, the security subsystem can govern the access permissions that the code has authority to access, including system resources and additional code. Permissions govern all access to these resources and the same code might be governed by different permissions when it is executed under different conditions. For example, a control hosted in a Windows Form application might have the capability to read and write to the file system but that same control in a Web Page might be denied access.

Code Access Security

Permissions are granted by the runtime to assemblies and managed by administrators. *Code access security* prevents less-trusted code from using highly-trusted code to do potentially damaging actions. In this case, the highly-trusted code is reduced to the security level of less-trusted code.

For code access security to work correctly, the system requires a policy-based management system. The use of policies allows users and administrators to specify what kind of permissions assemblies from varying locations have.

The .NET Runtime ships with a default policy that reflects common security permissions users and organizations give to applications running from locations such as the Internet, intranet, or a local hard drive.

Within code access security, specific permissions are given to resources. Resources include things such as the file system, display windows, the clipboard, network channels, and unmanaged APIs.

When code attempts to access a resource, the runtime must walk through the call stack to determine that all assemblies in the call chain have authority to access the resource in the manner that is being attempted. If any of the assemblies do *not* have access, an exception is thrown.

Identity Permissions

Another mechanism used by code access security is the ability to identify the caller. This is where the Internet site or zone, shared name of the assembly, and publisher become involved with the security subsystem.

Access to resources is controlled by permissions granted to the identity of the code. In this way, a trusted assembly in a Windows Form application can gain access to the file system, but the same assembly is denied access if run from a Web browser page that originated at a site not given high enough permissions.

Declarative Security

The .NET Framework security model has an integrated *declarative security* mechanism. This is a very powerful mechanism for controlling access to secure code at either load time or runtime of an assembly.

Using declarative security, a developer can use attributes to annotate classes, fields, or methods. This encoding is included in the assembly metadata and enforced at load time or runtime. This allows a developer to, for example, restrict a class to being called only by another assembly from a specific publisher.

Imperative Security

At a more granular level, the .NET Framework also allows a developer to make specific demands of the security subsystem through *imperative security*. Whereas declarative security can restrict access to a predetermined file directory on a machine, an imperative demand might be needed to check if permission is allowed for on a file that won't be known at load time.

Imperative security is most commonly used against resources such as the file system. It allows restrictions on resources when there are multiple access modes to the same resource. Thus a system can specifically ask whether the assembly has access to delete a certain file at a certain point in a process.

Role-Based Security

Within organizations, different individuals (or more likely groups) commonly have different authority to processes. When Microsoft introduced Microsoft Transaction Server in 1997, it introduced this concept to Windows application developers. It was the normal pattern to design access to a database via a database userid and password. With role-based security, users were assigned roles, which would govern the authority to enact actions that would affect data and other processes.

The .NET Framework builds role-based security into the platform. This allows developers to control actions via roles. Users are assigned to roles, and—depending on the role a user fits in—applications can control the process, deny access to resources, or allow access to special processes.

Remoting Security

One of the main problems that COM, COM+, and DCOM had was to deal with security across machine boundaries when a distributed method call was made. The NT security model could make passing security contexts across machines difficult.

The Remoting strategy in the .NET Framework supports the security model across machine, application domain, and even business identities. The Remote security infrastructure uses a variety of standards-based security mechanisms. Key-based authentication protocols, point-to-point authentication protocols such as SSL and IPSEC, and cryptographic security algorithms are built in to the security subsystem.

Cryptography

Not only are cryptographic algorithms built in to the security subsystem, but also cryptography classes are included in the .NET Framework for application developers to use.

The cryptographic classes included with the .NET Framework libraries give developers a very rich set of functionality to build secure applications.

Garbage Collection and Resource Management

One of the most controversial changes to VB.NET is the move from deterministic finalization to garbage collection as the memory, object, and resource management model in the .NET Framework. To most, the new model is a superior model. To VB developers, in some ways it is a superior model and in a few instances it is a complex, difficult, and painful change. Figure 11.2 depicts where Garbage Collection fits in the .NET Framework.

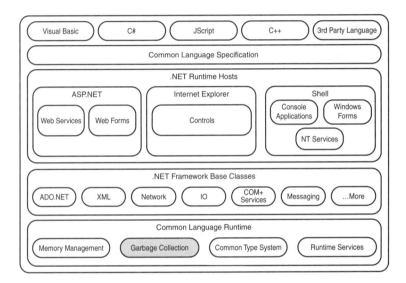

Figure 11.2

Where Garbage Collection fits in the .NET Framework.

COM-Based Resource Management

COM Resource Management is done using a method called deterministic finalization. Deterministic finalization is often referred to as reference counting. Basically a class keeps track of the number of references to it that are held by others. When the count hits zero, the object cleans itself up.

Deterministic finalization is code intensive in most languages, although Visual Basic has always hidden this code from developers. The COM implementation of deterministic finalization is built around the IUnknown interface, using a technique known as reference counting. The IUnknown interface supports three methods:

- AddRef—Increments the reference counter by one
- Release—Decrements the reference counter by one
- QueryInterface—Determines whether other interfaces are supported by an object (not used in deterministic finalization)

Internally, every object maintains a reference counter that it uses to determine whether it is time to clean up the object. It is the client's responsibility to call AddRef every time a reference is added to the object, and Release every time a reference is removed. This puts a heavy burden on the client to make sure that AddRef and Release are always called at the correct time.

In VB, this process has been hidden from developers by the VB Runtime. It has been hidden so well, in fact, that most VB developers don't even know that it is occurring or the ramifications of architectural decisions that they make, which affect how this works. One of these architectural decisions is circular references.

Deterministic finalization is the cause of one of the most common problems in VB systems—circular references. This is a very common object-oriented design. Circular references are when two objects hold references to each other (thus creating a circle).

As an example, consider Figure 11.3, which shows the object model for a typical Order Entry application, consisting of five types of objects: Customer, Orders, Order, Line Items, and Line Item. The arrows in the diagram indicate that each class implements a Parent property so that instances of the class can communicate back to their parent. When an instance of the Customer class creates an instance of an Orders class, it will pass it a reference to itself. This causes the AddRef method of the Customer class IUnknown interface to be called. This same pattern will be repeated all the way down the object hierarchy.

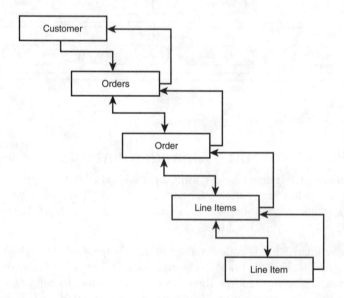

Figure 11.3

Circular Reference.

Now the expected behavior is that when the client who holds the reference to an instance of the Customer class sets the instance to Nothing, the complete hierarchy will be destroyed. What actually happens is the `Release` method of the Customer class `IUnknown` interface is called and the reference count is decremented by one. If the reference count hits zero, the instance of the Customer object will be destroyed. But in this example, because the instance of the Customer object created an instance of an Orders class and passed it a reference to itself, the reference count is still one. The result is a memory leak because after the client sets its reference to the Customer class to Nothing, the client cannot talk to the instance of the Customer class. But, the object and its children won't be destroyed.

A couple of methods can fix the circular reference problem. The most common techniques are the `CleanUp` method (officially designated the Dispose design pattern in Java and the .NET Framework), and the `WeakReference` method.

Of the two methods, `CleanUp` is the most commonly used. The basic technique is to add a `CleanUp` method to an object and call that method prior to releasing it. The `CleanUp` method, in turn, calls the `CleanUp` method of any child objects that it holds. The `CleanUp` method then sets any object pointers it holds to Nothing.

This method works quite well, if implemented correctly, but it is unfortunately very easy for a developer to forget to call `CleanUp` from the client application. In addition, if the client passes around the instance of the Customer class, it might be difficult to determine exactly when the `CleanUp` method should be called.

The other common technique is to use a `WeakReference` inside of the child classes to hold a reference to a parent. The only problem is that `WeakReferences` aren't supported by any native VB keyword or statement. A `WeakReference` is a reference that avoids `AddRef` being called (In reality what happens is that `AddRef` is called and almost immediately so is `Release`). This is done through the use of an undocumented (in the VB Manuals), unsupported function called `ObjPtr` and through an API Call. This method is the better method to use to avoid the problems associated with the `CleanUp` method. It does have its own problems though. It is very tricky code to write. (It looks deceptively simple, but it is very easy to use this technique and blow up the VB IDE.) You are also using a VB function that isn't supported or documented. (In fact, this function is gone in VB.NET.)

Encapsulating Cleanup

Deterministic finalization has its problems, but one of the things that it does provide is encapsulation of object cleanup. In most cases, this cleanup is trivial and there is no requirement that it be done immediately. But in a few cases, it is very important that the cleanup code should be executed as soon as an object is no longer referenced. This is usually the case with such things as files, handles to TCP/IP sockets, or other limited resources.

The deterministic finalization model makes this easy in Visual Basic, although in other languages the AddRef and Release logic is difficult to code. Listing 11.1 shows a simple class that controls when a hourglass is displayed and when it will be returned to the previous mouse pointer.

Listing 11.1   Encapsulating CleanUp—ChourGlass *Class*

```
Option Explicit
Private m_iPointer As MousePointerConstants

Private Sub Class_Initialize()
    m_iPointer = Screen.MousePointer
    If Not m_iPointer = vbHourglass Then
        Screen.MousePointer = vbHourglass
    End If
End Sub

Private Sub Class_Terminate()
    If m_iPointer <> vbHourglass Then
        Screen.MousePointer = m_iPointer
    End If
End Sub
```

Note that this class actually has no methods or properties, and it relies on the deterministic finalization functionality of COM and Visual Basic to control the mouse pointer. Without deterministic finalization, the Class_Terminate wouldn't fire and the mouse pointer wouldn't be returned to its original state.

.Net Framework Resource Management

Rather than the deterministic finalization model used by COM, the .Net Framework uses garbage collection, a relatively new method for Microsoft development tools (although it is used in Visual J++ and by other vendors).

The garbage collection models relies on a process, known as the garbage collector, monitoring resource utilization in an area of memory called the managed heap. When the garbage collector determines that a specific types of resource, such as memory, is getting scarce, it starts the garbage collection process.

The garbage collection process in the .Net Framework uses the "Sweep and Compact" method. This means that the garbage collector sweeps through all the objects, determining which ones to destroy, and, after they have been destroyed, it compacts memory to avoid fragmentation.

The garbage collector starts by assuming that all objects should be collected and destroyed. An application has a set of roots that tell the application where to find objects in the managed heap, or if the object is not referenced any longer the root will be set to null. When the garbage collector determines that an object is accessible from the roots, it will mark that object so that it isn't collected. It will then start looking at the objects and the roots that the object contains which point to objects that the object is using.

The garbage collector will recursively look through the roots of all the objects within a hierarchy, marking all the objects so that they aren't collected. After the garbage collector finishes walking the roots of the application, it knows which objects are being used and which ones can be collected.

Refer back to the object hierarchy shown in Figure 11.3. The reference to the Customer class held by the application is accessible from the roots. When the client reference goes out of scope or is explicitly set to Nothing, the pointer in the roots will be set to Null. The next time the garbage collector starts its work, it won't find the instance of the Customer class in the roots nor any of its children, so the whole hierarchy will be cleaned up. Thus, given the garbage collection resource management model, the circular reference problem disappears.

Unfortunately, however, other designs have different circular reference problems, some of which require using a new object in the .NET Framework known as a WeakReference. The WeakReference in the .NET Framework is different than a WeakReference from VB. It is a first class object in the framework and is supported and documented.

Nevertheless, garbage collection solves the most common circular reference problem without any code from a developer.

Table 11.1 Deterministic Finalization Compared to Garbage Collection

Issue	Deterministic Finalization	Garbage Collection
Circular Reference Problem Averted	Yes, through problematic code	Automatic
Encapsulated Cleanup	Class_Terminate Event	Finalize method or Dispose method
Immediate Cleanup of Objects	Yes	No, Cleanup is done when resources low
WeakReferences	Yes, via a hack	Built into Framework

Encapsulated Cleanup

In a garbage collection system such as the .NET Framework, objects are cleaned up after two things occur:

- Object references are set to Null
- A Garbage Collection is started

This means that unlike deterministic finalization, objects are not destroyed in any predictable order or at any predictable time. This greatly affects the idea of encapsulated cleanup. There are two methods for the cleanup of a VB.NET Framework object.

If cleanup must occur but need not be done immediately, a Finalize method will solve the problem, although at an expense beyond the code that executes in the method (see Chapter 5, "Creating and Destroying Objects"). The Finalize method causes an object to be marked for finalization, and when it has been determined that the object can be collected, it will first be put in a list of objects to be finalized. Some time later, the Finalize method will be executed and then the object will be put in a queue of objects to be collected.

The other technique for encapsulated cleanup in the .NET Framework, called the Dispose design pattern method, is similar to the CleanUp method of deterministic finalization. Unfortunately, similar to the CleanUp method, the Dispose design pattern method forces the client of the object to be responsible for calling it at the correct time. (Chapter 5 has more info on the Dispose design pattern.)

However, the Dispose design pattern method does ensure that any resources an object is using will be released or returned to their previous state. Listing 11.2 shows how the Dispose design pattern method might be used with the Hourglass class we examined earlier.

Listing 11.2   VB.NET Dispose Version of the ChourGlass **Class**

```
Public Class ChourGlass
    Implements System.IDisposable
    Private m_Pointer As Cursor = Cursor.Current()
    Public Sub New()
        MyBase.New()

        If Not m_Pointer.Current Is Cursors.WaitCursor Then
            Cursor.Current = Cursors.WaitCursor
        End If
    End Sub
    Public Sub Dispose() Implements System.IDisposable.Dispose
        If Not m_Pointer Is Cursors.WaitCursor Then
            Cursor.Current = m_Pointer
        End If
    End Sub
End Class
```

CHANGES TO GARBAGE COLLECTION

At the time of this writing, there has been much debate over the removal of deterministic finalization and the Terminate event in VB classes. Microsoft has been very open about this on VB Newsgroups, .NET Framework List Servers, and through other mechanisms. Microsoft has published a document from one of its architects about the problems with deterministic finalization and garbage collection and how they cannot play together. With that in mind, Microsoft has publicly stated a couple of ideas to alleviate (for example, not remove the problem). In my opinion, the most promising is an event that an object would receive if the object goes out of local scope. As of Beta 2, we haven't seen any implementation of this.

The thing to remember about this problem is that it is a rarely used design. However, some of the circumstances still make it important.

Performance Considerations

In this section I want to point out a few items to ensure that you start off building VB.NET applications that are scalable and perform well. There are a number of guidelines you will want to use to ensure acceptable performance of .NET applications.

Scalability Versus Performance

Sometimes it will be necessary to sacrifice performance to gain scalability. For example, in an ASP.NET application, you might choose to use session state for an application, and it will perform excellently. But in an effort to increase the scalability of you application, you might choose for the state to be maintained in SQL Server. This will dramatically increase your scalability, but the application won't perform as fast. But it will perform fast for many users rather than very fast for a few users. These are typical tradeoffs of building scalable applications.

Keep Interop to a Minimum

Calling Win32 APIs and COM components involvesgoing through an interoperability layer, which reduces performance. Note that this doesn't apply to COM+ Services, which aren't accessed via interop. Most importantly, avoid API calls that require a number of calls in succession. Instead, choose an API that accepts more parameters.

Use Value Types

Whenever possible, use a value type rather than a reference type. Value types are more efficient and require less overhead.

Don't Overuse the `Finalize` Method

As you saw in the last section, the `Finalize` method is the closest thing to the `Terminate` event in VB 6, but they do cost a great deal more than `Class_Terminate` events did because classes that have `Finalize` methods require two passes by the garbage collector to clean up. The first pass discovers the `Finalize` method and places the object in a special queue. A separate thread then runs the method. Finally, the garbage collector can collect the object next time it executes.

Unnecessary code placed in a `Class_Terminate` event in VB 6 didn't have any real effect on performance. This is no longer the case in the .Net Framework, so unless you are using a scarce resource or must save the state of an object before it is cleaned up, avoid using `Finalize` methods.

Avoid Using `On Error`

VB Developers are accustomed to using the `On Error` method of error handling. This is still supported in Visual Basic.NET, but will result in slower execution than a `Try...Catch...Finally` block. In addition, `Try...Catch...Finally` will continue to be optimized over the years. The same cannot be said for `On Error`.

Use the .Net Framework Class Library

You might be tempted to write every algorithm, every sort, and every piece of code yourself. After all, this is what you usually had to do with previous versions of Visual Basic.

In VB.NET, the .Net Framework Class Library contains a wealth of feature-rich classes that might provide exactly what you need. Look there first.

Architectural Considerations

A complete discussion of Visual Basic.NET application architecture would require another complete book. But in general, if you have been designing and building component-based applications, you will be ready to begin building .NET Framework solutions. The theory is still the same; only the implementation is different.

Windows DNA, DNA 2000, and .NET

Microsoft has been touting the Windows DNA and Windows DNA 2000 since 1997 as the architecture to use to build applications. People who have become confused to what Windows DNA means have said that DNA is dead with .NET. This isn't the case because Windows DNA isn't about server software, COM, or anything about implementation. Windows DNA is about designing your application in a layered or n-tiered approach. Microsoft marketing simply wanted to put a name on n-tiered design that was Microsoft-centric. You could think of the architecture of .NET Framework applications as Windows DNA 2001 because the .NET Framework should be released in 2001.

Fortunately, the naming is irrelevant. What *is* important is the separation of an application in to logical layers and the use of component-based implementation.

- Presentation Layer—This layer is made up of the actual user interface such as HTML/DHTML in ASP.NET Web Forms or Windows Forms. This layer also consists of components that support the presentation layer; for instance, in ASP.NET this would include ASP.NET Server controls and in Windows Forms it would include Windows Controls.
- Business Rule Layer—This layer is made up of components that control how data is persisted to a store and rules that govern how data is treated. Rules include validation, calculation, and regulations. These components also control interfaces with other systems.
- Data Persistence Layer—This layer is made up of components that control the data access and the data persistence mechanism itself such as SQL Server, Oracle database servers, or Exchange 2000.

The important thing to keep in mind is that although the applications are designed in a layered manner, it doesn't mean that they must be built in a layered component manner, nor does it mean that they must be deployed across multiple machines. A layered application can be built in one project in Visual Studio.NET and deployed on a single machine.

For example, you might build an ASP.NET Web Form application that has a Web Form class to control the presentation layer, classes to control the business rule layer, and classes that save and gather data from a SQL Server database that exists on the same machine. Later on, as the use of the application grows, you might move parts to components and parts to other machines to increase the scalability.

Layered Architectures in the .NET Framework

The Windows DNA Architecture translates quite easily to the .Net Framework.

Presentation Layer

The Presentation layer is perhaps the simplest layer in regard to what it is made up of. In most cases, this is HTML/DHTML with some client-side JavaScript to control user entry and simple validation, or it is a Rich Windows Form application or Windows Form application running inside a browser. In addition, the .NET Framework includes support for Pocket PC devices using the .NET Compact Framework, and wireless devices will also be services by Microsoft Mobile Information Server 2001.

Business Rule Layer

The Business Rule layer in the .NET Framework is much more complex and involves a great deal of services provided by the underlying platform. In a Windows implementation (the only implementation to date), the Business Rule layer consists of WebServices, Class Libraries, COM+ Services, and System Services (For logging, performance monitoring, application integration). In .NET Framework applications, you might use some of the following .NET Enterprise servers:

- SQL Server 2000
- Exchange Server 2000
- BizTalk Server 2000
- Commerce Server 2000
- Host Integration Server 2000
- SharePoint Portal Server 2001
- Mobile Information Server 2001
- HailStorm WebServices

You might also use services provided by other vendors, and—most importantly—by using WebServices you might use outside services over the Internet. Figure 11.4 illustrates where the .NET Enterprise servers and Visual Studio.NET fit together.

Data Layer

The Data layer not only can be the most complex, but also the simplest in structure. This layer controls the access to the data persistence mechanism (most likely a relational database). In the .NET Framework, this is where you will use ADO and ADO.NET to manipulate data and present data to other layers of the application—most likely in the form of XML. There are various methods that architects use to gather data and translate the data to other services. The Data layer might also take advantage of COM+ Services and WebServices to persist data.

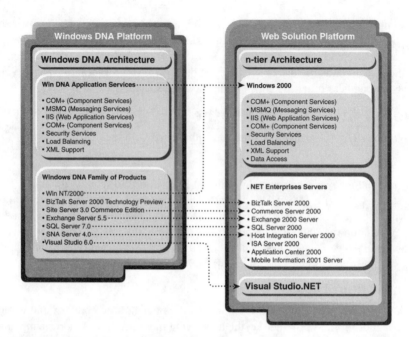

Figure 11.4

Windows DNA evolution to .NET.

.NET Enterprise Servers

Over the past year, Microsoft has released a great deal of server products that will be part of many .NET Framework applications. It is important to understand where they fit in and the services that they provide. In most cases, these servers are considered .NET Enterprise servers because they work with industry standard protocols such as HTML, XML, LDAP.

SQL Server 2000

Perhaps the simplest server to understand is SQL Server 2000. SQL Server 2000 is a relational database engine and will, in most circumstances, be the prime .NET Server used. SQL Server 2000 has a very deep integration with XML because of its capability to return data as XML and take updates to data in XML format.

Exchange Server 2000

Exchange Server 2000 provides messaging and workflow capabilities to applications, and, similar to SQL Server 2000, has a deep integration with XML and HTTP to service .NET Applications.

BizTalk Server 2000

BizTalk Server 2000 provides facilities to integrated Business Process Orchestration and XML document exchange between businesses (Trading Partners) and integrates with existing applications. I like to tell people who are familiar with *Electronic Data Interchange (EDI)* that BizTalk Server 2000 is a EDI translator on steroids.

BizTalk supplies services to translate incoming XML (and non XML data) into an internal processing format and again translate internal formats to external formats for Trading Partners. Also provided are tools to set up Trading Partners and to manage how communication is done between partners. BizTalk has a number of COM Components and Interfaces that .NET developers can use through COM Interop as well as methods to accept information via WebServices and HTTP.

Commerce Server 2000

Commerce Server 2000 provides facilities to deploy, manage, and develop commerce-related Internet and intranet applications. Commerce Server 2000 has a number of components that developers can access through COM Interop. Commerce Server 2000 also provides interfaces for analyzing sites and making promotion of products in many ways.

Host Integration Server 2000

Host Integration Server 2000 provides mechanisms for developers to talk to systems and data stores on AS/400 and MVS based mainframe systems. One of the mechanisms is *COM/Transaction Integrator (COMTI)*, which allows developers to expose CICS programs as COM+ Components.

Mobile Information Server 2001

Mobile Information Server 2001 is a new product, which allows integration of Mobile devices such as, hand-held devices, and cellular phones into solutions.

Sharepoint Portal Server 2001

Sharepoint Portal Server 2001 is another new product that Microsoft will be releasing shortly. The purpose of Sharepoint Portal Server 2001 is to make it easier for organizations to aggregate information from various sources into portals. Sharepoint Portal Server 2001 provides for facilities to control documents, integrated discussion, and instant mechanisms into portal solutions.

Application Center 2000

If you plan on building applications that are expected to scale into Web Farm scenarios, you will need to take a good hard look at Application Center 2000. Application Center 2000 is a tool to manage, deploy, administer, and troubleshoot multiserver applications as if they were on one server. It provides facilities for Component load balancing, and Network load balancing. When you need a new server in a farm, you simply install Windows 2000 Advanced Server (or later this year, Windows XP Advanced Server) and have Application Center 2000 install the server into the farm. Application Center 2000 will configure the machine to have all the same software and configuration settings that the other machines in the cluster have.

Internet Security and Accelerator Server 2000

Internet Security and Accelerator Server 2000 is a firewall server, and in the case of .NET provides for the caching of static content to relieve the load of Web Servers.

Hailstorm WebServices

On March 18, 2001, Microsoft introduced the first set of WebServices that it will provide for developers to use. These initial services provide for integration with Microsoft Passport for authentication and personalization, a XML modified Instant Messaging mechanism, and services for calendaring and inbox management. This will allow sites to integrate with a user's calendar and to send messages in the form of instant messaging or e-mail. Passport integration has been built in to Windows XP so that when a user logs in to a computer, she will also already be logged in to Passport. Any site she goes to and does business with will know who she is and information about her (as much information that the user wants to share).

XML Integration

Microsoft decided very early on in the development of the .Net Framework not only to support XML, but also to make it a key part of the architecture. XML is used throughout the .NET Framework in the following ways:

- Data transfer between objects
- Object serialization
- Application administration
- Internationalization
- Documentation
- Web services
- Data access

But the key XML technology in the .Net Framework is SOAP.

SOAP

One of the design goals of the .NET Framework was to integrate a cross-platform method of remote procedure calls. Microsoft was one of the first software firms to embrace XML when it first began making a storm in the Internet space. Along with Developmentor and David Winer, they married these two ideas and the result is the *Simple Object Access Protocol (SOAP)*.

SOAP was unveiled in September 1999 when Microsoft first publicly previewed Visual Studio.NET. SOAP 1.0 was submitted to the W3C in the Fall of 1999. During the winter, IBM and Lotus joined with Microsoft and helped author SOAP 1.1, which has also been submitted to the W3C. During the year 2000, Microsoft released a technology preview in the form of the Visual Studio 6 SOAP Toolkit, and IBM has released several releases for the Apache Web Server and Java. During the summer of 2000, Sun formally said it would support SOAP. Although SOAP was originally developed as a method of using XML and HTTP to do *Remote Procedure Calls (RPC)*, after IBM joined the effort SOAP has been generalized to support other methods of invocation.

SOAP is actually deceptively simple. It is built around stateless calls to a Web site, with both parameters and responses in the form of XML messages. Microsoft has built SOAP in to the remoting strategy of the .NET Framework. In the .NET Framework, creating a WebService is as simple as placing an attribute on a method stating that it is a Web method.

WebServices

WebServices allow outside clients to look at the data or to call functions that you are supplying. The most common example is in the form of an e-commerce shopping site that wants to provide to shipping information. In current sites, the most common way to provide this information is to link to the shipping companies' sites with the tracking number of the shipment. If the shipping company were to create a WebService to provide this information, then the e-commerce site could display it directly on the customer's order page.

The beauty of this model is that it doesn't matter what type of process is on the other side of the WebService. With SOAP, all that is required is a SOAP listener (A SOAP listener listens for incoming SOAP requests on a transportation protocol such as HTTP and routes the request to the appropriate component), which needs to be built to accept WebService requests. Behind the listener could be any sort of process, running on any platform.

One of the requirements for the successful adoption of SOAP was a standard way for a site to describe a WebService that it exposed for outside use. On September 25, 2000, IBM and Microsoft submitted to the W3C the specification for *Web Services Description Language (WSDL)* 1.0. The WSDL uses XML describe to a WebService to outside sources. (For developers familiar with COM, WSDL can be thought of as a TypeLib in XML.)

In addition, Microsoft, IBM, and Ariba recently disclosed the *Universal Description, Discovery and Integration (UDDI)* project. UDDI's purpose is to act as a Web-based repository of WebServices available on the Internet.

Finally, Microsoft has an early proposal for a technology called *Discovery of Web Services (DISCO)* that it published at the Professional Developers Conference in July 2000. DISCO is a technology to allow a Web site to be searched for the WSDL documents on the site so that a potential client of the WebService can find out how to use the WebService.

UDDI shouldn't be confused with DISCO. UDDI is a repository and DISCO is a discovery mechanism. When you create a WebService with .NET, the Web server you deploy it in will have a DISCO file created. When your WebService is complete you can choose to publish your service to UDDI. (Visual Studio.NET will provide tools to do this from directly inside of the development tool.)

Putting all the pieces together produces the following picture: Developers can search UDDI for a WebService meeting their needs. When a developer has identified the URL of a potential WebService, she can then use Visual Studio.NET (or another developer tool that understands DISCO) to search the WSDL documents at that URL to determine how to use the WebService. After Visual Studio.NET has a WSDL document for a WebService, it can be used the same as any other component in Visual Basic.NET.

IMPORTANT URL'S FOR SOAP TECHNOLOGIES

- Simple Object Access Protocol (SOAP) 1.1 Specification:

  http://msdn.microsoft.com/xml/general/soapspec.asp
- Web Services Description Language (WSDL) 1.0 Specification:

  http://msdn.microsoft.com/xml/general/wsdl.asp
- Universal Description, Discovery and Integration (UDDI) project:

  http://www.uddi.org
- Discovery of Web Services (DISCO):

  http://msdn.microsoft.com/xml/general/disco.asp

Creating Web Services

When a method is exposed as a WebService through the use of the `WebMethod` attribute, the *Common Language Runtime (CLR)* marshals information as XML. This allows a WebService to return objects serialized into XML.

By default, each piece of data in an object is stored as an XML element. Class attributes are used to customize the serialization, as shown in Listing 11.3 This might be necessary, for example, to force the serialization to conform to an existing XML Schema.

Listing 11.3   XML Serialization Attributes

```
Imports System
Imports System.Xml.Serialization
Public Class EmployeeInfo
    Private c_sFirstName As String
    Private c_sLastName As String
    Private c_sEmployeeNumber As String
    Private c_dtStartDate As Date
    Public Overloads Sub New()
        MyBase.New()
    End Sub
    Public Overloads Sub New(ByVal FirstName As String, ByVal LastName As
String, _
            ByVal StartDate As Date)
        MyBase.New()
        c_sFirstName = FirstName
        c_sLastName = LastName
        c_dtStartDate = StartDate
    End Sub
```

Listing 11.3   *Continued*

```
<XmlElement()> Public Property FirstName() As String
    Get
        Return c_sFirstName
    End Get
    Set(ByVal Value As String)
        c_sFirstName = Value
    End Set
End Property
<XmlElement()> Public Property LastName() As String
    Get
        Return c_sLastName
    End Get
    Set(ByVal Value As String)
        c_sLastName = Value
    End Set
End Property
<XmlAttribute()> Public Property StartDate() As Date
    Get
        Return c_dtStartDate
    End Get
    Set(ByVal Value As Date)
        c_dtStartDate = Value
    End Set
End Property
<XmlIgnore()> Public ReadOnly Property FullName() As String
    Get
        Return c_sFirstName & " " & c_sLastName
    End Get
End Property
End Class
```

CHAPTER 12

Interoperability

Interoperability is nothing new for VB developers; they have been using the Declare statement to call Windows APIs for years.

What is new to the .NET Framework is the total integration of interoperability into the .NET Framework. This isn't surprising because both the .NET Framework itself and .Net Framework application run inside of the *Common Language Runtime (CLR)*. There had to be a way to interoperate with traditional Windows APIs, COM Components, *Microsoft Transaction Server (MTS)*, and COM+ Services.

A great deal of effort went into making the interoperability components as seamless and powerful as possible. In addition, the syntax for calling Windows APIs from Visual Basic has been changed as little as possible in order to facilitate the use of legacy code.

The Declare statement is still the method for calling Windows APIs. In most cases, COM interoperability is simply a matter of creating metadata for the COM component. MTS and COM+ Services integration is achieved through attributes and a few optional utilities.

Calling the Windows API

Visual Basic has always tried to keep developers from hurting themselves. This principle has limited some of the Windows functionality that VB developers could access directly. Fortunately, there were methods to gain access to this functionality through the use of the Windows API.

In addition, developers could add functionality by building API-based components in other languages such as C, Fortran, Pascal, or others. VB could gain access to these components provided that they were used VB-friendly data types.

The .NET Framework allows the use of API-based components through the Platform Invoke (P/Invoke) technology. In VB.NET, P/Invoke is implemented by VB.NET using the familiar `Declare` statement.

It is extremely important to understand that direct calls to the Windows API won't be needed nearly as often in Visual Basic.NET as they were in previous versions of VB. Don't assume that just because previous versions didn't support some functionality it will still be necessary to resort to the Windows API. It's important to fully explore the .NET Framework before deciding to use an API call.

For example, one of the most common Windows API calls made in previous versions of Visual Basic is `SendMessage`. Typically Visual Basic developers use `SendMessage` to send messages to ActiveX controls to achieve functionality not directly exposed by the controls' COM interface. In the .NET Framework, any control that inherits from the `System.Object.MarshalByRefObject.MarshalByRefComponent.Control` has a `SendMessage` method. Therefore, all Windows Forms controls inherit the `SendMessage` method. This means that there is no reason to use Declare to use the `SendMessage` API. But, to illustrate the use of API calls in VB.NET, I will use `SendMessage` for my examples.

Listing 12.1 illustrates using the `SendMessage` method of a .NET Framework `ListBox` control to find the length of an item in a list box using VB.NET.

Listing 12.1   Use `SendMessage` **to Determine the Length of a List Box Item**

```
Private Function GetListBoxItemLength() As Integer
        Const LB_GETITEMLENGTH As Integer = &H18A
        Dim iLength As Integer

        iLength = ListBox1.SendMessage(LB_GETITEMLENGTH, _
         ListBox1.SelectedIndex, 0)
        msgbox("Length of Selected Item is " & CStr(iLength))
        Return iLength
End Function
```

The `Declare` Statement

The syntax of the `Declare` statement hasn't changed a great deal between VB6 and VB.NET, but there have been some significant changes in functionality related to using the `Declare` statement. The basic syntax of the `Declare` statement is as follows:

```
Declare Sub NameOfFunctionInDLL Lib "libraryname"
```

The syntax for calling a function that returns a value is shown in the following:

```
Declare Function NameOfFunctionInDLL Lib "libraryname" As ReturnValueType
```

The NameOfFunctionInDLL defines both the name of the function in the DLL and how you will call it in code. Note that this is case sensitive. If you want to call the function by another name code or if the function name is invalid in Visual Basic, you can use the optional Alias keyword, as shown in the following:

```
Declare Sub FunctionNameToUseInVB Lib "libraryname" Alias "NameOfFunctionInDll"
```

libraryname is the name of the library being called. In most cases, this will be a DLL.

Parameters are defined in the Declare statement just as they were in standard VB.NET Subs and Functions. Listing 12.2 illustrates the syntax of Declare with parameters, whereas Listing 12.3 uses SendMessage as an example.

Listing 12.2 Declare **with Parameters**

```
Declare Sub FunctionNameToUseInVB Lib "libraryname" _
        Alias "NameOfFunctionInDll" (ParameterList)
```

Listing 12.3 SendMessage **Example**

```
Declare Function SendMessage Lib "user32" Alias "SendMessageA" _
        (ByVal hwnd As Integer,
ByVal wMsg As Integer, ByVal wParam As Integer, _
ByVal lParam As String) As Integer
```

Specific rules must be followed when passing parameters. This book doesn't go into all the rules that a given API function might require. For more information on using the Windows API with VB.NET, read Daniel Appleman's *VB Programmers Guide to the Win32 API,* published by Sams Publishing.

A couple of other optional keywords are used with the Declare statement. Declare can have accessibility modifiers associated with it, as shown in Listing 12.4. The available accessibility modifiers for the Declare statement are Public, Private, Friend, Protected, and Protected Friend.

Listing 12.4 Declare AccessibilityModifier

```
AccessibilityModifier Declare Sub FunctionNameToUseInVB Lib "libraryname" _
Alias "NameOfFunctionInDll" (ParameterList)
```

Also a new set of optional keywords is to be used to indicate the marshaling behavior of strings, as shown in Listing 12.5. MarshalingBehavior can have one of three values: Ansi, Unicode, or Auto. Ansi specifies that all strings should be marshaled as ANSI strings. Unicode specifies that all strings should be marshaled as Unicode strings. Auto puts the decision into the CLR's control, based on .NET rules that are determined by the name of the function being called. If no MarshalingBehavior is specified, the default is Auto.

Listing 12.5   *Marshaling Behavior*

```
AccessibilityModifier Declare MarshalingBehavior Sub FunctionNameToUseInVB _
Lib "libraryname" Alias "NameOfFunctionInDll" (ParameterList)
```

One important change to the Declare statement in VB.NET is the removal of the Any keyword. In previous versions of Visual Basic, Any supported API functions that accepted more than one type of data for the same argument, as shown in Listing 12.6, using SendMessage again as the example.

Listing 12.6   *VB6* SendMessage *with* Any

```
Declare Function SendMessage Lib "user32" Alias "SendMessageA" _
(ByVal hwnd As long, _
ByVal wMsg As long, ByVal wParam As long, ByVal lParam As Any) As Integer
```

Using Any was never the recommended method because it allowed disabled type checking, and Microsoft has removed the keyword from VB.NET. In VB.NET, you must create multiple Declare statements to handle the multiple types, as shown in Listing 12.7. VB.NET allows you to use the new function overloading capability to call the declares the same name for different function signatures. The removal of Any does involve more work, but it is safer in the long run.

Listing 12.7   *VB.NET Declares without* Any

```
Overloads Declare Function SendMessage Lib "user32" Alias "SendMessageA" _
            (ByVal hwnd As integer,
ByVal wMsg As integer, _
             ByVal wParam As integer, ByVal lParam As integer) As Integer
Overloads Declare Function SendMessage Lib "user32" _
            Alias "SendMessageA" (ByVal hwnd As integer, _
            ByVal wMsg As integer, ByVal wParam As integer, _
            ByVal lParam As string) As Integer
```

Controlling Marshaling

The MarshalingBehavior keywords in the Declare statement tell the CLR exactly how to move strings in and out of API calls, but the .NET Framework provides a more elegant solution that can be used for any data type, not just a string.

This is done through the use of attributes. Attributes provide a declarative method for handling situations that used to involve a great deal of code. The Attribute class that you will use to influence data marshaling is System.Object.Attribute. MarshalAsAttribute, or MarshalAs for short. MarshalAs allows you to specify how to pass each parameter in the parameter list by adding an attribute to the parameter definition.

The example in Listing 12.8 illustrates the syntax of MarshalAs using the CopyFile function. Notice that the MarshalAs attribute receives a constructor for each use. In the example, both instances received a parameter of UnmanagedType.LPStr, which is a pointer to a null terminated array of ANSI characters.

Listing 12.8   Using Attributes to Influence Marshaling

```
Declare Auto Sub CopyFile Lib "Kernel32" (ByVal
<MarshalAs(UnmanagedType.LPTStr)> _
        existingfile As String, ByVal <MarshalAs(UnmanagedType.LPTStr)> _
        newfile As String, ByVal failifexists As Boolean)
```

A number of parameters can be passed to the MarshalAs constructor. The parameters
are contained in the System.Runtime.InteropServices.UnManagedType enumeration
following the members of UnManagedType. Table 12.1 lists the enumeration.

Table 12.1   MarshalAs Constructors

Constructor Value	Definition
AnsiBStr	ANSI character string that is a length prefixed, single byte.
AsAny	Dynamic type that determines the type of an Object at runtime and marshals the Object as that type.
Bool	4-byte Boolean value (true != 0, false = 0).
BStr	Unicode character string that is a length prefixed double byte.
ByValArray	A fixed length array. The UnmanagedFormatAttribute must contain the count of elements in the array. The UnmanagedFormatAttribute might optionally contain the unmanaged type of the elements when it is necessary to differentiate among string types.
ByValTStr	A string in a fixed length buffer. The type UnmanagedFormatAttribute must also contain the size of the buffer in bytes. The type of the characters is determined by the Charset used by the class.
CustomMarshaler	Custom marshaler native type. This must be followed by a string of the following format: "Native type name\0Custom marshaler type name\0Optional cookie\0" or "{Native type GUID}\0Custom marshaler type name\0Optional cookie\0".
Error	This native type associated with an I4 or an U4 will cause the parameter to be exported as an HRESULT in the exported typelib.
FunctionPtr	A function pointer.
I1	1-byte signed integer.
I2	2-byte signed integer.
I4	4-byte signed integer.
I8	8-byte signed integer.
IDispatch	A COM IDispatch pointer. This only applies to a generic object, not a derived class.
Interface	A COM interface pointer. The GUID of the interface is obtained from the class metadata.

Table 12.1 `MarshalAs` *Constructors*

Constructor Value	Definition
IUnknown	A COM IUnknown pointer. This only applies to a generic object, not a derived class.
LPArray	An array whose length is determined at runtime by the size of the actual marshaled array. Optionally followed by the unmanaged type of the elements within the array when it is necessary to differentiate among string types. When marshaling from managed to unmanaged, the size of the array is determined dynamically. When marshaling from unmanaged to managed, the size is always assumed to be 1.
LPStr	A single byte ANSI character string.
LPStruct	A pointer to a C-style structure. Used to marshal managed formatted classes and value types.
LPTStr	A platform-independent character string, ANSI on Win9x, Unicode on WinNT.
LPWStr	A double byte Unicode character string.
R4	4-byte floating point number.
R8	8-byte floating point number.
SafeArray	An OLE Automation SafeArray. The `UnmanagedFormatAttribute` might optionally supply the unmanaged type of the elements within the array when it is necessary to differentiate among string types.
Struct	A C-style structure, used to marshal managed formatted classes and value types.
SysInt	A platform-independent signed integer. 4-bytes on 32 bit Windows, 8-bytes on 64-bit Windows.
SysUInt	Hardware natural sized unsigned integer
TBStr	A length prefixed platform independent char string. ANSI on Windows 9x, Unicode on Windows NT.
U1	1-byte unsigned integer.
U2	2-byte unsigned integer.
U4	4-byte unsigned integer.
U8	8-byte unsigned integer.
VariantBool	2-byte OLE Boolean true = -1 false = 0
VBByRefStr	VB specific.

Formatting Structures for Declare

Many Windows APIs require a structure to be passed in the API call. In previous versions of VB, this could be a difficult task to accomplish because the data types available in VB often didn't match the data types that the API required.

This has changed with VB.NET. Structures don't have the problems that user-defined types had in the past with the data types not matching.

Two attribute classes in the .NET Framework allow you to control the way that structures are passed in Declare. Listing 12.9 illustrates the use of these attributes.

- StructLayout—Determines the layout method of the structure data and has three layout possibilities that are passed in the constructor. Listing 12.9 illustrates the use of this attribute.
- FieldOffSet—Used when the StructLayout is set to LayOutKind.Explicit. This lets a developer exactly control the offsets into the structure and how various pieces of data are placed. Listing 12.10 illustrates the use of this attribute.

Listing 12.9 Using StructLayout

```
Public Structure <StructLayout(LayoutKind.Sequential)> SystemTime
    Public Year As Short
    Public Month As Short
    Public DayOfWeek As Short
    Public Day As Short
    Public Hour As Short
    Public Minute As Short
    Public Second As Short
    Public Miliseconds As Short
End Structure
```

When you use the LayoutKind.Explicit enumeration with struct layout, you then use the FieldOffSet attribute. Notice that in Listing 12.10 not only are we using FieldOffSet, but we are also using unsigned types.

Listing 12.10 Using the FieldOffSet Attribute

```
Public Class <StructLayout(LayoutKind.Explicit)> SYSTEM_INFO
    <FieldOffset(0)> Private OemId As System.UInt64
    <FieldOffset(4)> Private PageSize As System.UInt64
    <FieldOffset(16)> Private ActiveProcessorMask As System.UInt64
    <FieldOffset(20)> Private NumberOfProcessors As System.UInt64
    <FieldOffset(24)> Private ProcessorType As System.UInt64
End Class
```

Using .NET Framework Components in COM Applications

.NET Framework interoperability allows .Net Framework components to be used from unmanaged COM code, including applications built with previous versions of VB, VBA, Active Server Pages, other COM languages, and scripting languages.

The .NET Framework will create a *COM Callable wrapper (CCW)* when a COM client creates an instance of a .NET Framework component. The CCW isn't visible to other .NET classes. It's purpose is simply to integrate with unmanaged COM code. To keep overhead low, each .NET Framework component instance will have only one CCW no matter how many outside references to the instance are held.

THE CCW makes .NET Framework components accessible to unmanaged COM clients via either IDispatch or IUnknown. This allows unmanaged COM code to make either early- or late-bound calls to .NET Framework components.

Creating Strong Names

.Net Framework components require a strong name, which is similar to a GUID in that it guarantees a unique name, but they are created by hashing a 128-bit encryption key against the string-based name of a component or assembly. Strong names are created using SN.exe, which creates a *keyfile* that is hashed with the component during compilation to generate the strong name.

Install into the Global Assembly Cache

To use a .NET Framework component from a COM application or component, the .NET Framework component needs to be installed into the Global Assembly Cache with the AL.exe (Assembly Linker Utility).

Registration

Before a .NET Framework component can be called from unmanaged COM code, it must first be installed into the registry. Registration is done through the register assembly utility, RegAsm.exe. Optionally, RegAsm.exe could also create a TypeLib and register it as well.

Creating a Type Library

In order to make early-bound calls to a .NET Framework component, a *type library (TypeLib)* needs to be created. TypeLibs can be created a number of ways:

- Via the TypeLib export utility TlbExp.exe
- Via the `System.Runtime.InteropServices.TypeLibConverter` class
- Via Visual Studio.NET when a COM component is referenced

A COM client can late-bind to a .NET Framework component using the IDispatch interface provided by COM. Support for IDispatch is automatically supplied by the CLR. This is one of the circumstances in which the CLR might create a TypeLib on-the-fly to provide an implementation of IDispatch.

Walkthrough

Listing 12.11 shows a simple Employee class that we'll use to walk through the process of calling a .Net Framework component from unmanaged code.

Listing 12.11   .NET Component to Use from COM

```
Public Class Employee
    Private c_sFirstName As String
    Private c_sLastName As String
```

Listing 12.11   Continued

```
    Private c_sSSN As String
    Public Property FirstName() As String
        Get
            Return c_sFirstName
        End Get
        Set(ByVal Value As String)
            c_sFirstName = Value
        End Set
    End Property
    Public Property LastName() As String
        Get
            Return c_sLastName
        End Get
        Set(ByVal Value As String)
            c_sLastName = Value
        End Set
    End Property
    Public Property SSN() As String
        Get
            Return c_sSSN
        End Get
        Set(ByVal Value As String)
            c_sSSN = Value
        End Set
    End Property
    Public Function ReverseString(ByVal TheString As String) As String
        Dim sReversedString As String
        Dim i As Integer
        For i = TheString.Length - 1 To 0 Step -1
            sReversedString = sReversedString & TheString.Substring(i, 1)
        Next
        Return sReversedString
    End Function
End Class
```

Before the component is compiled, a keyfile needs to be created so that the component can be compiled with a strong name.

We will call our sample strong name ComInterop.SNK. From the Windows Start menu, select Run and the Run CMD to Open the Command prompt. Set the directory to your project's BIN directory, and then run the following command:

```
SN.EXE -k ComInterop.SNK
```

Now that you have a strong name, go into Visual Studio.NET, right-click on the project in the Solution Explorer, and bring up the project properties (see Figure 12.1). In the Common Properties panel, click Sharing and check Generate Strong Name Using. Check the Key File option and type the Key File name (or browse to it)—for the example, it should be ComInterop.SNK. Now build the component.

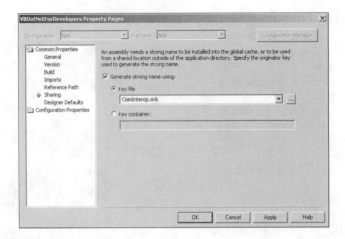

Figure 12.1

Set strong name in Visual Studio.NET.

Now we have a DLL to register (and create a TypeLib) and install into the *Global Assembly Cache (GAC)*. Run the following command from the command prompt:

```
RegAsm ComInterop.Dll /tlb:ComInterop.Tlb
```

Now you need to install the component into the GAC, using the following command:

```
AL.Exe /i:ComInterop.Dll
```

The component is now ready to use from unmanaged COM code. Give it a try using VB 6 or VB for applications. The code in VB 6 looks similar to what is illustrated in Listing 12.12. (First you need to reference the TypeLib.)

Listing 12.12   VB6 Calling .NET Component

```
Dim oEmployee as ComInterop.Employee
Dim sReversedString as String

Set oEmployee = New ComInterop.Employee
oEmployee.FirstName = "DotNet"
oEmployee.LastName = "Guru"
sReversedString = "Hello World"
Debug.Print oEmployee.FirstName
Debug.Print oEmployee.LastName
Debug.Print oEmployee.ReverseString(sReversedString)
```

Using COM Components from .NET Framework Applications

When moving applications into the .Net Framework, the best method will be to migrate applications component by component because you will still be able to use your existing COM components from within .Net Framework code.

Fortunately, using COM Components from .NET Framework applications is a great deal easier than using .Net Framework components from COM.

When .NET Framework code creates an instance of an unmanaged COM object, the object is exposed through a wrapper: in this case the *runtime callable wrapper (RCW)* that will act as the proxy for the real unmanaged object. This is roughly analogous to the CCW used to call .Net Framework components from COM.

To the .NET Framework code, the RCW appears to be just another managed .NET Component, but in fact its sole purpose is to marshal calls between the .NET Framework code and the unmanaged COM component. An instance of a COM object will have only one RCW no matter how many references to the unmanaged COM object are held.

Most of the time, Visual Studio.Net will do all the work that's needed to use an unmanaged COM component from .NET Framework code behind the scenes. When you select a COM component from the Add Reference dialog, Visual Studio.Net will automatically run the TypeLib import utility, TlpImp.exe, which creates an assembly containing all the metadata required for the .NET Framework to use the unmanaged COM component.

Figures 12.2–12.4 and Listing 12.13 walk you through the creation of a Windows Form application that uses ADO 2.6 to access SQL Server and load a list box.

First, you need to create a new Windows application. Then from the Solution Explorer right-click on References and add a reference. Figure 12.2 shows the Reference dialog box.

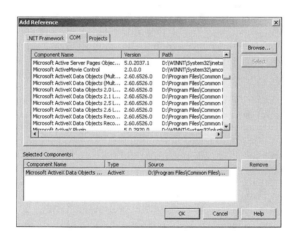

Figure 12.2

Reference dialog box showing ADO 2.6.

Now find ADO 2.6 and select it. Figure 12.3 illustrates the Reference dialog box with ADO 2.6 selected.

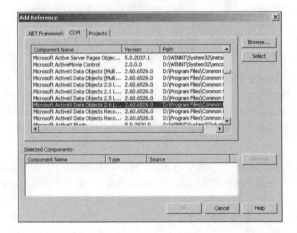

Figure 12.3

Select ADO 2.6.

Now drag a list box and a button onto the form and make it resemble the form in Figure 12.4. Name the button **btnLoad** and the list box **lstPublishers**.

Figure 12.4

A sample Windows form (before a call to ADO).

View the form in code view and add the code from Listing 12.13. (Change the connection information to point to your database server.)

Listing 12.13   Fill List with Information from the Pubs Database

```
Private Sub btnLoad_Click(ByVal sender As System.Object, _
        ByVal e As System.EventArgs) Handles btnLoad.Click
    Dim oPublishersRecordset As ADODB.Recordset
    Dim oPubsConnection As ADODB.Connection
    Dim sPubsConnection As String = "Provider=SQLOLEDB.1;Password='';" & _
        "Persist Security Info=True;User ID=sa;Initial Catalog=pubs;" & _
        "Data Source=red-leader2"
    Dim sGetPublisher As String = "Select pub_name from publishers " & _
            "order by pub_name"


    oPubsConnection = New ADODB.Connection()
    oPubsConnection.ConnectionString = sPubsConnection
    oPubsConnection.Open()

    oPublishersRecordset = New ADODB.Recordset()
    oPublishersRecordset.Open(sGetPublisher, oPubsConnection, _
        ADODB.CursorTypeEnum.adOpenForwardOnly,_
        ADODB.LockTypeEnum.adLockReadOnly)

    Do Until oPublishersRecordset.EOF
        lstPublishers.Items.Add( _
                oPublishersRecordset.Fields("pub_name").Value.ToString)
        oPublishersRecordset.MoveNext()
    Loop

    oPublishersRecordset.Close()
    oPubsConnection.Close()
End Sub
```

Now run the application, click the **btnLoad** button, and the application should resemble Figure 12.5.

Figure 12.5

A Windows form filled with data from ADO.

The .NET Framework provides mechanisms for calling unmanaged COM Components in a late bound fashion as well as using additional interfaces of a component. VB.NET continues to include a statement to create an object based on a string. This is accomplished through the `CreateObject` statement.

In VB.NET `CreateObject` is limited to creating ActiveX objects (or .NET Framework classes that are exposed as ActiveX objects). The `CreateObject` statement in VB.NET also supports the optional parameter to supply the server name that the component will run on.

When using COM components from VB.NET and when designing components that will be used by VB.NET, it is important to properly clean up in a manner that best supports Garbage Collection in the .NET Framework. COM component references are held by the CCW, and the CCW won't be destroyed as soon as the CCW goes out of scope. That is why in the code in Figure 8.20, I explicitly closed the connection and the recordset. I shouldn't wait for the GC to do this because they hold resources. If you use a COM component that has a cleanup method (or methods), use the method(s). If you design a COM component that will hold resources, add a cleanup method.

COM+ Services

Although interoperability with API based components is important, the most important part of the interoperability story in the .NET Framework is with COM+ Services. COM+ Services are still extremely important tools to use when building highly scalable .NET Framework applications. No matter if the applications are ASP.NET WebSites, ASP.NET WebServices, or Distributed Windows Form applications in order to make them scale, you need to take advantage of the services that COM+ Services provide.

Services Provided by COM+

It is important to understand what services that COM+ provides for .NET Framework applications. COM+ Services are an outgrowth of the introduction of Microsoft Transaction Server (MTS). MTS was introduced in 1997 and it provided a runtime environment for components. Although there was a great deal of confusion about MTS, most people simply thought by the name that it was a transaction processor, although in fact it provided a great deal of resource management to components. Some of the resource management that MTS provided was transaction management, thread pooling and reuse, connection pooling to databases, and object reuse (not object pooling). Transactions could span across various resource managers such as SQL Server, Oracle, DB2, or *Microsoft Message Queue (MSMQ)*.

In Windows 2000, Microsoft enhanced what was MTS and introduced COM+ Services. COM+ Services enhanced what MTS did in a number of ways. First and foremost, the services that MTS provided were integrated into the operating system. New services were also added in COM+ Services to improve the scalability, performance, and stability of Internet and distributed applications running on Windows 2000, as shown in Table 12.2.

Table 12.2   COM+ Services Provided in Windows 2000

Service	Description
Transaction Services	Provides services and resource managers for handling database and non-database transactions without resource specific coding
Automatic Transactions	Provides declarative syntax to transaction services rather than manual code based methods
Object Reuse and Pooling	Provides the ability to create a pool of reusable objects
Queued Components	Provides the ability to execute methods of components that will actually run at some other time
Just-In-Time Activation	For maximum scalability provides a mechanism to create objects (or reuse existing objects) as soon as a method is called and release the object as soon as the method is complete
Synchronization	Provides concurrency management
Shared Properties	Shares state between multiple instances of objects within a server process
Thread Reuse and Pooling	For maximum scalability provides a service that reuses threads and maintains a pool of threads rather then constantly creating and destroying threads for component execution
Connection Pooling	For maximum database scalability provides a service to reuse database connections that share the same properties rather then open a new connection for each database action
Declarative Construction	Provides a mechanism for administrator to provide construction information to components rather than build this information inside the component
Role Based Security	Provides a flexible mechanism to determine the authority that a group of individuals have access to
Compensating Resource Managers	Allows a component to implement transactions without a resource that provides transaction management services

Some of the services are automatically provided for components that are installed as COM+ Applications. Services such as Thread Reuse and Pooling and Synchronization are automatic services.

Writing .NET Framework Components That Interoperate with COM+ Services

The majority of interoperation between .NET Framework and COM+ Services is accomplished through the use of attributes. Attributes are used to install applications into the COM+ catalog, to show transaction information, to set the Object pooling properties, and to indicate the use of Constructor strings to name a few. The remaining interoperability is done through a number of classes provided by the System.EnterpriseServices Namespace.

Installing Applications into the COM+ Catalog

.NET Framework applications can use traditional COM components or .NET Framework components that make use of COM+ Services. .NET Framework components can also be installed into COM+ Services to be used by .NET Framework applications or traditional COM based applications. Using COM Components from .NET Framework applications and using .NET Framework components from COM applications will be covered in the next section. To use COM+ Services in a .NET Framework component, you need to get the component information into the COM+ Catalog.

To install a .NET Framework component into the COM+ Catalog, you need to do a few things. You need to supply via attributes information about the COM+ application that the .NET Framework component will be installed into. The attributes to do this are located in the System.EnterpriseServices Namespace. Table 12.3 depicts the application attributes.

Table 12.3   The Major COM+ Application Attributes Located in System.EnterpriseServicess

Attribute	Purpose
ApplicationName	Use this to name the COM+ application that the components of the assembly are installed into
ApplicationID	Indicates the GUID of the COM+ Application
ApplicationActivation	Indicates whether the component should be activated in a dedicated server process or in the process of the creator
ApplicationAccessControl	Allows configuration of security for the library or server application housing the application
ApplicationQueuing	Enables queued component support
Description	Description of Application
AssemblyKeyFileAttribute	Key File for Strong Name (This is required)

All the application attributes are used at the assembly level to define the application that the components will be installed into. Installation will be done automatically the first time a .NET Framework application runs the component. When the CLR loads the assembly for the first time, it will discover that it is inheriting from System.ServicedComponent and will use the information supplied to install the component into the COM+ Services catalog and the GAC. Because it is installed into the GAC, the `AssemblyKeyFileAttribute` is required. If the .NET Framework component needs to be installed prior to the first run, for instance so that a COM application can use it, the RegSvcs.exe utility can be used to register the .NET Framework component into the COM+ Catalog with the information in the assembly metadata. The application attributes must be the first items in the component file. Listing 12.14 illustrates assembly level attributes for a .NET Framework component installed into a COM+ application.

Listing 12.14   Install .NET Component into COM+ Services

```
<Assembly: ApplicationName("Employee Data Access")>
<Assembly: ApplicationID("ffdc6a80-d527-11d0-a32c-34af06c10000")>
<Assembly: ApplicationActivationAttribute(ActivationOption.Server)>
<Assembly: DescriptionAttribute("Sample Employee Data Access Component")>
<Assembly: AssemblyKeyFileAttribute("KeyFile.snk")>
<Assembly: ApplicationQueuing(Enabled:=True)>
```

Listing 12.14 creates a COM+ application named "`Employee Data Access`" that has an Application ID of "`ffdc6a80-d527-11d0-a32c-34af06c10000`". The application will run in a dedicated server process: security is enabled and the application supports queued components. To set a property of an attribute, you must use the name parameter approach as shown in the following, which is the last line of Listing 12.14:

```
<Assembly: ApplicationQueuing(Enabled:=True)>
```

This illustrates setting the `ApplicationQueuing.Enabled` property to `True`.

Using COM+ Transactions with .NET Framework Components

Now that we have an application installed into the COM+ Catalog, what does it do? Well let's look at how to configure COM+ transactions. First, all components that are going to be involved with COM+ Services must inherit from `System.ServicedComponent`. After that is done, you supply attributes on the class and method level. Table 12.4 shows which Transaction attributes are available.

Table 12.4   Major `EnterpriseServices` Transaction Attributes

Attribute	Purpose
Transaction	Indicates the type of transaction support that the component supports.
AutoComplete	Marks that the component method is set to AutoComplete, which means that if an exception is raised, the SetAbort will be called: otherwise, SetComplete will be called.
JustInTimeActivation	To use AutoComplete, you must also set JustInTimeActivation.

In COM+ Services components have a transaction setting property that can be set to any of the following:

- Disabled
- None
- Required
- RequiresNew
- Supported

To indicate the transaction setting in a .NET Framework component, you use the Transaction attribute and the `TransactionOption` enumeration. Listing 12.15 shows an example of class descriptions with different transaction settings.

Listing 12.15 Defining Transaction Settings

```
<Transaction(TransactionOption.Supported)> _
Public Class DataAccess
End Class
```

In Listing 12.16, two attributes are defined on the `DataPersistance` class.

Listing 12.16 Defining Two Attributes

```
<TransactionAttribute(TransactionOption.Required), JustInTimeActivation(True)> _
<Transaction
Public Class DataPersistance
End Class
```

Now that the component transaction setting is set, the next thing that you might do is set the AutoComplete setting on individual methods. This is done using the `AutoCompleteAttribute`. Listing 12.17 illustrates the `AutoCompleteAttribute`.

Listing 12.17 `AutoCompleteAttribute`

```
<AutoComplete()> _
Public Function GetEmployees() As DataSet
End Function
```

Alternatively, code can manually handle the transaction process using the `ContextUtil` object, which is supplied when you inherit from `System.ServicedComponent`. To indicate that the method completed and everything is ok, the following code in is used:

```
ContextUtil.SetComplete()
```

To indicate that something is wrong and the transaction shouldn't continue, the code should resemble the following:

```
ContextUtil.SetAbort()
```

`ContextUtil` supplies a number of other familiar (if your familiar with COM+ Services transactions) transaction and context related methods and properties. Some of the familiar methods and properties of the `ContextUtil` class are `IsInTransaction`, `EnableCommit`, `DisableCommit`, `OriginalCallerName`, and `IsCallerInRole`. In more complex scenarios—for instance when you will be using COM+ Roles for security—you will need to use the `ContextUtil` class for more granular security.

For the simple scenario that exists, the use of `AutoComplete` makes transaction programming incredibly simple. Simply mark the methods that are `AutoComplete`, raise an exception if a problem has arisen, and exit cleanly if everything was OK.

Using Object Pooling with .NET Framework Components

One of the new features of COM+ Services that wasn't available to VB developers prior to VB.NET is Object Pooling. Object Pooling requires that components support at a minimum Thread Neutral threading. VB 5 and 6 were only capable of building Apartment threaded components, which aren't supported. VB.NET creates Free threaded components, which is the best threading model for Object Pooling.

Object Pooling gives developers the ability to have COM+ Services establish a pool of instantiated objects of a given type service all requests for methods called on the object. In some cases, this is a great improvement over recreating objects repeatedly as Just-In-Time activation does. In most cases though, the actual creation of objects is insignificant.

Cases in which Object Pooling can help are when the actual object does a great deal of work when it is created. For instance, an insurance application might have a table stored in a database with rates. These rates don't change very often, but they are used quite often. In a Just-In-Time activation scenario, the component would be created, the database would be accessed to bring in the rates, and then a method would be called that used the rates for some sort of process. Every call to an object of this type would result in the database being hit for this information, which rarely changes.

Object Pooling can help in this type of situation. Declare that the component exists in a pool and structure the code so that once instantiated the data is loaded and then every call to the methods that use the data will use a pooled version of the object. This is great, but you need to be careful in your implementation so that, between every call, the state remains the same. In other words, you don't want one method changing the data and not reverting the data back to the way it received the data when the method started. Object Pooling is best for a state that is read-only and rarely changes. Because of the nature that there will be a number of instances of the class running, you want the state to be exactly the same so that it doesn't matter which instance your code gets when it makes a request. In a COM language, to use Object Pooling you need to implement the `IObjectControl` interface.

The `IObjectControl` interface consists of three methods: `Activate`, `Deactivate`, and `CanBePooled`. The .NET Framework version of the `IObjectControl` interfaces exists in the `System.EnterpriseServicess` namespace, but the better way to use

`IobjectControl` is to override the base class (ServicedComponent) implementations of the three methods involved with Object Pooling. The three methods give you the ability to do the setup and cleanup of state as well as saying that this instance is no longer valid for the pool.

Activate

`IObjectControl.Activate` is a method that will be called by COM+ Services when the object is about to be used from the pool. This method is where you will do any work to get the state in the proper working order for any methods that will be called. In the `ServicedComponent` class, this is the `Activate` method.

Deactivate

`IObjectControl.Deactivate` is the method that you should do any cleanup of your code so that the next user of the object gets the object in a valid state. In the `ServicedComponent` class, this is the `Deactivate` method.

CanBePooled

`IObjectControl.CanBePooled` is provided for you to indicate that the instance can or cannot be placed into the pool. The method should return a Boolean true if the object can be placed back in the pool or a false if it cannot. In the `ServicedComponent` class, this is the `CanBePooled` method.

Object Pooling in the VB.NET

In VB.NET, the method in which the use of Object Pooling is implemented is through attributes and by overriding the base class methods. The Object Pooling attribute is placed on the class definition. Listing 12.18 shows a class that uses Object Pooling, setting the pool to be between 2 and 5 instances of the class with a creation timeout of 20 milliseconds. The class has one method that retrieves an ADO.NET `DataSet` and stores it in a class-level variable. After it is retrieved the first time, every other time the method is called it simply returns the existing `DataSet`. The implementation of `IObjectControl` is pretty basic with nothing happening in the `Activate` or `Deactivate` methods, and the `CanBePooled` simply returning true.

Listing 12.18   Class That Supports Object Pooling

```
<ObjectPoolingAttribute(Enabled:=True, MinPoolSize:=2, MaxPoolSize:=10, _
        CreationTimeout:=20000), _
JustInTimeActivationAttribute(True)> _
Public Class PooledEmployees
    Inherits ServicedComponent

    Private m_oEmployees As DataSet

    Public Function GetEmployees() As DataSet
        Dim oDA As DataAccess
        If m_oEmployees Is Nothing Then
            oda = New DataAccess()
            m_oEmployees = oda.GetEmployees()
```

Listing 12.18   Continued

```
        End If
        Return m_oEmployees
    End Function
    Public Overrides Sub Activate()
    End Sub
    Public Overrides Function CanBePooled() As Boolean
        Return True
    End Function
    Public Overrides Sub Deactivate()
    End Sub
End Class
```

Using Constructor Strings with .NET Framework Components

One of the least complex, yet most functional, new services in COM+ Services is the capability to pass in a string to assist in the construction of a component. Constructor strings' largest use is for a data access component to pass in the connection string to the database. In the past, numerous methods were used for the connection string, such as hard-coding the string in the component (best performance, least flexibility), using a DSN (Poor performance), storing in the registry (Poor performance), or using some sort of text file to store the information (Poor performance. Often, one of the methods was used and then the string was stored in the shared property manager.

Now with constructor strings, the choice of database (or any other configuration setting that can be set by an administrator in the COM+ Catalog) and when the components run the information is brought into memory and passed into the components. Similar to Object Pooling, constructor strings involve an attribute placed on a class and over-riding the base class Construct method. Listing 12.19 illustrates using a constructor string.

Listing 12.19   Class Using Constructor Strings

```
<ConstructionEnabled(Enabled:=True, Default:="(local)")> _
Public Class ObjectConstruction
    Inherits ServicedComponent
    Private c_sConstructString As String
    Public Overrides Sub Construct(ByVal constructString As String)
        c_sConstructString = constructString
    End Sub
    Public Function GetConstructionString() As String
        GetConstructionString = c_sConstructString
    End Function
End Class
<ConstructionEnabled(Enabled:=True, Default:="(local)")> _
```

To use construction strings, the class needs to use the ConstructionEnabled attribute. In the example, construction is enabled and the default is set to "(Local)". When an instance of the class is loaded, COM+ will call the Construct method passing in the constructor string. This model is different from the model used in VB 6 where a class to use a constructor string had to implement IObjectConstruct.

Using Queued Components with the .NET Framework

In COM+ Services, Microsoft introduced to the COM world the concept of Queued Components. Queued Components were a mechanism to call components asynchronously. This is quite powerful. Developers could develop components that a process could use, but the actual execution would not be done immediately. The service used Microsoft Message Queue (MSMQ) to record all the actions that were applied toward a component. After the component process was started, MSMQ would play back the actions and the component processed them. To a developer, the actual calling of the methods and setting of properties were exactly the same as using a standard component.

Two attributes are associated with Queued Components, and they are shown in Table 12.5.

Table 12.5 COM+ Services Queued Components Attributes

Attribute	Purpose
ApplicationQueuing	Enable queued component support on a Assembly
InterfaceQueuing	Enable queued component support on a interface

Listing 12.20 illustrates a class that is enabled as a Queued Component.

Listing 12.20 .NET Framework Class That Supports Queuing

```
'Assembly level Attribute for Queued Component Support
<Assembly: ApplicationQueuingAttribute(Enabled:=True, _
        QueueListenerEnabled:=True)>
'Class Levelt Attribute for a Interface for Queuing
<InterfaceQueuingAttribute(True)> _
Public Interface IQueuedDataPersistance
    Sub SaveEmployee(ByVal SSN As String, ByVal FirstName As String, _
        ByVal LastName As String, _
        ByVal Title As String, ByVal Address As String, ByVal City As String, _
        ByVal State As String, ByVal Zip As String, ByVal Picture As String)
End Interface
Public Class QueuedDataPersistance
    Inherits ServicedComponent
    Implements IQueuedDataPersistance

    Public Sub SaveEmployee(ByVal SSN As String, ByVal FirstName As String, _
            ByVal LastName As String, ByVal Title As String, _
            ByVal Address As String, ByVal City As String, _
            ByVal State As String, ByVal Zip As String, _
            ByVal Picture As String) _
            Implements IQueuedDataPersistance.SaveEmployee
    End Sub
End Class
```

This example doesn't include the complete assembly registration. It just includes the enabling of Queued Component support. An assembly that enables Queued Component support can contain both Queued and standard components. In the example, the `IQueuedDataPersistance` interface is marked as enabled for Queued execution. An interface must be defined and enabled for Queued execution to use Queued Components, and of course the interface must be implemented.

Using the COM+ Event Service

Perhaps the most complex COM+ Service is the *Loosely Coupled Event Service (LCE)*. LCE allows a developer to create a mechanism to broadcast to subscribers that something has occurred. In previous versions of VB, LCE was supported in the following manner.

Create an interface that consists entirely of Subs. This will become the `Event` class: the Subs become the events. Compile this class into a DLL so that it can be installed into the COM+ Catalog.

In a COM+ Application, invoke the Add New Component Wizard from. In the wizard, choose to install a new `Event` class. Browse to where the compiled DLL is located to install it as an `Event` class.

Subscribers then must implement the interface defined in the `Event` class and subscribe to the event. Subscribing to an event can be done through the COM+ Component Services explorer for components that have been installed into the COM+ Catalog, or it can also be done through code.

After subscriptions are made, events are fired by another process, instantiating an instance of the `Event` class and calling one of the events. All the subscribers to the event will then be called.

In the .NET Framework, the process is basically the same. The difference is that to create an `Event` class in the .NET Framework, you use an attribute on a class to indicate that it is an `Event` class. Listing 12.21 illustrates an `Event` class.

Listing 12.21 *Sample* Event *Class*

```
'Event Interface
Public Interface IEmployeeEvents
    Sub EmployeeSaved()
End Interface
```

Now a class needs to expose the Event Interface. Listing 12.22 illustrates a class that implements the interface to expose the event defined in Listing 12.21.

Listing 12.22 Event *Class*

```
'Event Class
<EventClass(AllowInProcSubscribers:=False, FireInParallel:=True)> _<EventClass(
Public Class EmployeeEvents
    Inherits ServicedComponent
```

Listing 12.22   Continued

```
    Implements IEmployeeEvents
    Public Sub EmployeeSaved() Implements IEmployeeEvents.EmployeeSaved
    End Sub
End Class
```

After an event is exposed, another class can listen to the event. To do this, it needs to implement the Event Interface. Listing 12.23 illustrates a `Listener` class.

Listing 12.23   Client CodeEvent Sink

```
'Event Sink aka the Client
Public Class EmployeeClient
    Inherits ServicedComponent
    Implements IEmployeeEvents
    Public Sub EmployeeSaved() Implements IEmployeeEvents.EmployeeSaved
        'Do Logic here when the Employee is saved
    End Sub
End Class
```

Loosely coupled events are very powerful but easily misunderstood the first time that you look at them.

Using Role-Based Security

Introduced originally with MTS, role based security provides a rich declarative and programmatic method to determine whether a user has the authority to complete an action. Listing 12.24 depicts a simple Component using role based security.

Listing 12.24   Sample Role-Based Security

```
'Assembly level attributes2
<Assembly: SecurityRoleAttribute("Administrator")>
<Assembly: ApplicationAccessControl()>
'Setup roles at the class level
<SecurityRoleAttribute("Administrator")> _
public class RoleBasedSecurity
Inherits ServicedComponent
Public Function AmIInThisRole(ByVal RoleName As String) As Boolean
    Try
        If Not ContextUtil.IsSecurityEnabled Then
            Return False
        else
            If ContextUtil.IsCallerInRole(RoleName) Then
                Return True
            Else
                Return False
            End If
        End If
```

Listing 12.24   Continued

```
        Catch exp As Exception
        Return False
    End Try
End Function
End Class
<SecurityRoleAttribute("Administrator")> _
public class RoleBasedSecurity
    Inherits ServicedComponent
```

Compensating Resource Managers

You might find yourself in a situation in which you need to use something akin to transactions in a component. The problem occurs when the resource you are trying to supply transaction management over doesn't support COM+ Transactions. In COM+, Microsoft introduced the concept of Compensating Resource Managers for this case. Listing 12.25 illustrates the class that needs to use Transaction and Listing 12.26 illustrates the Compensating Resource Manager for this class.

Listing 12.25   Class Requiring Transactions

```
<TransactionAttribute()> _
Public Class TestWorker
    Inherits ServicedComponent
    Private c_clerk As CRM.Clerk
    Public Sub New()
        c_clerk = New CRM.Clerk(GetType(CRMCompensator), ".NET CRM  Sample",
➡CRM.CompensatorOptions.AllPhases)
    End Sub
    Public Sub DeleteFile(ByVal msg As String)
        If System.IO.File.Exists(msg & ".crmTmp") Then
            c_clerk.ForceTransactionToAbort()
        Else
            c_clerk.WriteLogRecord(msg)
            c_clerk.ForceLog()
            Try
                File.Move(msg, msg & ".crmTmp")
            Catch
                c_clerk.ForceTransactionToAbort()
            End Try
        End If
    End Sub
    Public Sub Commit()
        ContextUtil.SetComplete()
    End Sub
    Public Sub Abort()
        ContextUtil.SetAbort()
    End Sub
End Class
```

Because the resource used in Listing 12.25 doesn't have its own transaction manager, we define a Compensating Resource Manager in Listing 12.26.

Listing 12.26   Compensating Resource Manager

```
<Assembly: ApplicationName("CRMCompensationManager")>
<Assembly: ApplicationActivation(ActivationOption.Server)>
<Assembly: CRM.ApplicationCrmEnabled()>
<Assembly: AssemblyKeyFile("StrongName.snk")>


Imports System.ComponentModel
Imports System
Imports System.IO
Imports System.Reflection
Imports System.EnterpriseServices
Imports CRM = System.EnterpriseServices.CompensatingResourceManager


Public Class CRMCompensator
    Inherits ServicedComponent

    Public Override Function CommitRecord(ByRef rec as CRM.LogRacord) _
            as Boolean
        'delete file
        Try
            File.Delete(rec.Record & ".crmTmp")
            MsgBox("Deleted", rec.Record & ".crmTmp")
        Catch
            MsgBox("Could not deleted", rec.Record & ".crmTmp")
        End Try

        Return False

    End Function
    public Override AbortRecord(ByRef rec as CRM.LogRecord) as Boolean
        ' do something here - undelete file
        Try
            File.Move(rec.Record+".crmTmp", CTYPE(rec.Record,String)
            MsgBox("Aborting delete", CTYPE(rec.Record,String)
        Catch
            MsgBox("Could not abort delete", CTYPE(rec.Record,String)
        End Try

        Return false

    End Function
End Class
```

Summary

Microsoft has produced a very rich model of interoperating with API based components, COM components, as well as using COM+ Services from .NET Framework components. The interoperating story is also very good for using .NET Framework components from COM applications.

It is very important when you are using the Windows API through the P/Invoke mechanism to see whether there is a method of accomplishing the same task through the .NET Framework.

The .NET Framework supplies a great deal of options and utilities to ensure that nearly all .NET Framework components that you create can be used by unmanaged COM code and so that unmanaged COM components can be used by .NET Framework code. This chapter gives you an introduction to the COM interoperability story in the .NET Framework.

Coupled with the new scalability features of the .NET Framework, COM+ Services provide all the services that you need to create highly scalable, robust applications. In the future, you will see more and more of the Microsoft Platform moved to the .NET Framework so that the interoperability won't be needed.

CHAPTER 13

Migrating from VB 6

In the past, Visual Basic developers have usually been able to move code from one version of Visual Basic to another with little work. Controls have changed from VBXs to ActiveX, and the platform has moved from 16-bit to 32-bit, but the effect has never been truly drastic.

With the introduction of the .Net Framework, developers will not only be moving from one version of Visual Basic to another, but they will also be moving from one platform to another. The .NET Framework runs on top of Win32 and provides great interoperability, but the fact remains that the .NET Framework is a completely different operating environment.

What in VB 6 Has Been Removed in VB.NET

Throughout the chapters, I have told you what has changed and what is no longer available in VB.NET. In this section, I will again go over what projects, language syntax and capabilities have been changed or removed in the move from VB 6 to VB.NET.

Project Types

Most of the project types available in Visual Basic 6 map to Visual Basic.NET projects types, but a few are no longer available.

IIS Applications, more commonly known as WebClasses, were introduced in VB 6 to make the development of ASP Web applications easier.

Although WebClasses themselves have been removed, many of their innovations made it into the .NET Framework in the form of ASP.NET WebForms. Similar to WebClasses, WebForms do a great job of separating the graphic design of a Web application from the code that implements the applications.

DHTML Applications

DHTML applications provide a method for building applications that ran in Internet Explorer. Although the concept is pretty interesting, the design and debug environments are lacking, and DHTML applications are virtually non-existent.

The .NET Framework has moved to two models of client-side execution—JavaScript-based DHTML applications and Windows Forms clients, which share the deployment characteristics of HTML.

ActiveX Documents

ActiveX documents are similar to DHTML applications in that they were hosted inside of an application, but unlike DHTML applications, they are true Windows rich clients. Similar to DHTML applications, ActiveX documents have been replaced by Windows forms in the .Net Framework.

ActiveX EXE Applications

ActiveX EXEs are dedicated out-of-process server applications. The .Net Framework doesn't have a comparable project type.

However, because the .Net Framework is multi-threaded and doesn't suffer from the limitations of COM's threading model, the need for out-of-process server applications has largely disappeared. The only functionality that .NET Framework applications don't provide is a method of activating applications to be used via automation.

Data Projects

Data projects were primarily used to build reporting applications. All the capabilities of Data projects are available through the Visual Studio.Net data tools, typed DataSets, and the new Crystal Reports.NET.

Language Constructs

In VB.NET, Microsoft has attempted to clean up the Visual Basic language. Some developers feel that this is unwarranted, and others think Microsoft didn't go far enough. (I'm one of the latter.)

Many of the keywords that have been removed support old, unstructured programming constructs. Others are rarely used by developers. Most of the remaining keywords are simply no longer needed because the .Net Framework provides the same functionality in an alternative form. A very few have been removed because of the .NET rules in regard to how languages should work and interoperate between each other.

Table 13.1   Language Elements Removed

Discontinued Programming Element	Replaced by
As Any keyword phrase	Function Overloading
Calendar property	System.Globilization.Calendar Class
Currency data type	Decimal data type
Circle statement	System.Drawing.Graphics. DrawEllipse method
Date function and statement	Today property of the System.Date data type
Debug.Assert method	System.Diagnostics.Debug.Assert
Debug.Print method	System.Diagnostics.Debug.Write
Deftype statements	No replacement
DoEvents function	System.Windows.Forms.Application. DoEvents method
Empty keyword	Nothing keyword
Eqv operator	= operator
GoSub statement	No replacement
Imp operator	Instead of A Imp B use (Not A) or B
Initialize event	Constructors
Instancing property	Accessibility modifiers
IsEmpty function	No replacement
IsMissing function	Function overloading
IsNull function	Microsoft.VisualBasic.Information. IsDBNull method
IsObject function	Microsoft.VisualBasic.Information. IsReference method
Let statement	No replacement
Line statement	System.Drawing.Graphics.DrawLine method
LSet statement	System.String.PadLeft method
MsgBox function	MsgBox exists in compatibility library and Framework has MessageBox class
Null keyword	Nothing keyword
On ... GoSub construction	No replacement
On ... GoTo construction	No replacement
Deftype statements	No replacement
Option Base statement	No replacement
Option Private Module statement	Accessibility modifiers

Table 13.1   Continued

Discontinued Programming Element	Replaced by
Property Get, Property Let, and Property Set statements	New property syntax
PSet method	System.Drawing and System.Drawing.Design namespace
GoSub statement	No replacement
Rnd function	System.Math.Rnd method
Round function	System.Math.Round method
RSet statement	System.String.PadRight method
Scale method	System.Drawing and System.Drawing.Design namespace
Sgn function	System.Math.Sgn method
Sqr function	System.Math.Sqr method
String function	System.String constructor
Terminate event	Finalize method or System.IDisposable interface
Time function	System.Date.TimeOfDay property
Type statement	Structure statement
Variant data type	Object data type
VarType function	System.TypeCode
Wend keyword	End While statement

Undocumented Features

Many VB developers use undocumented and unsupported functions (despite repeated warnings against the practice). Many of these functions return the address of a variable.

These functions have been removed from Visual Basic.NET, but support for the functionality has been built into the .Net Framework. In fact, not only are the scenarios handled by the .NET Framework, but also in most cases the new methods are superior because of the added functionality provided.

Language Changes

Table 13.2 shows the language features that have been changed in VB.NET.

Table 13.2   Changes in VB.NET

Change	Description
Date and Time statements	VB.NET replaces the VB6 Date and Time statements with Today and TimeOfDay statements.
Pset and Scale methods replaced	In VB.NET, there is no direct equivalent for these statements.

Table 13.2   Continued

Change	Description
	The functionality supplied is available in the System.Drawing and System.Drawing.Design namespaces.
Calendar property extended	In VB.NET, the functionality provided by the Calendar property is now handled by the System.Globalization.Calendar and System.Globalization.CultureInfo classes.
Empty and Null replaced and IsEmpty isn't supported.	Empty and Null have been replaced by the Nothing keyword for checking for uninitialized variables or no valid data.
Functions using a $ to indicate string version are replaced by overloaded functions.	In VB 6, functions such as Trim had two versions: one for strings and one for variants. In VB.NET, only one version is overloaded.
Graphics functionality has been changed.	The System.Drawing namespace provides the functionally previously provided by the Circle and Line statements.
Mathematical functionality has been changed.	The System.Math class replaces the Atn, Sgn, and Sqr functions and provides much more comprehensive math functionality.
Functions to determine Null values and objects are moved into the Microsoft.VisualBasic.Information class.	The methods IsDBNull and IsReference of the Microsoft.VisualBasic.Information class and related classes supply many of the base tasks of a VB application.
Debug.Print and Debug.Assert replaced	The System.Diagnostics namespace provides the Debug class, which provides the Write, WriteIf, WriteLine, WriteLineIf, Assert, and Fail methods.
VarType function replaced	Functionality provided by VarType is now provided by the Value field of System.TypeCode.

Migrating from VB 6 to VB.NET

VB.NET provides a tool to assist in the migration of VB 6 code to VB.NET. It is important to understand that only in rare occasions will the migration tool be capable of upgrading complete applications. In general, applications architected according to Windows DNA guidelines will have the most success being migrated.

The migration will attempt to migrate the following types of applications:

- ActiveX DLLs—These have a good chance of migrating because they usually consist of mostly business logic.
- Standard EXEs—Applications built around connected data access will have the least success.
- ActiveX EXEs—If applications are built to be automated they are best left in VB 6.
- IIS applications—These can only be partially migrated.

The migration tool creates a new application, leaving the VB 6 version intact. In most cases, it will use COM interop to reuse existing COM components rather than converting them. So, for example, an application that references ADO won't be automatically converted to use ADO.NET. (You can, of course, convert to ADO.NET manually after using the migration tool.)

After it has finished, the migration tool will produce a DHTML-based report that describes any issues that it found in the application. In addition, all the issues will be added to the source as ToDo comments that show up in Visual Studio.NET's Task Window.

Tour of the Migration Process

The migration process is a wizard based process to determine which options should apply during the upgrade. To illustrate the wizard, I will use a VB 6 application that Microsoft supplied in the Visual Basic.NET Beta 1 Resource CD.

To start the migration wizard, all you need to do is open a VB 6 project from the Open Project dialog box. After you open the project, the VB Upgrade Wizard will start. Figure 13.1 illustrates the initial screen of the wizard.

Figure 13.1 simply depicts the start of the migration wizard but does not provide any functionality.

Figure 13.2 shows the upgrade choices that are available for a Windows application. You can also choose how to support existing arrays (changing arrays to zero based will increase performance) and generate default interfaces for exposed classes. Default interfaces will be needed if these components will still be used via COM clients that use Automation.

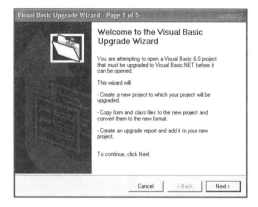

Figure 13.1

VB Upgrade Wizard—Welcome Screen.

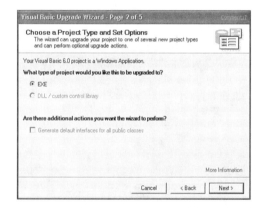

Figure 13.2

Choose a Project Type and Set Options screen.

Figure 13.3 simply asks you where to store the application.

Figure 13.4 is the last confirmation page prior to the migration process.

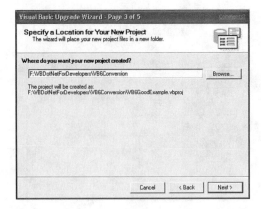

Figure 13.3

Specify a Location for Your New Project screen.

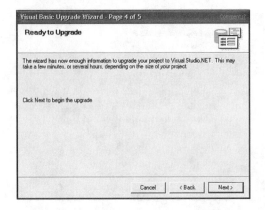

Figure 13.4

Ready to Upgrade screen.

Figure 13.5 illustrates the process of converting a project.

After a project has been migrated, a report similar to the one in Figure 13.6 illustrates information about the project and all the issues encountered while being migrated. The VB.NET team has stated that in addition to links to the Visual Studio.NET help system, the report will also place links to the Internet for more detailed information.

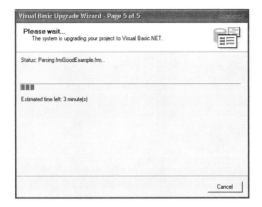

Figure 13.5

VB Upgrade Wizard—page 5.

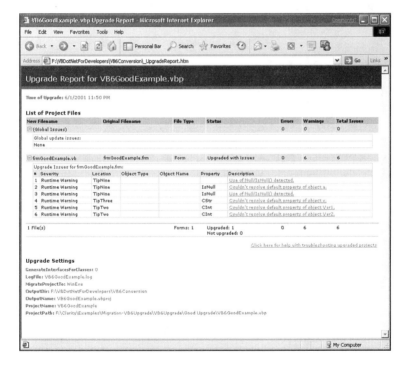

Figure 13.6

VB Upgrade Wizard Upgrade Report

Figure 13.7 illustrates the application inside of Visual Studio.NET with the Task list and the Migration report displayed. Double-clicking on items in the Task list will take you directly to the issue described in the Task list. In addition, comments are inserted into the code to indicate issues, to provide links to detailed information about the issue, and help to fix the issue.

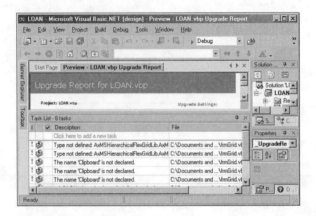

Figure 13.7

VB upgrade project in Visual Studio.

Migration Considerations

Because of the work involved, you should carefully consider whether to move existing applications into the .Net Framework, and only attempt to migrate those that need to be moved to the new .NET Framework platform. Determining what needs to be migrated to the .NET Framework is a difficult decision. Many factors will be involved such as the need to use applications or components from the .NET Framework and the difficulty in migrating the application. VB 6 applications will continue to be supported for a number of years. If your application needs to be enhanced to any great extent, it might be time to evaluate whether moving to .NET is warranted.

You should realize that not all types of applications fit in the .NET Framework. For example, applications that use DAO or RDO will be difficult to migrate without extensive changes.

The most drastic changes are going to be required in Windows applications, so you might choose to migrate only the business layer components and use interop prior to moving the user interface.

Building New VB 6 Applications

It's unlikely that you will be able to postpone new development until VB.NET has been released and adopted by your organization. But, certain techniques can be adopted now that will ease the migration process in the future.

Use a Standards Document

It has always been considered best practice for organizations to establish coding guidelines and standards. If you intend to migrate to VB.NET, it is especially important to create, publish, and enforce standards—even if you are a one-person shop—so that if someone new has to look at projects, he can get up to speed quickly. The standards document allows you to "code for the next guy." It will also help to keep code consistent because code is handed from programmer to programmer.

Education

No upgrade to Visual Basic has ever been so extensive. This means that education has never been as important. You cannot expect to simply start using VB.NET and enjoy its benefits without rethinking how you do things. The .NET Framework consists of over 6500 optimized class libraries. You shouldn't be reinventing the wheel unless you need some sort of functionality that isn't supported by a class.

Be Explicit

Previous versions of Visual Basic have been extremely forgiving. A great deal of this forgiveness is gone in Visual Basic.NET, at least by default, so the key to your eventual movement of code from VB 6 to VB.NET is being explicit:

- **Use Option Explicit on every module**—This will ensure that all variables are declared.
- **Strongly type all variables**—Strong types allow the migration tool to easily convert to the new types in the .NET Framework that are equivalent.
- **Explicitly convert all variables**—Don't rely on automatic type coercion.
- **Explicitly declare all variables**—A very common problem in VB and ASP applications is to simply rely on the ability to create variables just by using them in code. You should set all projects to Option Explicit On and Option Strict On.
- **Don't use default properties**—In VB.NET, most default properties have disappeared because default properties must have a parameter.
- **Use constants instead of literal values**.
- **Type variables correctly**—In VB 6, some data types can be used for multiple purposes. A `Date`, for example, can be used as a `Double`, and it is common to see Booleans stored in integers. In most cases, VB.NET won't support this usage.

Plan for Changes

VB.NET has numerous changes that require you to do things differently. Luckily, you can start doing most of these in VB 6. Doing so will allow the code to migrate to VB.NET more easily.

- **Use zero-based arrays**—VB.NET intrinsic arrays must be zero based. There is a method in the .NET Framework to use non-zero based arrays, but the code is ugly and much slower.

- **Don't rely on both sides of a logical operation being executed**—VB.NET operations can now be short-circuited.
- **Avoid using changed or removed language elements**—Keep a printout of these handy, perhaps posted in your office.

Use XML

Use XML to pass data between tiers of an application. XML will not only allow easy interoperability and flexibility between the layers of COM applications now, but will also allow COM applications and .NET applications to easily interoperate with each other.

You can simply use XML as the data that is passed back and forth between layers, go a little bit further and use the Microsoft SOAP Toolkit, which allows you to use SOAP as the protocol to call ASP.NET WebServices from COM applications, or vice-versa, as shown in Listing 13.1.

Listing 13.1 VB6 Calling WebService

```
Const WSDL = "http://localhost/HelloWorldWebService/HelloWorld.asmx?WSDL"
Dim oHelloWorldWebService as SoapClient
Dim sHelloWorld as String

Set oHelloWorldWebService = New SoapClient
oHelloWorldWebService.MSSoapInit WSDL
sHelloWorld = oHelloWorldWebService.HelloWorld
```

Summary

Moving applications and components from VB 6 to VB.NET will not be a simple recompile. Not only is the object model changed, but also the platform has changed. This will require significant work for many applications. In many situations, it will be more prudent to leave applications in VB 6 and enhance them by using Interop with VB.NET and the .NET Framework.

Microsoft has gone to a great effort to make sure that existing applications won't be broken when a new VB.NET application is installed on a machine with VB 6 applications. It will be your job as a developer to recommend to your management or customers when applications should be left in VB 6, when they should be ported to VB.NET, and when applications should be re-architected for the .NET Framework. Many applications should simply be left alone if there are no planned enhancements to the applications functionality. The .NET Framework will introduce many new options that in itself may merit applications migration though Interop or complete re-architecting applications. It will be your responsibility to understand the new capabilities and make choices that will benefit the applications and organizations.

CHAPTER 14

Future .NET Developments

So, what should developers expect in relation to .NET in the future?

Cross Platform .NET

Microsoft has submitted a portion of the .NET Framework class library, specifications for services and the C# language to ECMA in the hopes of having it adopted as a standard. If they are successful, other vendors will be able to implement the .Net Framework on other platforms.

But it is important to understand that only a subset of the library has been submitted. It will be up to developers to build to this subset of classes to ensure cross-platform capability. To be honest, unless third parties or Microsoft itself add additional framework classes, the cross-platform implementations won't be of great use.

Additional Base WebServices

One of the things that you should expect to see from Microsoft is additional WebServices. Hailstorm is the first release of WebServices by Microsoft, but it won't be the last. Expect to see more WebServices released as parts of future releases of software products.

Overview of Hailstorm

Microsoft is introducing what it calls "building block services" with a project code named *Hailstorm*. Hailstorm provides a number of WebServices built around .NET. Hailstorm WebServices are built at the core with Microsoft Passport and Microsoft Instant Messenger.

Microsoft Passport (Passport) is a user authentication system that is in use today. Passport allows users to sign in to one location and then be authenticated across many Web sites. Passport is being enhanced to be based on WebServices and to store a great deal of user controlled information. Microsoft Windows XP will include the capability to log directly in to Passport when a user logs in to her computer.

Microsoft Instant Messenger (MIM) is an instant messaging service in wide use today that allows people online to directly communicate with each other. Today you can send documents to each other through MIM, make phone calls through MIM, start netmeetings through MIM, in addition to the core text messaging features. MIM is being enhanced and built around WebServices to give applications the capability to send messages to users via SOAP and WebServices, and so the messaging services of Hailstorm to know which device of the user that notifications should be sent to.

At the core of Hailstorm is a great deal of information that a user will choose to store about herself and choose who has the authority to look at that information. With all of this information available to a user through WebServices, electronic business applications will be able to extend their functionality to enrich the user experience. Microsoft likes to use travel as an example of how Hailstorm and WebServices will make a user experience richer.

For example in a travel scenario, a user goes to a travel site such as Microsoft Expedia (Expedia) and because she is logged in to Passport, Expedia will have access to user information from Hailstorm. From this, Expedia can make assumptions about the user, such as where the user is traveling from, where she might be going, what kind of car she will rent, and so on. When a user is ready to make the travel purchase from Expedia, Expedia will use the payment methods that the user has set up in Hailstorm. This will make things much easier for the user. But Hailstorm won't stop there. We all know that after we make travel arrangements, things change. Expedia or other services acting on a user's Passport information will now know that the user is traveling somewhere and can provide additional services to the user. The airline that the user is flying on, for instance, can use the contact information to send instant messages to the user and e-mail messages when flight changes are made. Instead of a user needing to make phone calls and check the Internet for cancellations or delays, she will get instant messages or e-mail messages sent through Hailstorm to possibly all the users devices (cell phone, PC, PDA, and so on).

Initially, Hailstorm will include the set of services in Table 14.1.

Table 14.1   Initial Hailstorm Services (from Microsoft Hailstorm Documentation)

Service	Purpose
myAddress	Electronic and geographic address for an identity
myProfile	Name, nickname, special dates, picture
myContacts	Electronic relationships/address book
myLocation	Electronic and geographical location and rendezvous

Table 14.1   Continued

Service	Purpose
myNotifications	Notification subscription, management, and routing
myInbox	Inbox items such as e-mail and voice mail, including existing mail systems
myCalendar	Time and task management
myDocuments	Raw document storage
myApplicationSettings	Application settings
myFavoriteWebSites	Favorite URLs and other Web identifiers
myWallet	Receipts, payment instruments, coupons, and other transaction records
myDevices	Device settings, capabilities
myServices	Services provided for an identity
myUsage	Usage report for previous services

Hailstorm will certainly become a core set of services that most users will eventually simply take for granted. But it will make lives much easier in the Next Generation Internet. Because Hailstorm is built around SOAP based WebServices, the WebServices will be available across any platform on any device. Developers using Visual Studio.NET and, in particular, VB.NET will be at the forefront of Hailstorm usage.

Greater Integration of .NET with .NET Enterprise Servers

Currently the .NET Framework provides classes to use COM+ Services, system services such as the event log, and performance Monitors, MSMQ, and SQL Server 2000. To use other servers, developers need to use COM Interop. Expect Microsoft to expand direct support for enterprise servers in the future.

In some cases, the CLR will be integrated right into the product. For instance, at the July 2000 PDC in Orlando, Florida, Microsoft previewed the next version of SQL Server, code named Yukon, which allows developers to build stored procedures in any .NET language and to store objects built with the .NET Framework directly into SQL Server database tables. This will be a fantastic enhancement to SQL Server if we see it released.

Currently scheduled for 2002 is Microsoft Windows BlackComb, which is supposed to totally integrate the .NET Framework into the operating system. Exactly what this will mean is not fully understood at this time.

Summary

As a VB developer, you now have the development tool that can lead the development of the Next Generation Internet. You might hear developers who have never liked VB in the past continue to put down VB for reasons that today have no weight or merit.

It will be up to you to make sure that you have properly educated yourself in the .NET Framework to ensure that VB never becomes a second class language. The capabilities are there; you just need to take advantage of them.

APPENDIX A

Windows Form Application

This appendix illustrates a Windows Form application that uses an ASP.NET Web Service (built in Appendix B) to provide the middle tier. Sections of source code will be presented and the entire project(s) will be available to download.

The areas of the .NET Framework covered are depicted in Figure A.1.

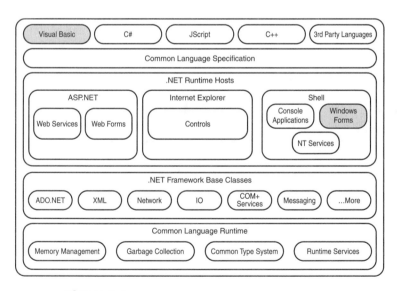

Figure A.1

Coverage of the .NET Framework.

Sports Statistics Data Entry

The purpose of the sample application is to collect baseball statistics. Figure A.2 is a database diagram that shows the table relationships in SQL Server 2000. Figures A.3–A.7 illustrate the forms that will be built for this sample application.

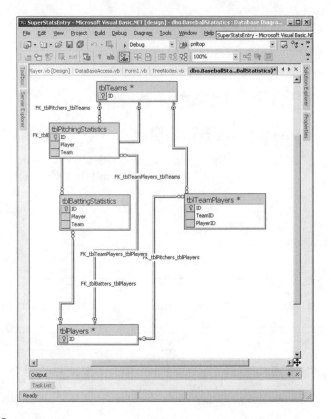

Figure A.2

A SQL Server 2000 database diagram for a Baseball Statistics database.

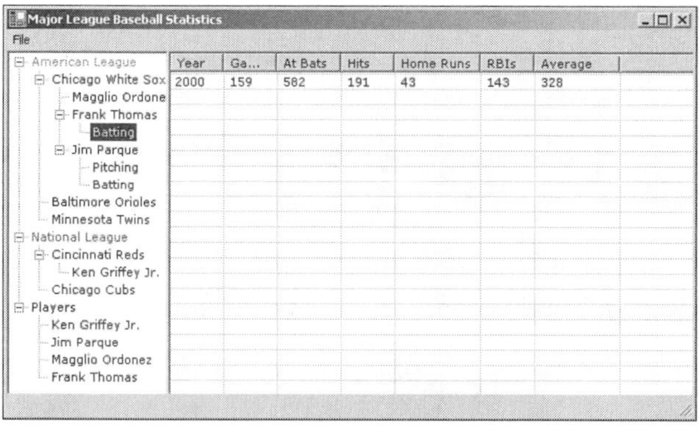

Figure A.3

Main form.

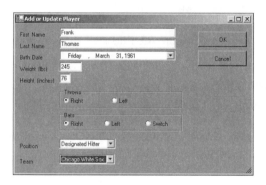

Figure A.4

Add or Update Team form.

Figure A.5

Add or Update Player form.

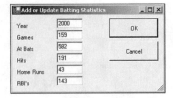

Figure A.6

Add or Update Batting Statistics form.

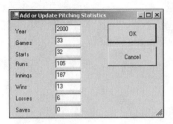

Figure A.7

Add or Update Pitching Statistics form.

Data Source of the Application

The data transfer for this application is handled by an elaborate typed dataset. The DataSet contains all the tables illustrated in Figure A.8. This might not be the ideal method in which applications should or will be architected, but it should give you an idea of the power of DataSets. Figure A.8 illustrates the XSD Schema that depicts the DataSet.

Loading the Tree

After the DataSet is retrieved from the middle tier, portions of the data are loaded into a System.Windows.Forms.Treeview (Treeview) control. Listing A.1 shows the code used to load the Treeview control. The code illustrates a number of techniques that developers will use with DataSets and Treeview controls. The code uses typed DataRows to more efficiently iterate through the tables in the DataSet.

Listing A.1   Load Data into a Treeview Control

```
Private Sub LoadTreeView()
    Dim oNode As PlayerNode
    Dim oNodePlayers As TreeNode
    Dim oNodeAmericanLeagueTeam As TreeNode
    Dim oNodeNationalLeagueTeam As TreeNode
    Dim oNodeTeam As TeamNode
    Dim oNodeTeamPlayers As TeamPlayersNode
    Dim oNodePlayer As PlayerNode
    Dim oNodePitching As PitchingNode
```

Listing A.1   Continued

```
    Dim oNodeBatting As BattingNode
    Dim oTeamRow As TeamsAndPlayers.TeamsRow
    Dim oTeamPlayers As TeamsAndPlayers.TeamPlayersRow
    Dim oPlayerRow As TeamsAndPlayers.PlayersRow
    Dim oPitchingRow As TeamsAndPlayers.PitchingStatisticsRow
    Dim oBattingRow As TeamsAndPlayers.BattingStatisticsRow
    Dim bFound As Boolean

    treeTeamsAndPlayers().Nodes.Clear()
    oNodeAmericanLeagueTeam = treeTeamsAndPlayers().Nodes.Add("American
League")
    oNodeNationalLeagueTeam = treeTeamsAndPlayers().Nodes.Add("National
League")
    oNodePlayers = treeTeamsAndPlayers().Nodes.Add("Players")
    For Each oTeamRow In c_oTeamsAndPlayers.Teams.Rows
        oNodeTeam = New TeamNode(oTeamRow.ID, oTeamRow.TeamName)
        If oTeamRow.League = "AL" Then
            oNodeAmericanLeagueTeam.ForeColor = System.Drawing.Color.Red
            oNodeAmericanLeagueTeam.Nodes.Add(oNodeTeam)
        Else
            oNodeNationalLeagueTeam.ForeColor = System.Drawing.Color.Blue
            oNodeNationalLeagueTeam.Nodes.Add(oNodeTeam)
        End If
        For Each oTeamPlayers In oTeamRow.GetTeamPlayersRows
            For Each oPlayerRow In c_oTeamsAndPlayers.Players.Rows
                If oPlayerRow.ID.Equals(oTeamPlayers.PlayerID) Then
                    oNodePlayer = New PlayerNode(oPlayerRow.ID, _
                        oPlayerRow.FirstName & " " & oPlayerRow.LastName)
                    oNodeTeam.Nodes.Add(oNodePlayer)

                    If oPlayerRow.GetPitchingStatisticsRows.Length > 0 Then
                        oNodePitching = New PitchingNode(oPlayerRow.ID)
                        oNodePitching.Text = "Pitching"
                        oNodePlayer.Nodes.Add(oNodePitching)
                    End If
                    If oPlayerRow.GetBattingStatisticsRows.Length > 0 Then
                        oNodeBatting = New BattingNode(oPlayerRow.ID)
                        oNodeBatting.Text = "Batting"
                        oNodePlayer.Nodes.Add(oNodeBatting)
                    End If
                End If
            Next
        Next
    Next

    For Each oPlayerRow In c_oTeamsAndPlayers.Players
        bFound = False
```

Listing A.1 Continued

```
    For Each oNode In oNodePlayers.Nodes
        If oNode.PlayerID.Equals(oPlayerRow.ID) Then
            bFound = True
            Exit For
        End If
    Next
    If Not bFound Then
        oNodePlayer = New PlayerNode(oPlayerRow.ID, _
            oPlayerRow.FirstName & " " & oPlayerRow.LastName)
        oNodePlayers.Nodes.Add(oNodePlayer)
    End If
Next

mnuNewTeam().Enabled = True
mnuNewPlayer().Enabled = True
mnuSave().Enabled = True
End Sub
```

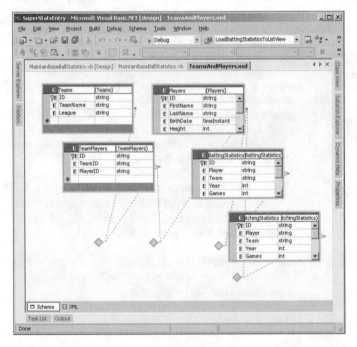

Figure A.8

TeamsAndPlayers DataSet.

This code also illustrates one of the ways that inheritance is used in Windows Form applications. You will notice that six different types of treenodes are defined: `TreeNode`, `PlayerNode`, `TeamNode`, `TeamPlayersNode`, `PitchingNode`, and `BattingNode`. All the nodes (except `TreeNode`) are derived from `System.Windows.Forms.TreeNode` (`TreeNode`). Listing A.2 shows the code for the five nodes that are derived from `TreeNode`.

Listing A.2 *Creation of* `NodeTypes` *Through Inheritance*

```
Imports System.Windows.Forms
Public Class TeamNode
    Inherits TreeNode
    Private c_oTeamId As System.Guid
    Public Overloads Sub New(ByVal teamID As System.Guid)
        c_oTeamId = teamID
    End Sub
    Public Overloads Sub New(ByVal teamID As System.Guid, _
                ByVal teamName As String)
        c_oTeamId = teamID
        Me.Text = teamName
    End Sub
    Public ReadOnly Property TeamID() As System.Guid
        Get
            Return c_oTeamId
        End Get
    End Property
End Class
Public Class TeamPlayersNode
    Private c_iTeamPlayerID As Integer
    Public Sub New(ByVal teamPlayerId As Integer)
        c_iTeamPlayerID = teamPlayerId
    End Sub
    Public ReadOnly Property TeamPlayerID() As Integer
        Get
            Return c_iTeamPlayerID
        End Get
    End Property
End Class
Public Class PlayerNode
    Inherits TreeNode
    Private c_oPlayerID As System.Guid
    Public Overloads Sub New(ByVal playerID As System.Guid)
        c_oPlayerID = playerID
    End Sub
    Public Overloads Sub New(ByVal playerID As System.Guid, _
            ByVal playerName As String)
        c_oPlayerID = playerID
        Me.Text = playerName
    End Sub
```

Listing A.2   Continued

```
    Public ReadOnly Property PlayerID() As System.Guid
        Get
            Return c_oPlayerID
        End Get
    End Property
End Class
Public Class PitchingNode
    Inherits TreeNode
    Private c_oPitchingStatisticsID As System.Guid
    Public Sub New(ByVal pitchingStatisticsID As System.Guid)
        c_oPitchingStatisticsID = pitchingStatisticsID
    End Sub
    Public ReadOnly Property PitchingStatisticsID() As System.Guid
        Get
            Return c_oPitchingStatisticsID
        End Get
    End Property
End Class
Public Class BattingNode
    Inherits TreeNode
    Private c_oBattingStatisticsID As System.Guid
    Public Sub New(ByVal battingStatisticsID As System.Guid)
        c_oBattingStatisticsID = battingStatisticsID
    End Sub
    Public ReadOnly Property BattingStatisticsID() As System.Guid
        Get
            Return c_oBattingStatisticsID
        End Get
    End Property
End Class
```

Menus

As mentioned in Chapter 9, "Error Handling," the Menu editor in VB 6 was pretty archaic. The following sample has a simple menu, and I also used a number of pop-up menus throughout. The pop-up menus are used on nodes in the Treeview and the Listview. The pop-up menus are built dynamically in two methods that are automatically invoked when the control is right-clicked. For a control to have a pop-up menu, its `ContextMenu` property must be set. Listing A.3 shows the code in the forms constructor to set the `ContextMenu` property. The `ContextMenu` property is set to an instance of `System.Windows.Forms.ContextMenu`, which is typed `WithEvents`.

Listing A.3   Create the `ContextMenus`

```
c_oTreeViewContextMenu() = New ContextMenu()
treeTeamsAndPlayers().ContextMenu = c_oTreeViewContextMenu()
c_oListViewContextMenu() = New ContextMenu()
lvwStatistics().ContextMenu = c_oListViewContextMenu()
```

Listing A.4 shows the event handlers for the ContextMenu's PopUp event. This code dynamically builds and—through the use of the AddressOf operator—creates delegates for the menu event handler.

Listing A.4 ***Handle the*** ContextMenu PopUp ***Event***

```
Private Sub TreeViewPopupHandler(ByVal sender As Object, _
                ByVal e As System.EventArgs) Handles
c_oTreeViewContextMenu._
                Popup
    Dim oMenuItemChangePlayer As MenuItem
    Dim oMenuItemChangeTeam As MenuItem
    Dim oMenuItemAddBatting As MenuItem
    Dim oMenuItemAddPitching As MenuItem

    Select Case c_oClickedNode.GetType.ToString
        Case GetType(TeamNode).ToString
            oMenuItemChangeTeam = New MenuItem("Update Team", _
                    AddressOf UpdateTeamMenuSelected)
            With c_oTreeViewContextMenu().MenuItems
                .Clear()
                .Add(oMenuItemChangeTeam)
            End With
        Case GetType(PlayerNode).ToString
            oMenuItemChangePlayer = New MenuItem("Update Player", _
                AddressOf UpdatePlayerMenuSelected)
            oMenuItemAddBatting = New MenuItem("Add Batting Statistics", _
                AddressOf AddPlayerBattingStatistics)
            oMenuItemAddPitching = New MenuItem("Add Pitching Statistics", _
                AddressOf AddPlayerPitchingStatistics)
            With c_oTreeViewContextMenu().MenuItems
                .Clear()
                .Add(oMenuItemChangePlayer)
                .Add(oMenuItemAddBatting)
                .Add(oMenuItemAddPitching)
            End With
    End Select
End Sub
```

Creating New Records

One of the interesting features of DataSets is the ability to create new DataRows that aren't tied to a DataSet, fill the fields, and then add the DataRow to a DataTable. I use this to pass data to all the dialogs used throughout the application. For instance, Listing A.5 shows the code that is used to create a new player and pass the DataRow to the dialog as part of the constructor.

Listing A.5   Creating a New Player

```
Private Sub mnuNewPlayer_Click(ByVal sender As System.Object, _
            ByVal e As System.EventArgs) Handles mnuNewPlayer.Click
    Dim oPlayerRow As TeamsAndPlayers.PlayersRow
    Dim oNewPlayer As AddUpdatePlayer
    Dim oTeamPlayerRow As TeamsAndPlayers.TeamPlayersRow
    'Use the NewPlayersRow method of the typed dataset
    'Player table to create an empty record
    oPlayerRow = c_oTeamsAndPlayers.Players.NewPlayersRow()
    'Pass the new record and the Teams table to the dialog box constructor
    oNewPlayer = New AddUpdatePlayer(oPlayerRow, c_oTeamsAndPlayers.Teams)
    oNewPlayer.ShowDialog(Me)
    If Not oPlayerRow.IsNull(0) Then
        c_oTeamsAndPlayers.Players.AddPlayersRow(oPlayerRow)
        If oNewPlayer.TeamID.ToString.Length > 0 Then
            oTeamPlayerRow = c_oTeamsAndPlayers.TeamPlayers.NewTeamPlayersRow()
            oTeamPlayerRow.ID = System.Guid.NewGuid
            oTeamPlayerRow.TeamID = oNewPlayer.TeamID
            oTeamPlayerRow.PlayerID = oPlayerRow.ID
            c_oTeamsAndPlayers.TeamPlayers.AddTeamPlayersRow(oTeamPlayerRow)
        End If
        Call LoadTreeView()
    End If
End Sub
```

Visual Inheritance

To illustrate Visual Inheritance, I created a base form for the gathering of the statistics for players. After I created the base form class, I then inherited from that class to create the `AddUpdatePitchingStatistics` form and `AddUpdateBattingStatistics` form. In Figure A.9, you can see the base class. Figures A.10 and A.11 show the classes that derive from A.9.

Before the base form class could really be used correctly, I needed to define that the `btnOK_Click` event could be overridden by a derived class, and I created two new properties for the Years and Games text boxes. Listing A.6 illustrates the code to do this.

Listing A.6   Expose the Button Click and Properties to Derived Form Classes

```
Protected Overridable Sub btnOK_Click(ByVal sender As System.Object, _
        ByVal e As System.EventArgs) Handles btnOK.Click

End Sub
Protected Property Year() As Integer
    Get
        Return CInt(txtYear().Text)
    End Get
```

Listing A.6   Continued

```
    Set(ByVal Value As Integer)
        txtYear().Text = Value.ToString
    End Set
End Property
Protected Property Games() As Integer
    Get
        Return CInt(txtGames().Text)
    End Get
    Set(ByVal Value As Integer)
        txtGames().Text = Value.ToString
    End Set
End Property
```

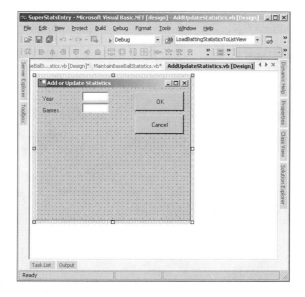

Figure A.9

The AddUpdateStatistics form.

Figure A.10

AddUpdateBattingStatistics *is derived from* AddUpdateStatistics.

Figure A.11

AddUpdatePitchingStatistics *is derived from* AddUpdateStatistics.

Summary

In this example, I illustrated a number of items that make the new Windows Forms library extremely powerful and extensible. You can take this example as a base and add new functionality to learn more about the .NET Framework. One thing that you should do is attempt to "bulletproof" the application with better exception handling.

The example used inheritance in a number of ways. Typed DataSets, which are derived from the Class Library DataSet class, were used. Visual Inheritance was used for the two statistic dialog boxes. Finally, the new Treeview control uses TreeNodes that are inherited from the base TreeNode class.

In Appendix B, "ASP.NET Web Service and Web Forms Applications," I will illustrate a middle-tier component that was used in this application and illustrate an ASP.NET Web Form application.

APPENDIX B

ASP.NET Web Service and Web Forms Applications

You were introduced to a Windows Forms application in Appendix A, "Windows Form Application." This appendix contains three related applications. The ASP.NET Web Service was used as the middle tier in Appendix A. You will also be shown two ASP.NET Web Forms applications that use the same Web Service (actually a set of services). The complete source code is available to download from the book's site (www.samspublishing.com).

The Web Service provides access to the Baseball statistics SQL Server 2000 database defined in Appendix A.

One of the Web Forms applications is meant for a user at a baseball game to update the statistics as the game is going on. It is a simple one-page ASP.NET Web Form application that shows some of the extremely powerful features of the ASP.NET DataGrid control.

The other Web Form's application is a possible use of a public Web Service. In this application, a fictional person (I call him Bob) has used the Web Service to display statistics about players on his fantasy baseball site.

In this appendix, the areas of the .NET Framework covered are depicted in Figure B.1.

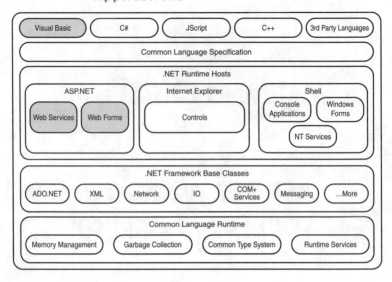

Figure B.1

Coverage of the .NET Framework.

Sports Statistics Web Service

The middle tier of the sample application involved in the application in Appendix A and in the applications in this appendix is serviced by an ASP.NET Web Service application.

This Web Service consists of a public set of methods that provide read access to data in the SuperStats database. Figure B.2 illustrates the SQL Server 2000 database used by this appendix. In addition, a set of methods can be secured so that only internal users can use these services. (Securing Web Services is outside the scope of this book.) Figure B.3 illustrates the publicly accessible Web Service and Figure B.4 illustrates the private Web Service.

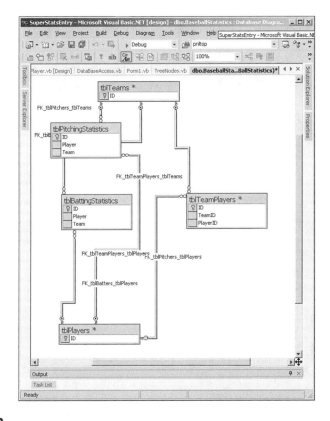

Figure B.2

A SQL Server 2000 database diagram for a Baseball Statistics database.

Figure B.3

Public Web Services.

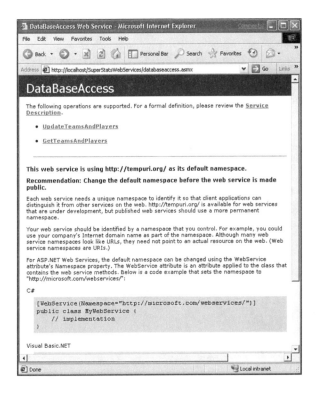

Figure B.4

Private Web Services.

The SuperStats Web Service is made up of two ASMX files that contain the Web Methods. Let's take a look at one of the Web Methods. The code in Listing B.1 illustrates one of the more complex methods in the sample Web Service. The code builds the complex DataSet depicted in Figure B.5.

Listing B.1 GetTeamsAndPlayers *Web Method*

```
<WebMethod()> _
Public Function GetTeamsAndPlayers() As TeamsAndPlayers

    Dim oConnection As SqlConnection = New
➥SqlConnection("server=localhost;uid=sa;pwd=;database=BaseBallStatistics")
    Dim DS As New TeamsAndPlayers()
    Dim oDataAdapter As SqlDataAdapter

    oConnection.Open()
    DS.EnforceConstraints = False
    CreateTeamAdapter(oConnection).Fill(DS, DS.Teams.TableName)
    CreatePlayersAdapter(oConnection).Fill(DS, DS.Players.TableName)
    CreateTeamPlayersAdapter(oConnection).Fill(DS, DS.TeamPlayers.TableName)
    CreatePitchingAdapter(oConnection).Fill(DS,
```

Listing B.1 Continued

```
DS.PitchingStatistics.TableName)
    CreateBattingAdapter(oConnection).Fill(DS, DS.BattingStatistics.TableName)
    DS.EnforceConstraints = True
    oConnection.Close()
    Return DS
End Function
```

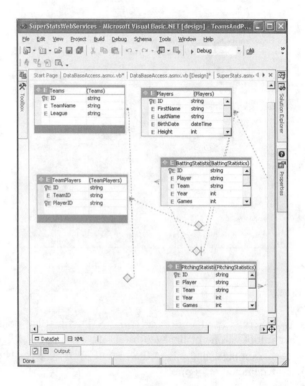

Figure B.5

TeamsAndPlayers *Typed* DataSet *in the schema designer.*

The code in Listing B.1 uses a number of helper functions similar to the one in Listing B.2 to create SQLDataAdapters for each of the ADO.NET DataTables that will be built for the complex typed DataSet. The helper function creates command objects and assigns them to the SelectCommand, InsertCommand, UpdateCommand, and DeleteCommand. The four commands use stored procedures for data access. These same helper functions are also used by the UpdateTeamsAndPlayer Web Method.

Listing B.2 `CreateTeamsAndPlayerDataAdapter`

```
Private Function CreateTeamPlayersAdapter(ByRef oConnection As SqlConnection) _
    As SqlDataAdapter
    Dim oDataAdapter As New SqlDataAdapter()
    Dim oCommand As SqlCommand
    oCommand = New SqlCommand()

    With oCommand
        .CommandType = CommandType.StoredProcedure
        .CommandText = "GetTeamPlayers"
        .Connection = oConnection
    End With

    oDataAdapter.SelectCommand = oCommand

    oCommand = New SqlCommand()

    With oCommand
        .CommandType = CommandType.StoredProcedure
        .CommandText = "InsertTeamPlayer"
        .Parameters.Add(New SqlParameter("@ID", SqlDbType.UniqueIdentifier, _
            16, System.Data.ParameterDirection.Input, True, 0, _
            0,"ID",System.Data.DataRowVersion.Original, Nothing))
        .Parameters.Add(New SqlParameter("@TeamID", SqlDbType.UniqueIdentifier,
            ➥16, System.Data.ParameterDirection.Input, True, 0, _
            0, "TeamID", System.Data.DataRowVersion.Original, Nothing))
        .Parameters.Add(New SqlParameter("@PlayerID",
SqlDbType.UniqueIdentifier, _
            16, System.Data.ParameterDirection.Input, True, 0, _
            0, "PlayerID", System.Data.DataRowVersion.Original, Nothing))
        .Connection = oConnection
    End With

    oDataAdapter.InsertCommand = oCommand

    oCommand = New SqlCommand()

    With oCommand
        .CommandType = CommandType.StoredProcedure
        .CommandText = "UpdateTeamPlayer"
        .Parameters.Add(New SqlParameter("@TeamPlayerToUpdateID",_
            SqlDbType.UniqueIdentifier, 16,
System.Data.ParameterDirection.Input_
            , True, 0, 0, "ID", System.Data.DataRowVersion.Original, Nothing))
        .Parameters.Add(New SqlParameter("@TeamID", SqlDbType.UniqueIdentifier,
```

Listing B.2 *Continued*

```
        ➡16, System.Data.ParameterDirection.Input, True, 0, _
           0, "TeamID", System.Data.DataRowVersion.Current, Nothing))
     .Parameters.Add(New SqlParameter("@PlayerID",
SqlDbType.UniqueIdentifier,
           16, System.Data.ParameterDirection.Input, True, 0, _
           0, "PlayerID", System.Data.DataRowVersion.Current, Nothing))
     .Connection = oConnection
   End With

   oDataAdapter.UpdateCommand = oCommand

   oCommand = New SqlCommand()

   With oCommand
     .CommandType = CommandType.StoredProcedure
     .CommandText = "DeleteTeamPlayer"
     .Parameters.Add(New SqlParameter("@TeamPlayerID",_
        SqlDbType.UniqueIdentifier, 16,
System.Data.ParameterDirection.Input,_
        True, 0, 0, "ID", System.Data.DataRowVersion.Original, Nothing))
     .Connection = oConnection
   End With

   oDataAdapter.DeleteCommand = oCommand

   Return oDataAdapter
End Function
```

One item of interest is how ADO.NET provides support for various forms of concurrency control. I created the update stored procedures with a very optimistic concurrency model. (I don't check at all if someone else has changed the data prior to updating.) In the setup of the stored procedures that change the data, one of the parameters when creating an ADO.NET SQLParameter is the sourceVersion. Use this to tell what version of a field to send to the stored procedure parameter. The most common values passed to this parameter are System.Data.DataRowVersion.Original and System.Data.DataRowVersion.Current. Original tells ADO.NET to pass the field value that was originally retrieved from the database. Current tells ADO.NET to pass the current value of the field to the stored procedure. You can use these to pass any number of parameters to the database to control concurrency using any of the common methods.

- Use a timestamp—This is a method that I use often. The idea is to update a timestamp each time that the row is changed. Then in the stored procedure, use the timestamp field to ensure that the timestamp that was selected is the same as the timestamp on the row.
- Pass in all fields—Then compare them to ensure that all the fields are still the same as they were when the data was retrieved from the database.

The remainder of the Web Methods create untyped `DataSets` that return data from stored procedures.

Super Stats Live Entry

The first ASP.NET Web Form application that I built was to allow a user to update the current season's statistics. It is a simple one-page Web Form, yet it showcases a couple of powerful features of ASP.NET and the ASP.NET `DataGrid` control. Figures B.6 and B.7 illustrate the Web Form in various modes.

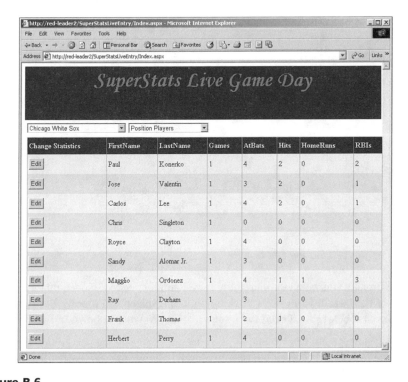

Figure B.6

Web Form in Browse mode.

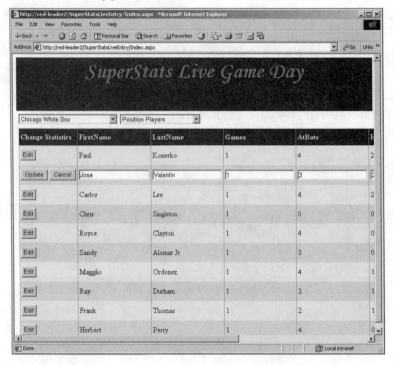

Figure B.7

Web Form after clicking the Edit button.

ASP.NET makes this behavior incredibly easy. I simply needed to open up the Property
Builder of the DataGrid by right-clicking on it and selecting Property Builder. A few
properties of the DataGrid need to be set according to what's shown in Figure B.8.

After you set the column's properties, you then need to provide server-side events for
the Edit, Cancel, and Update buttons. Listing B.3 shows the three event handlers that
I created to handle the DataGrid events.

- EditCommand—Puts the grid into edit mode
- CancelCommand—Resets the grid back to browse mode
- UpdateCommand—Applies the changes back to the database

Listing B.3   Code to Handle Server-Side Events for DataGrid

```
Protected Sub OnGridPlayersStatisticsEdit(ByVal sender As System.Object, _
    ByVal e As DataGridCommandEventArgs) _
    Handles gridPlayersStatistics.EditCommand
    Call BindGridDataSource(dropTeams().SelectedItem.Value)
    'Indicate to grid which row needs to be put in edit mode
    gridPlayersStatistics().EditItemIndex = e.Item.ItemIndex
    gridPlayersStatistics().DataBind()
End Sub
```

Listing B.3 Continued

```
Protected Sub OnGridPlayersStatisticsCancel(ByVal sender As System.Object, _
    ByVal e As DataGridCommandEventArgs) _
    Handles gridPlayersStatistics.CancelCommand
    Call BindGridDataSource(dropTeams().SelectedItem.Value)
    'Indicate to grid that now rows are being edited
    gridPlayersStatistics().EditItemIndex = -1
    gridPlayersStatistics().DataBind()
End Sub
Protected Sub OnGridPlayersStatisticsUpdate(ByVal sender As System.Object, _
    ByVal e As DataGridCommandEventArgs) _
    Handles gridPlayersStatistics.UpdateCommand

    If dropPlayerType().SelectedItem.Value = "1" Then
        Call UpdateBattingStatistics(e)
    Else
        Call UpdatePitchingStatistics(e)
    End If

    ' Switch out of edit mode.
    Call BindGridDataSource(dropTeams().SelectedItem.Value)
    'Indicate to grid that no rows are being edited
    gridPlayersStatistics().EditItemIndex = -1
    gridPlayersStatistics().DataBind()

End Sub
```

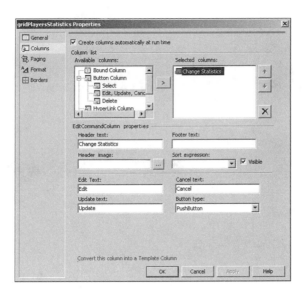

Figure B.8

Property Builder for DataGrid.

The rest of the code in the project is of some interest. (You will need to take a look at `UpdateBattingStatistics` or `UpdatePitchingStatistics` to see how to retrieve the updated values.)

Since I adopted a Web Service architecture, I decided to also build a sample application that consumes a Web Service.

Bob's Fantasy Baseball

Fantasy baseball and sports statistics are big on the Internet, so my fictional company (SuperStats) wants to provide Web Services.

In the second Web Form application, I created the beginning of a fantasy baseball site that consumes some of the Web Services. Figures B.9 and B.10 show the application in Internet Explorer.

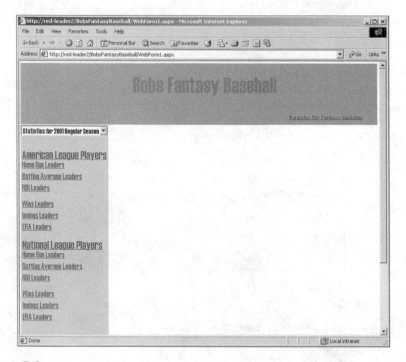

Figure B.9

Bob's Fantasy Baseball.

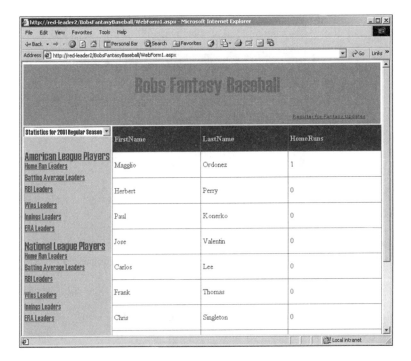

Figure B.10

American League leaders in homeruns.

The key to this application is the fact that all the data is retrieved from a external data source using Web Services and SOAP. The code to build the table is again using the ASP.NET DataGrid control to display the information. Listing B.4 depicts the code for each one of the hyperlinks on the left.

Listing B.4 *Code to Load* DataGrid

```
Protected Sub lnkNLBattingAverage_Click(ByVal sender As System.Object, _
    ByVal e As System.EventArgs) Handles lnkNLBattingAverage.Click
    Dim iYear As Integer = CInt(dropYear().SelectedItem.Value)
    gridPlayers().DataSource = _
    databaseaccess.GetBattingAverageLeaders("NL", iYear)
    Page().DataBind()
End Sub
```

To build this Web Form you need to simply adding a couple of Web Form panels (the top and left) to the form. To complete the menu, a number of hyperlinking buttons need to be added. Add the code to handle the events as shown in Listing B.3 and drop a DataGrid control onto the form. After the grid is dropped on to the form, you can format the form by right-clicking the form and choosing AutoFormat. Figure B.11 illustrates the AutoFormat dialog box.

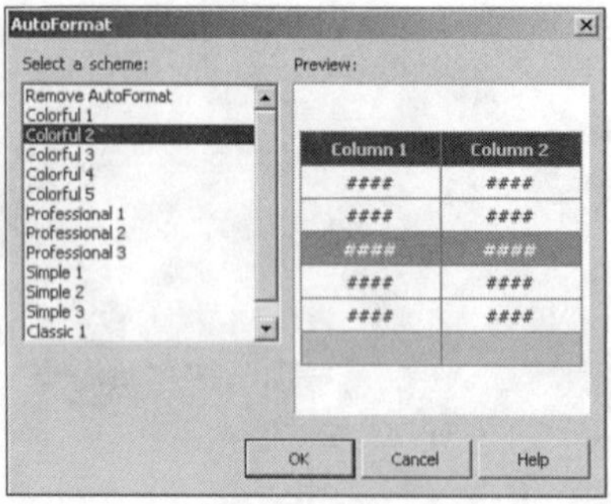

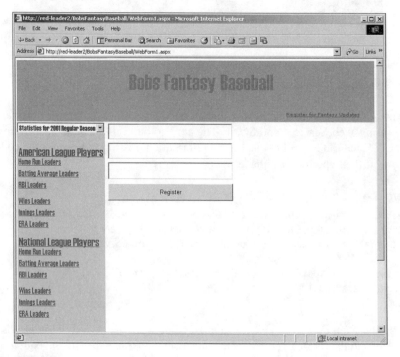

Figure B.11

The AutoFormat dialog box.

The application also allows a user to register to receive update information via e-mail. This simply is a registration process that allows him to enter a name and e-mail address. Figure B.12 illustrates the form to register the visitor.

Figure B.12

E-mail registration.

Listing B.5 shows the code behind the Click event that takes the data entered and inserts it into the database (using a stored procedure setup in another class).

Listing B.5 btnRegister Click ***Event***

```
Protected Sub btnRegister_Click(ByVal sender As System.Object, _
    ByVal e As System.EventArgs) Handles btnRegister.Click
    Dim sFirstName As String
    Dim sLastName As String
    Dim sEmail As String

    'Shows how easy it is to get the entered values
    sFirstName = txtFirstName().Text
    sLastName = txtLastName().Text
    sEmail = txtEmail().Text

    'Call Stored Procedure to insert registration
    BobsFantasyBaseballDBA.AddRegistration(sFirstName, sLastName, sEmail)

    'Hide the registration controls and show the datagrid
    Call HideRegistration()

    'Fill the Grid with the American League Players
    Call ShowALPlayers()
End Sub
```

To ensure that users have entered data into all three fields of the registration form, I used the ASP.NET RequiredFieldValidator control. This control will validate if data has been entered into a control. Depending on the browser, it will display messages as soon as a user tabs out of the control or after he clicks the Submit button (which is Register on my form). This is extremely easy to use and flexible, and its shows another one of the new powerful features of ASP.NET.

Summary

In this example, I illustrated a number of items that make the new ASP.NET development platform revolutionary. It has never been easier to build highly dynamic Internet applications. Couple this with the new capabilities of Web Services, and the third generation of Internet applications is ready to take shape.

The examples used the new ASP.NET DataGrid to display and edit data. The ASP.NET DataGrid control is one of the incredible powerful new ASP.NET Server controls. These controls and Visual Studio.NET brings the VB method of building applications to the Internet in the form of Web Forms and Web Services.

INDEX

O